T0305380

RETHINKING
FINANCIAL BEHAVIOUR

Rethinking Work, Ageing and Retirement

Series Editors: **David Lain**, Newcastle University,
Sarah Vickerstaff, University of Kent and
Mariska van der Horst, Vrije Universiteit
Amsterdam

This multidisciplinary series brings together researchers from a range
of fields including management and organisational studies, gerontology,
sociology, psychology and social policy, to explore the impact of extended
working lives on older people and organisations.

Find out more about the new and forthcoming titles in the series:

bristoluniversitypress.co.uk/
rethinking-work-ageing-and-retirement

RETHINKING FINANCIAL BEHAVIOUR

Rationality and Resistance in the Financialization of Everyday Life

Ariane Agunsoye

BRISTOL
UNIVERSITY
PRESS

First published in Great Britain in 2025 by

Bristol University Press
University of Bristol
1–9 Old Park Hill
Bristol
BS2 8BB
UK
t: +44 (0)117 374 6645
e: bup-info@bristol.ac.uk

Details of international sales and distribution partners are available at bristoluniversitypress.co.uk

© Bristol University Press 2025

British Library Cataloguing in Publication Data
A catalogue record for this book is available from the British Library

ISBN 978-1-5292-3225-7 hardcover
ISBN 978-1-5292-3227-1 ePub
ISBN 978-1-5292-3228-8 ePdf

Cover design: Andrew Corbett
Front cover image: Getty Images/Sezeryadigar
Bristol University Press uses environmentally responsible print partners.
Printed and bound in Great Britain by CPI Group (UK) Ltd, Croydon, CR0 4YY

FSC
www.fsc.org
MIX
Paper | Supporting
responsible forestry
FSC® C013604

To Mutti and my late Papa

Contents

Series Editors' Preface

David Lain, Sarah Vickerstaff and Mariska van der Horst

The 'Rethinking Work, Ageing and Retirement' book series explores the impact of extended working lives and changes to welfare states and labour markets on people, organizations and society. The radical changes affecting work and retirement were an impetus for the series. In particular, rising state pension ages, shifts towards individual responsibility and risk in private pensions saving, and the abolition of mandatory retirement ages in a number of countries now frame decisions about retirement. In theory, these policy developments extend individual discretion about continuing in employment, which may create new opportunities for those who want – and are able – to work. In practice, however, it arguably makes retirement timing only a hypothetical choice that people can be held more accountable for. Individuals must now assume greater financial responsibility for remaining in work as long as they need to. For significant numbers of older people this may be difficult to achieve, however, given evidence of widespread age discrimination in the labour market and reduced employment opportunities for this group. This is in addition to difficulties individuals experience in the labour market at any age – for example, due to racism or ableism, or constraints on time and energy stemming from outside paid work, such as care responsibilities. Work itself also appears to be getting more precarious, albeit to differing degrees across countries, and the management of older workers is becoming less straightforward given uncertainties around retirement.

It is in this context that we are delighted to welcome the excellent volume on financial behaviour by Ariane Agunsoye. The landscape of occupational, private and state pensions has changed dramatically in the last twenty years, placing ever more responsibility on the individual to save and to save wisely. This book focuses on the neglected topic of household financial behaviour and the wider financialization of everyday life against the backdrop of the neo-liberal agenda of financial deregulation. It contributes to debates on household finances, reviewing a large volume of literature and going on to use Foucault's analytical perspective in an original way to examine how people make sense of their new financial responsibilities and develop strategies of performance and resistance as 'everyday asset managers'. The book makes key theoretical and empirical contributions to our understanding of how individuals and households understand and navigate the increasingly important need for personal pension management as part of planning for retirement.

List of Figures and Tables

Figures

Tables

Acknowledgements

I would like to take this opportunity to express my sincere gratitude to the many people who have contributed in different ways to this book and its journey. I am forever grateful to Dimitris P. Sotiropoulos and Andrew B. Trigg for their input towards my academic development. Not only have they helped me academically with insightful comments on my work, but they have also provided guidance on a personal level. Their trust in my abilities during difficult times has enabled me to keep on going. I would like to thank particularly my friend Dimitris who has supported me over the past ten years. Our discussions always give me new aspects to think about and motivate me to go this one step further. Moreover, I will always be thankful to Claus Thomasberger, who inspired my interest in critical studies and my desire to enter academia.

I would also like to thank Bristol University Press, whose editorial team has been amazing. A particular thanks to Paul Stevens who has started my interest in developing this book and connected me with David Lain, Sarah Vickerstaff and Mariska van der Horst so that it could be included in the book series 'Rethinking Work, Ageing and Retirement'. I am particularly grateful for David's and Sarah's comments and guidance during the process of finalizing the book. I would also like to thank the Open University, Claire Brewis and Linda Plowright-Pepper for their support in the data collection process. I am deeply indebted to my interview participants, who have given me their trust and without whom this research would not have been possible.

I would like to express sincere gratitude to my friend and co-author Hayley James for our insightful discussions throughout the years. The book provides a summary of my research on everyday financialization over the past seven years and therefore integrates previously published material of mine. I am grateful that I was able to use extracts or revised versions from the following sources:

Agunsoye, A. (2021) ' "Locked in the rat race" – variegated financial subjectivities in the UK', *Environment and Planning A: Economy and Space*, 53(7): 1828–48.

Agunsoye, A. (2024) 'Lived experiences of everyday financialization: A layered performativity approach', *Critical Perspectives on Accounting*, 100(102756): 1–16.

Agunsoye, A. and James, H. (2022) '"I had to take control": gendered pension strategies in the articles UK', *Review of International Political Economy*, 30(4): 1486–509.

Agunsoye, A. and James, H. (2024) 'Irrational or rational? Time to rethink our understanding of financially responsible behavior', *Economic Geography*, 100(2): 191–212.

Agunsoye, A., Monne, J., Rutterford, J. and Sotiropoulos, D.P. (2022) 'How gender, marital status, and gender norms affect savings goals', *Kyklos*, 75(2): 157–83.

Hillig, A. (2019) 'Everyday financialization: the case of UK households', *Environment and Planning A: Economy and Space*, 51(7): 1460–78.

Hillig, A. (2019) 'Everyday financialization: the case of UK households', PhD Thesis, The Open University.

Throughout the years I have received many insightful comments on draft sections for this book. I wish to thank in addition to those mentioned earlier Paul Auerbach, Giorgos Galanis, Susan Himmelweit, Daniel W. Richards and Hadas Weiss.

I am most thankful to my family and friends, and particularly my husband, whose support and belief in me has been unwavering throughout. His calmness helped me to focus during the most stressful and emotionally challenging times. I would also like to pay my sincere gratitude to my late father and my mother for going above and beyond for me, taking away the fear of trying out new things and enabling several changes in my career: my father, who saw the beginning of this journey towards the book, remains with me always, having taught me to be determined and to always work hard for my goals; and my mother, to whom I am forever grateful for having instilled in me the desire to learn and explore new things. To my dear friends Eurydice Fotopoulou and Ilona Schön whose words of encouragement and their tremendous belief in me have inspired me to continue on this journey.

Preface

When I was approached by Bristol University Press after a seminar I gave, I was delighted to have the chance to synthesize my different strands of research in a book. This book draws on my experiences within the private sector but also on my interdisciplinary background, having studied international business, business administration and economics. My interest in the everyday perspective of financialization arose after having studied financialization and its impact on the household within the economics literature. The majority of these investigations have tended to focus on exploring how structural changes in the economy have led to changes in household behaviour. Wanting to introduce the perspective of the household, I sought to research everyday financial behaviour and its underlying reasoning, which eventually led my research to centre on the intersection between political economy and personal finance, exploring how people across different social and demographic groups respond to the rising pressure to manage financial risk. This research agenda has accompanied me for the last ten years, ranging from my PhD research to a range of papers published since then. The book has given me the opportunity to develop a coherent narrative which questions recent theorizations of everyday financial practices and brings to the forefront everyday financial practices as rational responses to an unequal system, highlighting the inefficiencies of the current system and its underlying power mechanisms.

The concept of finance rationality has underpinned many welfare policies in developed capitalist societies, promoting private asset ownership rather than publicly funded cash transfers to circumvent risks of income shortfalls when becoming unemployed or sick, or in retirement. Rational individuals are knowledgeable about financial concepts, conduct regular investments throughout their working life, and build a diverse asset portfolio to generate income during non-working periods. Behaviour deviating from these norms is categorized as irresponsible and corrective policy measures are introduced. While behavioural economics has put forward the notion that people use irrational heuristics when making financial decisions such as prioritizing current consumption over future consumption, financial literacy has attributed non-conforming behaviour to a lack of financial knowledge.

Both literature strands see finance rationality as an ideal which one should strive to achieve. This understanding of finance rationality assumes that it is possible to accumulate assets as expected if individual behaviour is adjusted, ignoring factors outside an individual's control such as having to take a break from work due to caring duties or being affected by unemployment or underemployment. Even when acknowledging contextual factors such as income or career status, discussions revert back to how individuals can behave more in line with finance rationality.

Critical studies instead have put attention on structural inequalities inherent in a capitalist welfare state where income constraints and gendered work patterns prevent individuals to conform to norms of asset accumulation. However, less is known about how people who face these constraints within savings and investments respond to them. Studies which have tackled this space, adopting an everyday financialization lens and unveiling the underlying capitalist relations, have shown that individuals transform (and are transformed by) the imposed rationality of finance and integrate their own everyday rationalities, such as uncertainties, relationships and moral understandings. While some of this literature has addressed how social groups are exposed to structural inequalities in the social, economic and institutional landscape within debt behaviour, the work has not explicated the role of these constraints in the meaning-making processes of asset accumulation and the conceptualization of variegated financial subjects.

This book builds on these bodies of work, exploring the interaction of active meaning-making processes within savings and investment decisions and constraints and contradictions inherent in asset-based welfare. It moves beyond identifying deviations to rational behaviour and reveals everyday financial practices as logical responses to a dysfunctional system. Proposing a typology of everyday financialization and a new way of thinking about rationality, it seeks to challenge current theoretical discussions and policy approaches. My wish is that these discussions will contribute to changing the current policy discussions, highlighting the need to establish equitable starting points for pension savers, balancing out inequalities due to occupational constraints, unpaid care work and income constraints, and reducing the reliance on individual investments for financial security in retirement.

PART I

Everyday Financial Subjects

1

Introduction

Since the end of the 1970s, successive Conservative and Labour governments have based policies on the belief that widening asset ownership results in an 'opportunity society where all have an equal chance to succeed' (Blair, 2004).[1] As part of this turn towards asset-based welfare, the focus of government policies has shifted away from providing public insurance against potential future risks to an emphasis on personal responsibility, as can be seen in a statement by Margaret Thatcher from 1987:

> I think we have gone through a period when too many children and people have been given to understand 'I have a problem, it is the Government's job to cope with it!' or 'I have a problem, I will go and get a grant to cope with it!', 'I am homeless, the Government must house me!' and so they are casting their problems on society and who is society? There is no such thing! There are individual men and women and there are families and no government can do anything except through people and people look to themselves first. It is our duty to look after ourselves. (Thatcher, 1987a)

Whereas the goal of providing publicly funded welfare is to support consumption during periods of income shortfall, asset-based welfare aims to increase economic participation and rests on the assumption that by accumulating assets everyone can gain a stake in the economy (Cutler and Waine, 2001; Sherraden, 2015). In line with this belief, the publicly funded welfare state has been continuously dismantled over the past four decades and social responsibilities which used to be borne by the state are increasingly carried by individuals. Consequently, the UK has one of the lowest social welfare provisions among OECD countries (OECD, 2015, 2017). Unemployment benefits, sick pay and state pensions have been reduced to the degree of solely providing poverty relief, and socially reproductive activities[2] such as caring for family members, domestic work and maintaining communities have been increasingly privatized (Fraser, 2017; Chzhen et al, 2019).

To enable UK individuals to take on these new responsibilities, *responsibilization*[3] has been accompanied by the introduction of asset-based welfare measures. Access to financial products such as mortgages, pension funds, savings and investment products has been widened and people are called upon to accumulate financial assets to draw upon during periods of income shortfalls instead of relying on income support by the government (Langley, 2006, 2008). One pillar of this transformation is private pension provision. Workplace pensions, alongside personal pensions and financial investments, have been established as key mechanisms to provide financial security (Grady, 2015). At the same time, defined-benefit (DB) workplace pensions, where employees are guaranteed a fixed pension income, have been largely replaced with defined-contribution (DC) pensions, where the pension income depends on the performance of the asset portfolio and the choice of investment package, thus transferring the risk of sufficient retirement income from the employer onto the individual (Lowe, 2010; PPI, 2017). To support asset accumulation, tax reductions and subsidies for savings and investments are put in place, such as a tax rebate for personal pensions or more recently a pause on stamp duty during the COVID-19 pandemic (Kempson and Collard, 2012; Osborne, 2021).

This transformation of society 'requires ... new identities and forms of calculation from its citizens' (Froud et al, 2010, p 340), calling upon people to internalize the subject position of the everyday investor. An everyday investor aims to earn returns in financial markets guided by finance rationality, defined as embracing risk willingly and adopting financial strategies such as diversification (Martin, 2002; Langley, 2008). Assuming people behave rationally and want to maximize their life-time income, they offset an expected income drop during retirement by means of developing a diversified portfolio of financial assets and choosing a workplace pension package and contribution amount in line with their desired retirement income, taking into consideration inflationary expectations, interest rate developments and tax implications (Langley, 2008; Strauss, 2008). Through mitigating future risks with the help of investments, the everyday investor increasingly interacts with financial products, and financial motives enter more and more aspects of everyday life. This has been referred to as the *financialization of daily life* (Martin, 2002), where 'individuals adopt new modes of self-governance and reflexivity to monitor their investments' (Lai, 2016a, p 3).

Yet, for having promoted prosperity for all, asset-based welfare has failed large groups of society miserably, as revealed by recent events. Wealth inequalities, which have been soaring since the Global Financial Crisis due to stagnating wages and austerity measures, have intensified since the pandemic. The top 10 per cent of UK households have become richer while middle- to lower income households lag behind in living standards compared to comparable OECD countries (Resolution Foundation &

Centre for Economic Performance, 2022). During the pandemic, high-earning individuals were able to pay off their debt and conduct further investments, while lower earning individuals were disproportionately affected by a fall in employment, deepening financial hardships (Allen and Rebillard, 2021; Bell, 2021). Policy solutions intensified these inequalities further. The pause on stamp duty pushed up already high property prices, pricing out younger and low- to medium-income individuals from the housing market, and lockdown measures impacted largely manual and service jobs rather than higher paid jobs (Pratley, 2021; Powell et al, 2022).

The current cost-of-living crisis originating from stagnating wages, rising inflation and high energy costs has deepened these inequalities further and illustrated once again the limitations of UK households providing financial security for themselves. The Office for Budget Responsibility now predicts a real disposable income fall in the next few years of dimensions which we have not seen since records began (OBR, 2022). This in turn has a detrimental effect on pension savings, with recent studies already showing that pension savers have stopped contributing to pensions or reduced their contributions (PMI, 2022). Even before the pandemic and cost-of-living crisis, studies have revealed the mismatch between the expectation of actively saving for retirement and the actual behaviour of individuals, with 12 million UK employees undersaving (DWP, 2017) and evidence of 'sub-optimal savings choices' (Strauss, 2008, p 139), such as not investing in a diversified asset portfolio including stocks and shares and bonds, not actively engaging with pensions and choosing investment options which are not in line with the needed future retirement income (PPI, 2017; DWP, 2017, 2018).

'Misbehaving' subjects?

Realizing that individuals are underinvesting with regards to their retirement needs, measures have been implemented that seek to nudge people into adopting the correct course of action, for example by automatically enrolling them in workplace pensions and introducing financial education campaigns (Altman, 2012; FinCap, 2021; MaPS, 2021). These policy initiatives are based on the assumption that the everyday person employs 'irrational heuristics' (Altman, 2012, p 680) as shortcuts when making financial decisions, such as not informing themselves sufficiently about their pension investments or overly relying on 'passive' financial products (Lai, 2016b, p 38) such as fixed-income savings products (Mitchell and Lusardi, 2012; Elliehausen, 2019).

In recent years, these measures have been increasingly combined with a call to make financial products and education more inclusive by providing access to financial products within a wide range of income and employment levels and encouraging lower income individuals, women and people with a minority ethnic background to adopt 'financial self-governance' (Loomis,

2018, p 144). These financial inclusion initiatives – including interventions based on financial education and wider access to financial products – seek to, on the one hand, increase confidence in managing personal finances over the life cycle and, on the other hand, give people the possibility to engage with financial products (Prabhakar, 2021; FCA, 2022). Yet, even with such measures in place, there remains a staggering wealth gap in place. Over the past decade, the top 10 per cent income earners have increased their wealth 574 times faster than the lowest 10 per cent income earners and now own more than half of the UK's wealth (Singer, 2022; Chaudhuri and Xu, 2023). Moreover, the UK has the second largest gender wealth gap within Europe, with women's wealth representing only 71 per cent of men's wealth (WTW, 2022), and displays a persistent ethnicity wealth gap where wealth is lowest among Bangladeshi, Black African and Pakistani headed households (ONS, 2021a).

More critical studies have therefore argued that financial inclusion initiatives, while seeking to establish equal access, ignore factors outside an individual's control, implicitly employing 'blame strategies' (Finley, 2021, p 126; see also Hamilton and Darity Jr, 2017) and making financial challenges seem like an individual problem. The UK's asset-based welfare system is built around a stereotypically well-earning, male life trajectory, that is, having a full-time job throughout one's working life and earning a decent salary from a single place of employment. The full state pension of £203.85 per week is based on 35 years' contributions (first tier) while the workplace pension only applies when a person earns at least £10,000 in one place of work and is over 22 years old (second tier, Strauss, 2014; PPI, 2017; HMRC, 2023). If moving away from these in-built assumptions, one does not have access to the first two tiers of the UK's pensions system, which results in 10 million people being excluded from workplace pension schemes due to earnings and age criteria (Morley, 2014; PPI, 2017; DWP, 2018). Now, finance rationality assumes that a third tier in the form of personal financial investments could be used to balance out this lack of state and workplace pensions. However, to be able to achieve the same level of wealth as someone who has access to a full workplace pension with its employer's contributions, one would be required to save and invest substantially more, which is unlikely when not being able to meet the earnings criteria. Moreover, someone experiencing income constraints, an interrupted work history, relying on several jobs, or being self-employed often cannot contribute continuously to private pensions and conduct additional financial investments for retirement. Even when being able to contribute to a workplace pension on a continuous basis, the inherent uncertainty of investments undermines future pension income (Langley, 2006; Storper, 2014), and income constraints limit its benefits as the minimum monthly contributions of 8 per cent (3 per cent from the employer and 5 per cent from the employee) of the income would not be sufficient for an adequate retirement income (PPI, 2017; DWP, 2018; PMI, 2022).

Despite its apparent limitations, current policies reinforce instead of question asset-based welfare by seeking to bring actual behaviour closer to theoretical expectations through financial literacy programmes and widening access to financial products. These measures, however, would not go far enough to address inequalities inherent in asset-based welfare. Having access to financial products will not overcome disadvantages due to income limitations, and having better knowledge of financial concepts will not smoothen limitations inherent in the current asset-based welfare system. The constraints of the current asset-based welfare state is once again highlighted in the current cost-of-living crisis, where even money advisers have 'run out of tools to help people' and call on the government to provide more support since 'it's not something money management can fix' (Lewis, 2022).

Notwithstanding, advice for dealing with the current rise in living costs while trying to save for retirement concentrates on individual responsibility, such as focusing on helping people understand how to plan for later life (MaPS, 2021) and providing guides on how to reduce spending and 'boost your income' (MoneyHelper, 2023a). This guidance includes, among others, renting out a spare room, taking on an additional job (increasing the workload of individuals), paying bills on time and seeking ways to reduce transport costs (GOV.UK, 2023a; MoneyHelper, 2023a). These measures ignore once again systemic constraints such as having the ability to have a spare room, to pay bills on time when already struggling to pay the basics and an environment of rising fuel and train costs. As recent studies have shown, lower income earners are at their limits, not turning on their heating on a regular basis, reducing the number of meals they eat per day and eating food beyond its use-by date (Peachey, 2023a). That persistent constraints inherent in the asset-based welfare system are ignored seems rather striking in a system which has portrayed the change in society from publicly funded to asset-based welfare as creating 'popular capitalism' (Thatcher, 1986) where everyone can become a capitalist by means of accumulating assets. However, it is less surprising when taking into consideration how norms of asset accumulation have intensified the power imbalances embodied in capital–labour relationships.

The profitable everyday capitalist

Despite its claim of seeking to enable people to become capitalists, critical studies have unveiled the underlying power mechanisms at play within asset-based welfare. Putting more responsibility onto individuals not only creates more asset ownership but also increases the pressure on labour while enabling the dismantling of the welfare state and creating profit opportunities for financial institutions (Belfrage and Kallifatides, 2018; Huber et al, 2020).

'Offloading' risks and responsibilities from the government and companies onto the 'increasingly fragile balance sheets of workers and their families' (Hacker, 2008, p ix) has introduced new financial and social risks into everyday life without people being equipped to manage these. In contrast to companies, households do not have limited liability and their portfolios are weighted towards non-tradable, illiquid assets. The largest component of the household balance sheet, which for the majority of households is the house (see Table 1.1), can be considered to be an illiquid asset which cannot be easily sold in a crisis situation due to declining demand and due to it being the home. At the same time, financial institutions have benefitted from widening access to mortgages through earning interest incomes and securitizing debt. Since in the securitization process ownership is not transferred but a future income stream promised, the constant income stream coming from households' long-term financial contracts makes them attractive as an asset base (Bryan et al, 2009, 2015; Beggs et al, 2014; Lysandrou, 2016).

A similar unequal relationship can be found when looking at the second largest asset in most households' balance sheets, namely pension provisions, which also cannot be easily accessed or traded in case of income

Table 1.1: Exemplary household balance sheet

Assets	Liabilities
Property	Property debt
Home	Main residence
Other property	Other property
Pension wealth	Financial liabilities
Transaction accounts	Personal loans
Bank account savings	Student debt
Savings certificates and bonds	Hire purchase
Investment trusts/unit trusts	Credit card debt
Stocks and shares	Store cards
Business assets	Business debt
Home contents	Overdraft
Vehicles	Overdue household bills
Other assets	Other debt

Note: While some categorizations of household balance sheets include human capital, defined as the skills and knowledge of individuals used to generate income (Schultz, 1961), this concept has been criticized for its underlying assumptions (Tan, 2014). Since generated income translates into consumption and investments, this book follows the household balance sheet approach incorporated in empirical studies (Guiso et al, 2002) and the government approach adopted when analysing wealth (ONS, 2021b, 2022a).

Source: Author's illustration based on Guiso et al (2002); ONS (2021b, 2022a)

shocks. The change from defined-benefit pensions (DB) to defined-contribution pensions (DC) has resulted in not guaranteeing a pension income during retirement and the need to prop up workplace pensions by additional asset accumulation (Webber, 2018), which is only possible if one earns sufficient income, thus increasing the pressure on labour. Even if individuals sufficiently invest in pensions and are increasingly involved in the accumulation process, they are in a disadvantageous position because of living in a 'snakes and ladders world where earnings, wealth effects and final values are unpredictable' (Erturk et al, 2007, p 562). Incomes fluctuate to a greater degree due to rising job insecurity and financial investments remain inherently uncertain, making it more difficult to plan ahead (Langley, 2007). Crises over the past 20 years, including the dot-com bubble, the Global Financial Crisis, the COVID-19 pandemic and numerous wars, have shown that financial values are extremely volatile, and declining asset values since 2008 have resulted in DC pensions being at risk of underperforming with regards to retirement provision (Cribb and Karjalainen, 2023). Meanwhile, the transfer of pension risks from the employer and state onto the individual has enabled the dismantling of the welfare state, reduced the financial liabilities of employers and generated huge fee incomes for the financial sector without ensuring adequacy of future pension incomes (Lebaron, 2010; Ayres and Curtis, 2015; Webber, 2018).

The persistence on individual solutions such as more accessible, simplified financial products and financial education reinforces the belief that people can achieve sound financial management despite the constraints inherent in asset-based welfare. These financial inclusion measures ensure that individuals who struggle with the system's inherent constraints continue to meet financial commitments without retreating back to the welfare state (Allon, 2014; Loomis, 2018). Financial education programmes thus 'at once empower and discipline individuals' (Langley, 2007, pp 68–9).

This book's approach

As the book delves into the concept of asset-based welfare, it thoroughly examines decisions pertaining to assets and the accompanying debt, thus mortgages, but does not include a discussion of debt management, which has been extensively explored in the everyday financialization literature (Di Feliciantonio, 2016; Fields, 2017; Garcia-Lamarca, 2016). While the discussions on debt practices give valuable insights into everyday financialization, for instance showcasing how debt works as a disciplining mechanism, increasing the pressure for labour to generate future income, much less is known about households' overall interaction with assets, including not just one aspect of asset ownership such as homeownership, but several aspects such as savings, homeownership, investments and pensions.

Even though asset-based welfare has been criticized for its reliance on unrealistic assumptions of finance rationality (Clark, 2014; Thaler and Sunstein, 2021) and lack of attention to structural inequalities (Grady, 2015; Fraser, 2017), these studies tend to fall into the same trap as financial inclusion initiatives by either perceiving it as an ideal which one should strive to achieve or by paying little attention to everyday practices. What explanations for deviant financial behaviour ignore is the potential for *irresponsible* financial behaviour being a logical reaction to contradictions immanent within asset-based welfare. This is where this book intervenes, seeking to make a contribution to more just policies by way of challenging existing explanations of deviating behaviour and theorizing a novel concept of finance rationality. The uniqueness of the project lies in integrating assumptions originating from everyday discourses and practices and in perceiving actions taken by individuals not as irrational or solely constrained by structures, but rather as logical responses, resisting an increasingly unequal welfare system. Bridging a gap between theorizing rationality and the practical decisions made about assets, with their accompanying liabilities, the book acknowledges the variegated, immanent nature of resistance.

For this purpose, the project takes up the conceptual category of resistance, also named counter-conduct, defined within social theory (Foucault, 1978, 2004, 2007) and integrates the concept of variegated forms of everyday financialization (Lai, 2017; Pellandini-Simanyi and Banai, 2021). Variegated subjectivities show how everyday rationalities become intertwined with finance rationality, for instance, emotions and family members influence investment decisions which deviate from the 'ideal financialized subject position' (Pellandini-Simanyi and Banai, 2021, p 787). Whereas norms of asset accumulation and deviations to these are often treated as conceptually different concepts, integrating Foucault's understanding of counter-conduct helps to reveal the mutually constitutive relationship between norms of asset accumulation and resisting these, allowing for differential life trajectories rather than conforming and non-conforming financial behaviour and showcasing how resistance is essential for financialized subjectivities to form, albeit different to what might be theoretically expected. In other words, resistance is not perceived as solely rising up against power but as a fluid concept with various facets including discursive rejection and practical amendments of asset norms.

Throughout the book, I will argue that a mutually constitutive relationship exists between norms of asset accumulation and their being amended, allowing for differential life trajectories rather than conforming and non-conforming financial behaviour. The following two key assumptions will therefore guide the book:

(a) Despite asset-based welfare being presented as leading to prosperity for all, I will argue in this book that it intensifies power relationships embodied in capitalist relationships, working as a disciplining mechanism for labour while creating more profit opportunities for capitalists. Norms of asset accumulation shape and are reshaped by everyday practices, resulting in self-disciplining strategies to achieve asset ownership while also changing social relationships. This mutually generative relationship between norms of conduct and everyday practices enables a welfare system based on individual responsibility.

(b) Asset-based welfare is plagued with imperfections such as the inherent uncertainty of financial investment or constraints inherent in accumulating assets. The resultant diverse forms of resisting asset norms and finding one's own unique approach to providing financial security in the future should not be seen as irrational. Instead, they represent logical responses to an increasingly unequal welfare system. Strikingly, adjusting norms of asset accumulation to one's own needs provides not only a sense of agency but also reinforces an asset-based welfare system based on individual responsibility.

Both aspects are essential in challenging existing policies and building just policies, enabling us to identify coping mechanisms developed within existing constraints, and when acts of resistance risk contributing to the very system they aim to contest. This book thus moves beyond identifying deviations to rational behaviour and reveals everyday financial practices as logical responses to a dysfunctional system. I suggest this should be conceptualized as lived finance rationality, where variegated subjectivities and practices are understood as logical responses to personal contexts, while they also reinforce wealth inequalities. Proposing a typology of everyday financialization and a new way of thinking about rationality, the book seeks to challenge current theoretical discussions and policy approaches.

The methodological approach

To explore everyday financialization in the UK context, three levels of analysis consisting of practice (financial practices and their impact on everyday life), context (institutional changes) and language (media/policy discourses and everyday financial discourses) are included within an embedded mixed methods approach where qualitative research in the form of interviews is the guiding methodology. The integrated analytical approach is considered beneficial here because it helps to establish a link between interviewees' statements and institutional changes.

Semi-structured interviews aid in revealing the motivations and conflicting factors driving asset accumulation. To ensure a diversity of participants, the interview recruitment was based on purposive sampling which is prominent in qualitative, empirical research (Bryman and Bell, 2007). With the goal of exploring asset management by individuals who are 'able to manage at least an awkward performance of the financial subject positions they have been assigned' (Kear, 2013, p 940), medium- to high-income households were recruited. As a result of the employed recruitment strategy (for details on the recruitment strategy and interview profiles please see Appendix A), 58 semi-structured interviews with 63 household members and 57 households were conducted in 2016–2017. Focusing on medium- to high-income households resulted in interviewing household members who were the main income earners and in a relatively seen good income position, and in interviewing lower income household members who were more constrained in their ability to individually contribute to pension investments. Interviews lasted on average between 60 and 90 minutes, were digitally recorded, transcribed verbatim and anonymized. After having been given examples of assets and liabilities, interviewees were asked to fill in a provided balance sheet. A total of 45 interviewees either followed the request of providing an overview of their assets and liabilities or gave the relevant data during the interview. The assets and liabilities from the households were listed as overall assets and liabilities when living with a partner.

The unique approach in this research project lies in that data from a UK household survey is combined with the data provided by interviewees. Through combining UK balance sheet structures with statements and balance sheets of interviewees, the rationalities behind balance sheet compositions can be suggested and a wider perspective in relation to the UK provided. For this purpose, the Wealth and Asset Survey (WAS), which is a survey providing information about households' balance sheets including property, pension and financial wealth as well as debt, is employed to showcase UK household financial behaviour over time and compare interviewees' responses to the wider development in the UK. The survey data underlining the interview data should, however, not be understood as a generalization but more as a helpful mechanism to position participants' self-reported balance sheets and statements within UK household balance sheets.

To elucidate the effects of institutional changes and discourses on everyday practices, a document analysis accompanied the interviews. Document analysis can provide an overview of the wider social context including key events and discourses during the time period under investigation and can expose 'themes, images and metaphors' which help to understand the phenomenon (Hammersley and Atkinson, 2007, p 125). In other words, the relationship between media and policy discourses constructing norms of asset accumulation and individuals' engagement with these norms can be explored. Recognizing the importance of media as an 'informal education apparatus' (Greenfield and Williams, 2007, p 418), this study specifically concentrates on discourses constructed in newspapers and websites. Due to wanting to explore the impact of the existing discourses on households' practices, the focus lay on documents which were mentioned by the majority of interviewees, resulting in three newspapers (*Financial Times* [FT], *The Guardian* [TG] and *The Daily Telegraph* [TDT]) and one website (moneysavingexpert.com). In line with previous media studies, the document selection captures a broad sample of newspapers representing different political viewpoints including liberal, centre-left and centre-right (Berry, 2016; Samec, 2020). Following Sanders and Schroder (2008) and Taylor (2013), snapshots of historical moments which show the 'circumstances of repetition' of a discourse (Foucault, 1972, p 221) and illustrate the main content of the discourse have been chosen for analysis. Relating to peaks and troughs of personal finance mentioned in the media and interviewees' statements, the following time periods were selected: 1984–1987, 1997–2002, 2006–2010 and 2016–2018.[4]

Organization of the book

The structure of the book is divided into four parts. After having been introduced to the concept of everyday financialization and the methodology employed in this book, the second chapter of Part I provides a critical overview of the existing literature strands exploring financial subjects and introduces a theoretical framework which is employed to analyse the empirical data. Chapter 2 therefore sets the scene for the subsequent chapters where the empirical data is discussed in interconnection with previously suggested theoretical viewpoints, highlighting the novel insights the empirical data provides and challenging previous assumptions of rationality. Following the theoretical discussions, the second part of the book first outlines how norms of asset accumulation are constructed (Chapter 3) and then shows how individuals engage with these institutional changes and discourses (Chapter 4). While Chapter 3's objective is to depict how policy changes and media discourses have constructed norms of asset accumulation and show how these changes have reinforced power relationships embodied in capital–labour relationships, Chapter 4 unpacks how interviewees engage with these asset norms.

Building upon the previous two chapters, the third part moves on to show the impact of the adopted norms of asset accumulation on everyday life. Chapter 5 begins with charting the impact of financialization on the asset structure using data from the UK Wealth and Assets Survey and interviewees' balance sheets and underscoring these with interviewees' underlying reasoning for their chosen asset strategy. The particular focus of Chapter 6 then lies on how asset norms impact everyday practices and relationships, uncovering the mutually generative relationship between social relations and asset norms. More specifically, it charts self-governing measures which are adopted by individuals to achieve asset ownership, focusing on four areas within everyday life: saving strategies, consumption practices, work relationships and the intersection between family relations and emotions.

After having seen how asset norms interact with everyday life, the chapters integrated in Part IV take the discussion further and highlight how contradictions and constraints inherent in asset norms result in variegated subjectivities. Chapter 7 discusses how constraints built into an asset-based welfare system impact everyday financial practices. The key empirical insights are then brought together in Chapter 8, which introduces unique variegated financial subjectivities. Bringing in an understanding of resistance being immanent in power technologies, it is shown how these deviations of norms of conduct not only represent ways of dealing with contradictions inherent in asset norms and their constraints but are also necessary for everyday financialization to work. Due to its inherent imperfections, everyday financialization could not take place without amending norms of asset accumulation to one's own rationalities.

The concluding chapter synthesizes the different levels of analysis and highlights its relevance to current literature but also makes policy suggestions. Taken together, the findings presented in the book point to a rethink of the theorization of everyday financialization and what constitutes financially rational behaviour.

Willing and Unwilling Subjects of Everyday Financialization

Since the 1980s, households in English-speaking countries in particular have been increasingly called upon to internalize the subject position of the everyday investor. An everyday investor mitigates potential income shortfalls during non-working periods by way of investing in financial assets and adopting finance rationality, defined as 'techniques of calculations' (Greenfield and Williams, 2007, p 415), which enables them to 'self-fund non-wage work' (Bryan et al, 2009, p 462). That means everyday investors embrace risk in the quest to earn financial returns, are knowledgeable about financial concepts such as diversification and hedging, and build a diverse asset portfolio by means of regular investments throughout their working life (Campbell, 2006; Langley, 2006; Strauss, 2008). Yet, individuals are not behaving as expected, for example, private pension savings in the UK fell steadily up until 2012 (PPI, 2017; DWP, 2018).

To provide depth to explanations of deviating financial practices and how the processes of financialization have impacted the life of the everyday person, this chapter synthesizes key literature within the financialization of daily life, comprising the following fields: (1) behavioural approaches to finance and the accompanying financial literacy research seeking to nudge people to behave as theoretically expected, (2) political economy studies investigating how the increasing importance of finance has changed capitalist relations within society and intensified its inherent inequalities, and (3) interdisciplinary research on the everyday financialization of individuals which examines how the expansion of finance and associated financial motives become enmeshed with everyday rationalities such as emotions and moral understandings. The connections between these strands of discussion are explored, their limitations identified, and potential directions for future research are proposed and then taken up in the empirical sections.

These literature discussions will be presented within key themes of the conceptual framework employed in this book. To elucidate the formation of variegated dimensions of financial subjects, this book makes use of Foucault's work on governmentality (1980, 2004, 2007), which is used extensively in the financialization literature (Langley, 2008; Hardt and Negri, 2009; Sotiropoulos et al, 2013), and merges it with the concept of variegated subjectivities defined within the everyday financialization literature (Lai, 2017; Pellandini-Simanyi and Banai, 2021). In line with Foucault's conceptualization of counter-conduct being immanent in norms of conduct, the concept of variegated subjectivities has countered the uniform theorization of finance rationality and allows for active meaning-making processes. This is taken up here and extended by showing not only these unique approaches to asset accumulation and the resultant variegated financial subjects but also by revealing how these emerge from the interplay between experiencing constraints and the pressure to provide financial security. This project thus seeks to bridge a gap between theorizing rationality and practical decisions made about assets and liabilities, giving insights into how diverse forms of resistance configure varied financial subjects and identifying the implications of constraints on these variegated subjectivities. Both aspects are essential in furthering the critique of finance rationality and suggest an alternative to the classical interpretation of finance rationality, an endeavour towards which this book contributes.

Researching everyday financial practices: the normalizing society

To understand the interaction between asset norms and everyday life, I develop a link to Foucault's concept of governmentality and his discussion on power relations (Foucault, 1978, 2003, 2004). Employing a governmentality approach is helpful here due to the importance ascribed to resistance and enabling the exploration of how individuals engage with asset norms while recognizing the unequal capital–labour relationship immanent in asset-based welfare.

Governmentality emphasizes that power is not exercised in a direct, disciplining way, but by establishing the environment, conditions and discourses leading to individuals conforming to created norms (Foucault, 2008). Inherent in Foucault's elaborations are two key concepts, namely conduct ('how to be governed' [Foucault, 2004, p 127]) and counter-conduct ('how not to be governed like that' [Foucault, 2007, p 44]). The term 'conduct' incorporates the double sense of the French terms 'conduire' and 'se conduire', where the former refers to the 'activity of conducting' and the latter to 'the way in which one conducts oneself' (Foucault, 2004, p 258). Individuals are, in other words, governed and govern themselves based on two mechanisms operating as power technologies – a disciplinary and a regulatory mechanism. Whereas the former seeks to influence individuals' behaviour through laws and restrictions, the latter has 'much more to do with the manner in which the individual needs to form himself' (Foucault, 1978, p 67) based on interests and desires.

The disciplinary technology of power seeks to construct 'docile bodies' which are 'subjected, used, transformed, and improved' (Foucault, 1980, p 136) by introducing rules, restrictions and rewards, hence households are 'subject to someone else by control and dependence' (Foucault, 1982, p 781). This mechanism has an individualizing effect, concentrating on the individual rather than the overall population. It starts from the norm and distinguishes between normal and abnormal – trying to get people to conform to the norm with the help of individual measures such as rules and punishments. Whilst in the case of the 'disciplinary technology of labour' (Foucault, 2003, p 242) this means ensuring workers' productivity, for example, through supervision, in the case of 'the activity of conducting' (Foucault, 2004, p 258) within asset accumulation this means draining labour by putting more costs of social reproduction onto individuals rather than the employer or state (Hardt and Negri, 2009; Fraser, 2017; Stevano et al, 2021). Dismantling the welfare state makes it costlier for individuals not to save for periods of income shortfalls, forcing individuals to accumulate assets or risk poverty.

The regulatory mechanism focuses on collective, or 'massifying', effects (Foucault, 2003, p 243). It operates on the population as a whole,[1] and not the individual. In lieu of directly prescribing behaviour through making some activities costlier than others, the regulatory mechanism is based on interests and desires where subjects choose to adhere to constructed norms. This is not a binary distinction between normal and abnormal: there are different levels of 'normalities' where 'the operation of normalization consists in establishing an interplay between these different distributions of normality and [in] acting to bring the most unfavourable in line with the more favourable' (Foucault, 2004, p 91). In the case of financial behaviour, this would mean creating the norm of accumulating assets and leading to different ways, that is levels of normalities, of achieving asset ownership. Important correlates of the regulatory mechanism are notions of freedom, autonomy and self-actualization, which incentivize people to change their behaviour in line with established norms (Grey, 1997). Power is thus exercised through 'a mode of action which does not act directly on others. Instead, it acts upon their actions' (Foucault, 1982, p 789). Foucault (2007, p 503) calls this concept 'conduct of conduct', where the government shapes individual behaviour by means of discourses of empowerment and freedom of choice.

The disciplinary mechanism with a focus on individualizing effects and the regulatory mechanism with a focus on massifying effects construct an overall norm – for example, the norm of asset ownership. Whereas the disciplinary mechanism influences behaviour directly by risking old-age poverty if not accumulating assets, the regulatory mechanism operates through the transformation of individual behaviour by creating a desire to become asset owners as a means of empowerment. The constructed norms are internalized, thereby leading individuals to adapt their behaviour according to what they have learned is desirable by reflecting on their actions, evaluating them and adjusting them accordingly; that is, they adopt self-governing measures. Put differently, individuals could align their behaviour with the goal of achieving norms of asset accumulation by, for example, restricting consumption in order to conduct investments. This governmental reasoning brings with it an understanding of power not only as repressive ('it doesn't only weigh on us as a force that says no'), but also as productive of subjectivity ('what makes it accepted, is that it ... produces things' [Foucault, 1980, p 119]), where the subject is constructed through being 'tied to his own conscience or self-knowledge' (Foucault, 1982, p 781).

However, this should not be understood as a top-down approach in which practices are transformed without resistance. A will to be governed necessarily entails with it also the opposite, the will not to be governed in that manner, representing the second key concept of Foucault's discussion on power: counter-conduct. Through giving autonomy to subjects to make a choice from a 'field of possibilities' (Foucault, 1982, p 790), norms are not only made admirable but they also implement the opportunity to adjust them. Foucault rejects a binary categorization of domination and resistance ('power is not one side and resistance on the other' [Foucault et al, 2012, p 108]), but instead emphasizes the immanence of resistance in power relationships: 'there are no relations of power without resistances' (Foucault, 1980, p 142). Indeed, relations of power 'depend on a multiplicity of points of resistance: these play the role of adversary, target, support, or handle in power relations' (Foucault, 1978, p 95) and can represent 'ruptures' or 'innovation' (Hardt and Negri, 2009, p 59), for instance investing in silver rather than stocks because of distrusting the financial system. Rather than trying to eradicate power, resistance aims to harness power: where subjects transfigure subject positions that they are called upon to internalize and adjust them to their own needs. To reflect this multiplicity of resistance, Foucault (2007, p 75) employs the term counter-conduct, that is, 'the will not to be governed, thusly, like that', and departs from the narrower meaning of resistance, such as 'breaking all the bonds of obedience' (Foucault, 2004, p 453).

By moving away from the conventional dichotomy between power and resistance, an analysis of governmentality is enabled whereby the mutually constitutive relationship between conduct and counter-conduct can be shown to be productive in creating variegated subjectivities in place of deviant subjectivities and practices, allowing for different ways of achieving norms of behaviour. Here, counter-conduct is an essential part in the formation of subjects through problematizing governmentalities but also reproducing them, thus being a productive power in constructing financialized subjects.

Before returning to this framework within the empirical discussions, I give insights into previous research and how this is integrated in the framework.

'Conduct': the everyday investor

Foucauldian-inspired studies reveal how mechanisms of governance – institutional changes (for example, reduction of state pensions), discourses (for example, policy discourses) and financial products (for example, private pensions) – shape the conduct of the everyday investor (Martin, 2002; Aitken, 2003; French and Kneale, 2009). With the dismantling of the publicly funded welfare state, asset-based welfare measures have been introduced, seeking to turn 'passive pension-savers into active-capitalists' (Davies et al, 2018, p 486). Access to means of asset accumulation has been widened and 'people are being asked to think like capitalists' (Martin, 2002, p 12), appropriating money from their investments to mitigate future risks. This means that they need to make decisions between the percentage of wages going into accumulation and the ratio going into consumption (Bryan et al, 2009). In the transformation of society to one based on norms of self-governance, discourses are employed to induce people to become 'active investor-subjects' (Kear, 2013, p 15). Here, 'language is not simply a medium in which ideas and intentions are communicated' (Jacobs and Manzi, 1996, p 543), but seen as constructing subject positions. Everyone is portrayed as being able to own and grow wealth, and thus escape 'the tyranny of earned income as unpropertied subjects' (Froud et al, 2010, p 5) by means of developing 'a portfolio of financial market assets that, carefully selected by the individual through the calculated engagement with risk, holds out the prospect of pleasure through returns' (Langley, 2006, p 923).

This understanding of everyday investors entails two components. On the one hand, everyday investors actively plan the use of money over their lifetime and accumulate financial assets for retirement (Langley, 2008). Here, it is posited that everyday investors are rational agents with optimal expectations with regard to their lifetime income and wealth (Modigliani and Brumberg, 1954; Friedman, 1957). Due to anticipating an income drop at retirement, everyday investors plan how much wealth should be accumulated to offset this drop, resulting in sacrificing current consumption for future consumption and in assets accumulated for retirement being proportional to income and wealth earned during the working life. Consequently, they do not solely rely on 'passive forms of financial practices' (Lai, 2016b, p 38) such as savings products with a guaranteed return but include higher risk products such as bonds, stocks and investment portfolios (Guiso et al, 2002; Coppock, 2013). On the other hand, everyday investors adopt sophisticated financial strategies and 'embrace, and bear risk as opportunity' (Langley, 2006, p 919). A key aspect of financially rational behaviour is diversification, where individuals are expected to develop a diversified asset portfolio, taking into consideration current and future risk–return relationships, interest rates, tax and inflationary impacts (Campbell, 2006; Mitchell and Lusardi, 2012). According to this line of reasoning, everyday investors are confident and knowledgeable investors and emotions are perceived as disturbances to rational decision-making (Murdoch, 2017; Pellandini-Simanyi and Banai, 2021). Employing a competitive stance in dealing with personal financial decisions and aspiring financial growth drives this subject (Weiss, 2015; Samec, 2018). While accumulating financial assets highlights the will of the everyday investor to provide financial security, adopting finance rationality reveals that this is someone who enjoys investing.

Whereas the Foucauldian-inspired literature undoubtedly makes a substantial contribution by revealing technologies of power at play and giving valuable insights into how households are induced to deal with financial matters such as financial services (French and Kneale, 2009) or pensions (Langley, 2006), the majority of these studies focus on one aspect of asset ownership, rather than taking into consideration asset ownership in general, and implicitly assume an 'inescapability of finance' (Hall, 2012, p 405). The work of Langley (2006, 2008) provides here an additional window into governance mechanisms by acknowledging contradictions inherent in the investor subject. Rising insecurity in the workplace is argued to militate against the ability to contribute to pensions on a continuous basis. The increasing precariousness of work in the form of uncertain work contracts and pay undermines the ability of people to make regular pension provisions over a long time period. Even if individuals invest in financial assets as expected, these investments remain uncertain. This inherent uncertainty in financial market investments where 'freedom and security in retirement is simply determined by luck and timing' (Langley, 2007, p 81) undercuts labour's ability to perform the role of the investor subject. As a consequence, individuals are argued to be 'pushing at the frontiers of investment' (Langley, 2006, p 932) by mainly investing in property or retreating to savings, thus rejecting the subject position of the everyday investor.

Though this Foucauldian-inspired literature acknowledges contradictions incorporated in the construction of investor identities, conduct and resistance are treated as conceptually different categories, with the everyday investor on the 'savings side' and the property investor on the 'borrowing side' where the question remains what 'the place of the residential property investor [is] in neoliberal society' (Langley, 2008, pp 199–205). Yet, if one follows the Foucauldian logic of the immanence of resistance, not only seeking to subvert norms of conduct but also being productive of conduct, it is not sufficient to shed light on power mechanisms and resistance without exploring how the interplay between conduct and counter-conduct constructs a multiplicity of subjectivities. Research so far has also not adequately accounted for the impact of asset norms on worker identity. For instance, we have little empirical knowledge of how being self-employed, working part-time or experiencing a patchy work history shapes variegated financial subjectivities. These gaps are due, in part, to the fact that studies of subjectification within asset accumulation rely to a large extent on an analysis of policy or media documents (Martin, 2002; Maman and Rosenhek, 2019) rather than primary data – despite recognizing that subject positions are manifested in 'reflective, intentional and aspirational practices' (Langley, 2007, p 73).

'Activity of conducting': the financially capable investor

Contrary to the theoretical assumptions built into the norm of the everyday investor outlined in the previous section, evidence shows that people tend to not only underinvest but also underdiversify (Guiso et al, 2002; Erturk et al, 2007), which has intensified the 'activity of conducting' (Foucault, 2004, p 258) within policy measures.

One argument put forward to explain discrepancies between theory and actual behaviour is the concept of bounded rationality, which suggests that individuals are limited in processing information and are therefore unable to collect and process all the necessary information to make financially rational decisions (Becchio, 2019; Elliehausen, 2019). Behavioural economics has integrated this concept and put forward the notion that because people experience cognitive limitations, they employ heuristics and intuitions based on past experiences when making decisions (Strauss, 2008; Altman, 2012). As a consequence, retirement decisions are shaped by issues of 'self-control, procrastination (which produces inertia), and nominal loss aversion' (Thaler and Benartzi, 2004, p S170). People, for instance, are considered to be biased as they prioritize current standard of living and needs over long-term savings (Thaler and Sunstein, 2021), 'make irrational decisions about joining (or not joining) company plans' and 'overestimate the income their pension will provide in retirement, not understanding the tax implications of their savings behaviour, and failing to plan' (Strauss, 2008, p 146). These shortcuts are cast as 'error of judgement' (Kahneman and Tversky, 1982, p 493), resulting in strategies to nudge individuals to act according to economic theory, for instance by being automatically enrolled in a workplace pension scheme (Thaler and Shefrin, 1981; Thaler and Sunstein, 2021).

Similarly, the field of financial literacy has sought to educate people on the best way to collect and assess information and 'to better control their emotive side ... since emotion and intuition are regarded as key culprits in driving irrational decision-making' (Altman, 2012, p 682). Financial education scholars argue that 'the failure to plan for retirement' and 'lack of participation in the stock market ... can all be linked to ignorance of basic financial concepts' (Lusardi, 2015, p 260) and thus advocates conscious rather than intuitive decisions, seeking to bring behaviour closer to the ideal of finance rationality. Financial literacy is measured by a person's understanding of inflation, compound interest rates and risk–return relationships on future investment values, including knowledge of key financial concepts such as diversification and how workplace pensions provide higher and tax-efficient income during retirement in contrast to other savings or investment products (Mitchell and Lusardi, 2012). More recently, these insights have been extended by financial capability campaigns arguing that even if people receive financial education and have access to financial products, they also need to have the 'behavioural disposition' (Prabhakar, 2021, p 27) and confidence to make responsible financial decisions (Bucher-Koenen et al, 2016).

These initiatives have detected differences between groups where women and people from minority ethnic groups have displayed a lower level of financial literacy, are argued to be less financially confident and less inclined to conduct long-term planning (Lusardi et al, 2010, 2015; Hasler and Lusardi, 2017; Nam et al, 2019). Research has found, for instance, that women spend less time thinking about retirement than men and are more risk averse and pessimistic than men (Lusardi and Mitchell, 2008; Neelakantan, 2010; Jacobsen et al, 2014), all factors detrimental for accumulating assets for retirement. Similarly, it has been put forward that 'race and ethnicity was another predictor of financial literacy' (Lusardi et al, 2010, p 370), with people from minority ethnic backgrounds having a lower knowledge of key financial factors, depicting lower levels of savings and choosing less beneficial investments (Boshara et al, 2015). Much research in this vein has failed to interrogate the reasons for these differences and advocated for individual solutions such as increasing engagement with financial products by means of 'more targeted and effective financial education' (Clark et al, 2021, p 5). Moving beyond a 'one-size-fits-all' approach is argued to address the financial fragility of 'women, minorities, such as Blacks and Hispanics' (Lusardi, 2010, p 377), implicitly blaming individuals for 'deficient knowledge' (Hamilton and Darity Jr, 2017, p 59).

Economic geography studies have criticized these policy suggestions for ignoring context. Being in a junior position, in a lower paid job, being younger and a single woman are portrayed as factors which coincide with a lower risk tolerance and distrust of managed products, culminating in a tendency to discount the future and using property in a non-strategic manner (Clark, 2010, 2014). This work posits the financial literacy agenda as impossible due to spatial and context-specific dimensions of financial literacy, highlighting the need to develop financial education programmes which recognize socio-economic specificities (Clark, 2014; Prabhakar, 2021). Yet, akin to recent suggestions within financial literacy research, instead of questioning the ability of asset-based measures to deliver financial welfare and its underlying assumption of rationality, measures are suggested which attempt to bring 'the most unfavourable in line with the more favourable' (Foucault, 2004, p 91), thus normalizing asset norms and depicting deviating behaviour as simply flawed. Norms of asset accumulation are engineered as desirable and achievable for everyone, if only one accepts personal responsibility and adjusts financial practices in line with one's own circumstances.

There is, however, little evidence to suggest that a high degree of financial sophistication and access to financial products will be enough to overcome the inequality inherent in asset-based welfare. Having access to financial products and better knowledge of financial concepts will not overcome the unequal starting point due to income limitations or smoothen systemic limitations within an asset-based welfare system. In the context of fundamental uncertainty (such as those involving long-term financial investments like pensions), where it is not possible to identify possible future outcomes, even financially capable individuals cannot predict the future (Altman, 2012; Storper, 2014). Perhaps most importantly, the focus on changing behaviours to fit the expectations of the financial system distracts from the inherent unequal nature of asset-based welfare and closes down the possibility to meaningfully challenge it.

'Counter-conduct': unwilling subjects?

Critical studies exploring the impact of financial education have shown that these financial inclusion interventions, even if furthering equal access, obscure the political nature of the capitalist welfare state, which has enabled the dismantling of the welfare system, established profit opportunities for financial institutions (Allon, 2014; Belfrage and Kallifatides, 2018; Huber et al, 2020) and reproduced labour market inequalities based on class, gender and race (Strauss, 2014; Loomis, 2018; Karagaac, 2020).

Rather than property investments being a deviation from the everyday investor subject, it is seen here as 'functionally useful' (Lysandrou, 2016, p 450) for the capitalist welfare system. On the one hand, in the process of financialization the house has been assigned a welfare function, becoming a site of accumulation that can be used for an 'individualized life course risk management' (Bryan and Rafferty, 2014, p 404), culminating in debt-financed homeownership. This enables capitalists to realize financial profits out of households' income streams based on earned interest and securitization which allows financial institutions to move high-risk debt off their balance sheets and realize future income streams early (Schwartz, 2012). As a result, new ways of including households in the financialization process by offering credit have been sought (Keasey and Veronesi, 2012). On the other hand, the concomitant rising indebtedness ties labour to capital not only in the present but also in the future, by having to generate income to service debt

(Karacimen, 2015). Specifically, debt-financed homeownership puts pressure on households as they are susceptible to swings in financial markets and house price changes. A drop in house values accompanied by an increase in interest rates can lead to negative equity. Because households want to maintain their lifestyles, they are committed to comply with debt service obligations. This can result in avoiding strike action which would mean a loss in wages (Bonefeld and Holloway, 1996), more work hours and acceptance of precarious work (Bryan et al, 2009; Karacimen, 2015).

Whereas this first literature strand takes into consideration homeownership, the main focus lies on relative indebtedness rather than on assets per se. Assets, however, represent a significant aspect of financialization of which income and wealth inequality have been a defining feature (Huber et al, 2020), as shown in a persistent gender and ethnicity income and wealth gap in financialized countries (Vlachantoni et al, 2014; Szymborska, 2019). A second strand of literature has therefore shown how individuals are in a disadvantageous position, having to carry more responsibilities without being equipped to do so (Lebaron, 2010; Loomis, 2018), being constrained rather than unwilling in adopting asset norms. Women often cannot contribute in the same way to workplace pensions and investments as men due to caring duties (Strauss, 2014; Grady, 2015) and unequal starting points caused by intergenerational wealth inequalities and discriminatory employment practices often limit asset accumulation for people from a minority ethnic background (Hamilton and Darity Jr, 2017; Finley, 2021).

As social reproduction has been increasingly privatized and individualized in 'financialized capitalism' (Fraser, 2017, p 34), it is predominantly women that have been absorbing the rise in non-state-funded caring duties (Ghodsee, 2019), as demonstrated once again during the COVID-19 pandemic (Stevano et al, 2021; Mezzadri et al, 2022). This burden goes unrecognized in a pension system built around a stereotypical life trajectory of a man. While women experience breaks in employment and often work in part-time or low-income employment due to socially reproductive activities (Anxo et al, 2006; Loretto and Vickerstaff, 2013; Grady, 2015), financialized pension systems assume that members have a full-time job, earn a decent income and can make continuous pension contributions throughout their working life, disadvantaging anyone whose experience diverges from this. Having less time available for work not only affects access and participation in pension savings but also impacts wealth accumulation through a lower income potential, as also reflected in the persistent gender pay gap (Frericks et al, 2009; Steiber and Haas, 2012).

In addition to having benefitted from putting the burden of social reproductive activities from the governing onto the governed, financialized capitalism has profited from 'systemic racism and structural discrimination in labour and credit markets' (Szymborska, 2022, p 25), disadvantaging people belonging to minoritized ethnic groups within the frame of asset accumulation (Folbre, 2020). Financial inclusion initiatives depict lower average wealth holdings among Blacks in the US as a consequence of behavioural deficiencies on their part, without the acknowledgement of the role of race-based employment and income discrimination in constraining asset accumulation in Black communities (Blau and Graham, 1990). Racialized hierarchies within the labour market have led to lower wages, less job protection for minoritized ethnic groups and the likelihood of being under-employed, increasing profits for capitalists while reducing the income base for asset accumulation, thus resulting in lower wealth holdings throughout generations (Darity, 2005; Flynn et al, 2017).

Financial inclusion interventions do not tackle these unequal relationships within a capitalist welfare system, yet they serve to create new income sources for financial institutions. Calls for active engagement with pensions does little to tackle the structural disadvantage for women (Strauss, 2014; Grady, 2015) and employing smart financial practices cannot resolve the unequal starting points caused by intergenerational wealth inequalities and discriminatory employment practices (Finley, 2021). Instead, policy measures seek to ensure that constrained individuals continue to meet financial commitments without having to rely on the welfare state. Perhaps even worse, they reinforce stereotypes about financial behaviour. Women and minority ethnic groups are constructed as inherently risk averse and worse at dealing with financial concerns (Halko et al, 2012; Hamilton and Darity Jr, 2017), ignoring the potential impact of internalized stereotypes on financial behaviour (Booth and Nolen, 2012; Eswaran, 2014; Kim, 2020). Due to the importance ascribed to capitalist relations within everyday financialization, capitalist relationships will be included in the introduced conceptual framework, depicting an extension to Hardt and Negri's (2009) and Sotiropoulos et al's (2013) elaborations on governmentality and capitalist relations.

'Self-conduct': variegated dimensions of financial subjectivity

Even though the studies introduced earlier draw attention to structural inequalities in the capitalist welfare state, less is known about how people who face these constraints engage with them, reflecting a 'tendency to portray individuals devoid of bodies' (Karagaac, 2020, p 8). For the purpose of 'afford[ing] subjects a greater degree of agency to determine their own identity' (Coppock, 2013, p 496), a recently growing strand within the everyday financialization literature addresses the differentials in engagement with finance from a different angle, unveiling the other sense of conduct apart from the 'activity of conducting' (Foucault, 2004, p 258), namely mechanisms of self-conduct. Conceptually, researchers in this field delineate everyday financial practices and discourses into dimensions of the 'ideal financialized subject' (Pellandini-Simanyi and Banai, 2021, p 787) which is defined here as having internalized the everyday investor subject position and having adopted 'a morally permissive approach to debt' (Pellandini-Simanyi and Banai, 2021, p 786). Employing predominantly qualitative research, these studies have shown that subjects do not only succumb to or reject categories offered to them but 'conform, diverge or subvert top-down neoliberal forms of financial subjectification' (Coppock, 2013, p 481).

Whereas research into debt behaviour has concentrated on the first meaning of resistance, namely subversion, and unveiled how inequalities inherent in a capitalist society have culminated in the overt contestation in the form of non-payment, alternative borrowing networks or blocking evictions (Di Feliciantonio, 2016; Montgomerie and Tepe-Belfrage, 2019), studies exploring asset management have focused on the second meaning, namely divergence, without focus on capitalist inequalities. Integrating one's own rationalities in the form of emotions, moralities and temporalities is argued to lead to selectively draw on one of the two components of the investor subject – namely accumulating financial assets or finance rationality (also coined as behaviour versus subjectivity within this literature strand) – but not resisting the investor subjectivity wholeheartedly (Pellandini-Simanyi et al, 2015; Guermond, 2022). Individuals reject investing in financial assets but perform pervasive calculations when conducting alternative investments (Lai, 2017) or they accumulate financial assets but have not internalized finance rationality (Pellandini-Simanyi and Banai, 2021). People, for instance, might not invest with the intention of financial gain but for social motivations such as to deepen personal relationships or invest in financial products which support their religious beliefs (Pollard et al, 2016; Bandelj et al, 2017).

What these insights into 'variegated outcomes of financialization' (Lai, 2017, p 915) highlight is that contrary to viewing resistance as solely opposing, it is a rather fluid concept with various facets. Despite not investing in the advised financial products, individuals should not be categorized as 'passive savers or non-investors' (Lai, 2017, pp 927–8), as these individuals often perform more complicated and pervasive calculations when investing in alternative investments. And while emotions and relational meanings are seen within behavioural economic approaches as a disturbance to the investor subject driving 'economically irrational decisions' (Bandelj et al, 2017, p 43), within everyday financialization literature they are understood as an element of variegated financial subjectivity where intimacies such as relationships and emotions can form part of assuming personal financial security (Lai, 2017; Hall, 2019).

Strikingly, despite acknowledging that individuals engage with aspects of the investor subject to a differing degree (Pellandini-Simanyi and Banai, 2021) and should not be categorized as 'risk-averse or passive' (Lai, 2017, p 927) when not accumulating financial assets and choosing instead to invest in properties, a consequent conceptual development of differential subjectivities and practices into varied financial subjects is missing. One underlying reasoning might be that qualitative studies, similar to Foucauldian studies focusing on secondary data, have tended to focus on debt practices (Penaloza and Barnhart, 2011; Di Feliciantonio, 2016) or one aspect of asset ownership, such as homeownership (Pellandini-Simanyi et al, 2015; Samec, 2018) or non-professional trading (Ailon, 2019; Roscoe, 2015), without integrating a broader set of investment decisions. Much less is known about people's interaction with asset norms in general and its impact on everyday life. Research within this vein has also not sufficiently recognized the impact of socio-demographic factors on one's capacity to either contest, subvert or perform the investor subject. Whilst studies exploring everyday debt behaviour have integrated the underlying inequalities inherent in a capitalist society, everyday financialization studies concentrating on asset accumulation have not explored how constraints, meaning structural barriers and inequalities in the social, economic and institutional landscape, might be part of this meaning-making process, shaping practices that build into 'variegated financialized subjects' (Pellandini-Simanyi and Banai, 2021, p 796).

Building upon the work on everyday financialization and extending this with insights into counter-conduct, the book thus attempts to develop a wider project by not only revealing pathways of resistance but also exploring subjectivities based on a holistic view of asset management and its impact on everyday life. Employing the concept of counter-conduct means to look within norms of asset accumulation and its inherent contradictions and identify how diverse forms of resistance are intertwined with the power relationships they aim to challenge. Such an analysis unveils coping strategies being at play and recognizes that counter-conduct is necessary to the process of everyday financialization. The book thus moves beyond identifying subjectivities deviating from an 'ideal financialized subject position' (Pellandini-Simanyi and Banai, 2021, p 787) where some aspects are rejected while others are drawn upon and sheds light on the 'multiple subject positions' (Coppock, 2013, p 480) within the realms of everyday financialization. Unveiling the complex interplay between conduct and counter-conduct helps to understand the persistence of variegated instead of uniform subjects and highlights limitations of current policy solutions.

Concluding remarks

This chapter has set out to synthesize the literature on everyday discourses and practices with regards to asset accumulation within the theoretical framework introduced. Inquiries into conduct have been particularly influenced by a Foucauldian governmentality framework, revealing not only how mechanisms of governance construct the subject of the everyday investor but also how contradictions inherent in the investor subject have led to individuals 'pushing back the frontiers of what it means to be an investor' (Langley, 2007, p 81) by investing in property or simply saving. In response, behavioural economic and financial literacy campaigns have sought to nudge people to the correct course of behaviour, thus intensifying the activity of conducting. Strikingly, these initiatives ignore how constraints immanent in asset-based welfare culminate in counter-conduct. Ignoring constraints is not surprising when recognizing the power relationships inherent in asset-based welfare. More critical studies have argued that financial inclusion initiatives work as a disciplining rather than empowering mechanism, solving the tension between 'capital's need for workers compelled to commodify their labour' (Strauss, 2014, p 524) and labour needing to reproduce itself by individualizing risk. Putting responsibility on the individual without recognizing constraints puts more pressure on labour while creating new profit opportunities. Drawing 'more and more households into disciplinary and exploitative financial relations' (Roberts and Zulfiqar, 2019, p 589), the capitalist welfare state reproduces and intensifies 'manifold forms' (Folbre, 2020, p 451) of exploitation based on class, gender and race.

Both explanations for deviating behaviour construct individuals who face constraints as passive in asset management, and either being depicted as flawed in their decision-making, which needs to be rectified, or simply constrained by the unequal system they are faced with. In contrast, a recently growing strand within the everyday financialization literature has raised awareness of the contingency in financial subject formation and has revealed the ways in which individuals are transformed through governance mechanisms while integrating their own rationalities. Yet, despite calling 'for variegated subjectivities rather than just financialised or non-financialised subjects' (Lai, 2017, p 914), these studies stop short of a resultant development into variegated financial subjects and have not explored how constraints, meaning structural barriers and inequalities within capitalist welfare, might be part of this meaning-making process.

This book thus seeks to address the interconnectedness between asset norms and power relations, extending recent elaborations on governmentality and capitalist relations. Approaching the study from a Foucauldian understanding of resistance being immanent in power relationships enables a conceptualization of these variegated subjectivities and practices not only as deviating from a theorized investor subject but also as essential for everyday financialization. The study conducted here thus supplies empirical insights into the differential nature of financial subject formation by revealing the complex relationship between norms of conduct and counter-conduct within capitalist relations. Moreover, establishing a dialogue between literature on everyday financial practices and critical studies on constraints allows us to identify the implications of constraints on variegated financial subjects, ultimately contributing to the critique of finance rationality.

PART II

Construction of the Everyday Asset Manager

3

Normalizing Asset Accumulation

After having seen in the previous chapter how processes of financialization are portrayed within the literature, the following discussions will look at how dynamics of everyday financialization play out in the UK. Following from the conceptual framework introduced in Chapter 2, the normalization of asset accumulation takes place by constructing an environment which induces everyone to accumulate assets and by creating discourses surrounding asset ownership.

Since the 1980s, a 'regime of truth' (Foucault, 1980, p 131)[1] has been established in which it is seen as normal that households save, own a house and conduct financial investments, and thus build an asset stock – 'diversified across a range of different asset classes (e.g. equities, bonds, property)' (DWP, 2011, p 17) – on which they can draw upon during periods of income shortfalls. As the UK was argued to be a 'capitalist country with too few capitalists' (Davies et al, 2018, p 486), the stated aim was to create a society with more capitalists – that is, 'more successful entrepreneurs' (LM, 1997). In line with this argument, social protection is presented as contradicting a free and prosperous society, being only possible to fully realize in an authoritarian regime: 'Our capitalist system produces a far higher standard of prosperity and happiness because it believes in incentive and opportunity, and because it is founded on human dignity and freedom ... No country can flourish if its economic and social life is dominated by nationalisation and state control' (Thatcher, 1975). Thus, assuming that a successful society is based on 'profits and the wider distribution of property' (Thatcher, 1984a), deregulation and privatization have consequently been promoted.

However, this regime of truth 'isn't outside power, or lacking in power' (Foucault, 1980, p 131), but rather enables the government to dismantle the welfare state. A discourse centred on entrepreneurial freedom puts the responsibility on the individual (Cutler and Waine, 2001) and has led to, as suggested in Chapter 1, systematic attempts to reverse previously introduced social policies. By emphasizing that there is 'no such thing as public money – there is only taxpayers' money' (Thatcher, 1983), and thus focusing on 'sound public finances' (May, 2017), publicly funded welfare measures in the form of unemployment benefits, sick pay and state-funded pensions have been continuously reduced (disciplinary mechanism) and 'replaced by risk represented as opportunity or reward for individuals' (regulatory mechanism) (Langley, 2006, p 921). Finance is established as a solution to deal with the increasing responsibilities arising from the disciplinary mechanism, culminating in financial concerns entering everyday life while increasing profit opportunities for companies. These policy changes with regard to responsibilization (disciplinary mechanism) and financialization (regulatory mechanism) are introduced in this chapter.

The responsibilization of UK households

The responsibilization of UK households has taken place by means of decreasing welfare support and weakening labour laws. Based on the belief that only households who have been working hard deserve access to welfare, policy changes were introduced which placed the burden of social reproduction onto households (Hardt and Negri, 2009; Fraser, 2017). At the same time, a deregulation of the labour market took place, seeking to incentivize businesses to hire more workers, but which instead has created rising job insecurity while reducing the costs for the employer.

Growing money insecurity

In the 1980s, a discourse of individual responsibility emerged, suppressing the belief in collective responsibility as it was perceived that people had exploited the benevolence of the welfare state. This is exemplified in a quote from Margaret Thatcher:

> [T]here are some people who have been manipulating the system and so some of those help and benefits that were meant to say to people: 'All right, if you cannot get a job, you shall have a basic standard of living!' but when people come and say: 'But what is the point of working? I can get as much on the dole!' You say: 'Look! It is not from the dole. It is your neighbour who is supplying it and if you can earn your own living then really you have a duty to do it'. (Thatcher, 1987a)

A similar discourse can be seen in today's discussion where it is argued that it is essential to have a 'welfare system that rewards work, that supports people who do the right thing' (Watts, 2013). Rather than questioning potential problems in the overall economy, a dichotomy between the responsible, self-reliant hard worker who deserves welfare provision and the undeserving welfare recipient misusing funds is constructed. This discourse of hard work and responsibility is then used to justify a dismantling of the welfare state and creating 'incentives' for households not to rely on the state but seek 'financial independence' (LM, 1997).

Such incentives include workfare – also called 'welfare-to-work' – which attaches welfare payments to obligations (White and Lakey, 1992, pp 195–6), including, for instance, having to provide proof that one is actively looking for a job (Jessop, 2003, p 11). With the Jobseeker's Act 1995, the terminology of being unemployed also changed, with the adoption of the active word 'jobseekers', reflecting the evolving perception of unemployed persons being responsible for finding a new job. If jobseekers did not follow the terms set out in a signed 'jobseeker's agreement', the benefits were reduced (The National Archives, 1995). When the New Labour government took over, this policy strategy was intensified by focusing on 'self-improvement' and the effort to be made by people themselves ('reforming welfare so that government helps people to help themselves' [Blair, 1997]). Policies were implemented aiming at bringing the unemployed back into the labour market, even in lower paid, part-time or temporary jobs (Jessop, 2003). That meant that unemployed persons could no longer decline an offered job, even when it would devalue their resume. These measures of workfare have been accompanied by a continuous reduction of benefit payments, which has led to the UK's unemployment benefit being ranked as one of the lowest of the OECD countries. Only when housing benefits are taken into consideration does its ranking improve, moving up one place (CIPD, 2015; OECD, 2015).

In addition to workfare, education funding, sick pay, maternity leave as well as pay, and state-funded pensions were continuously reduced. For example, whereas between 1962 and 1998 there were no tuition fees and maintenance grants were offered for higher education, tuition fees of £1,000 were introduced in 1998 and continuously increased to £9,250 in England in 2017 (Dearden et al, 2011). This has led to rising student debt levels with 1.5 million students holding around £20 billion in student debt (Parliament, 2022).

In the case of income provision during health issues, the main responsibility falls onto individual companies now, it having been argued that this will incentivize employers to reduce absences. Whereas up until the 1990s the risk of sick pay was carried on a collective basis where employers were fully refunded any sick pay they had to finance, the refunds were first reduced before being abolished completely. To counterbalance the increase of employers' responsibility for sick pay, employers' national insurance contributions and the amount of sick pay workers are entitled to were reduced (Harrop, 2021). As a result of these changes, employers are only required to provide six months of statutory sick pay based on a flat-rate (as of 2022, £109.40 per week) rather than it being income-related as in other

European countries (GOV.UK, 2022). This can, however, be topped up by company-linked sick pay if it is offered (European Commission, 2018). Employees who have already had 28 weeks of company-related sick pay cannot claim it again and have to ask for sickness benefits. These benefits are one of the lowest among OECD countries, namely 13 per cent of average earnings for six months compared to the majority of countries providing above 50 per cent for 12 months (Gaffney, 2015). This results in employees working in companies without an additional sick pay scheme or without private insurance being in a disadvantageous position in case of sickness, as the statutory sick pay is not sufficient to sustain oneself.

A similar picture can be seen with regards to maternity pay and leave. The UK has the second lowest maternity pay and the second highest childcare costs among OECD countries (35.7 per cent of average earnings for a two-wage earning couple with two children compared to 14.5 per cent OECD average [Chzhen et al, 2019; Fleming, 2019]). While statutory maternity pay is paid for up to 39 weeks, only the first 6 weeks are covered by a rate of 90 per cent of average weekly earnings, which reduces to a maximum of £156.66 for the remaining time unless the company has a separate support system in place. At the same time, childcare costs for children under two years old have increased by 44 per cent since 2010, which leaves mothers with a low maternity pay while being faced with rising childcare costs, often resulting in women having to take a break from work for the time period before government support of 30 hours of free childcare is offered when a child is three years old and both parents are working (GOV.UK, 2023b; TUC, 2022).

Finally, the state pension has been continuously reduced, eventually resulting in the UK state pension being among the lowest within developed countries (OECD, 2021a). The basic state pension provides a weekly provision if an individual is above the state pension age and has made sufficient national insurance contributions. A regular adjustment of the state pension was introduced in 1973 and was based on average earnings until 1980 when Thatcher's government adjusted it to thereafter adapt solely to price changes. This led to a decoupling from pension and wage development, culminating in the state pension only representing 15 per cent of average earnings by the mid-2000s (Rutherford, 2013). Because of the falling pension values, the government introduced a return to indexing pensions to wages in 2007 and then introduced a triple lock in 2011. Whilst the majority of OECD countries protect pensions from falling relative to wages and have introduced a basic level of indexation, the UK now increases the pension based on the largest rise in three components: average earnings growth, inflation and a minimum increase of 2.5 per cent (Bozio et al, 2010). Moreover, the UK is one of the few countries of the OECD which does not have a mandatory retirement age (OECD, 2017).

In addition to the basic state pension, individuals who made national insurance contributions through work were able to top up the basic state pension with an additional pension in the form of the State Earnings Related Pension Scheme (SERPS) between 1978 and 2002. After 2002, this was replaced by the state second pension (S2P) which was introduced to help people who cannot work due to disability, or who are caring for someone else or who earn a low income set up a pension (Disney, 2016). However, with the introduction of the second state pension, the government also removed the earnings-related component and moved towards an investment related one. In other words, rather than having a guaranteed pension income based on earnings, the second state pension was then based on investment performance, increasing the risk for the individual. In 2016, additional state pensions were abolished and a single basic state pension was introduced, comprising £203.85 per week based on 35 years national insurance contributions through full-time work (HMRC, 2023). Whilst prior to the new state pension it was possible for women to receive a state pension of up to 60 per cent, based on the national insurance contributions of their husband, this was abolished in 2016, the argument being that it would make women more independent of their partner. Instead, it has left women with caring duties more vulnerable due to a restricted recognition of maternity leave and often having to take a break from work or working part-time (DWP, 2021). Moreover, the piecemeal legislative changes introduced in the UK over time have resulted in one of the most complex pension systems (Ginn et al, 2001; Curry, 2021).

Rising job insecurity

In synergy with draining labour by putting more costs of reproduction onto households rather than onto the welfare state, the disciplinary technology of labour puts pressure on households to accumulate assets by increasing job insecurity. Since the 1980s, the labour market has been continuously deregulated and emphasis has been placed on 'flexible employment laws' and making 'it easier for companies to hire and manage staff' which 'should encourage employers to create new jobs' (DfBIS, 2013).

A first step in the deregulation of the labour market was weakening the power of the 'enemy within', identified as trade unions, who 'are out there to destroy any properly elected government' (Thatcher, 1984b). Several changes to strike laws were implemented which are still relevant today. Whereas in the past it was possible to support strike actions by other companies, call a strike at short notice and support political strikes, strike action can now only take place if the employer is informed in advance and a secret strike ballot is carried out prior to the strike and approved by a majority of union members. Equally important, regulations promoting non-unionist behaviour were established, where individuals are allowed to keep working during a strike without being disciplined and are able to apply in court to restrain strike actions (HoC, 2017). This new stance towards unions has been taken over by successive governments since then, independent of party affiliation. Whereas in the past, Labour had drawn attention to work inequalities, Labour since Blair's government has adopted a pragmatic approach with a commitment to businesses and putting the 'relations with the trade unions on a modern footing where they accept they can get fairness but no favours from a Labour government' (LM, 1997). Further strike restrictions were introduced in 2016 setting up a 50 per cent turnout requirement for votes on strikes to be valid and two weeks' notice for the employer (HoC, 2016), and as a reaction to the wave of strikes taking place in 2023 in response to real wage decline and the rise in living costs, the government has introduced a law requiring a minimum service provision when employees from sectors considered essential go on strike (Hollingrake and Merriman, 2023). As a result of these policies, union membership decreased from 70 per cent in 1979 to 22.3 per cent in 2022 (OECD, 2018; Newson, 2023), the lowest percentage since records began, and reducing the means to request an improvement of work conditions.

The weakening of the trade unions was accompanied by labour market deregulation, aimed at increasing the flexibility of the labour market and reducing wage costs. This entailed reduced rights for workers, for example, having to be employed for a longer time period before being able to make a claim when being fired under unfair conditions (a rise from six months to two years). In addition to that, wage councils which had set minimum wages, holiday pay and wage premiums on specific shifts in industries with low wages such as the retail sector were abolished (HoC, 1995; Gregory, 1998). This was done in the belief that minimum wages destroyed jobs ('job destroying notion of a national minimum wage'), and exemplified the prioritization of businesses ('lift regulatory burdens from the shoulders of those who create jobs' [Thatcher, 1985]). The New Labour government then promised to keep promoting 'a flexible labour market' where 'flexibility alone is not enough' but 'flexibility plus' is needed (LM, 1997). Even after having incorporated the EU directive on working conditions into British law, only its minimum requirements were implemented, for instance, the maximum average working week was limited to 48 hours (HoC, 1998). However, this is not a strict regulation since workers can decide to opt out, which has led to this option being commonly used to weaken the rights of the worker (Barnard et al, 2003). Consequently, the structure of the labour market changed, where, as noted by *The Guardian* in 1997, 'jobs are no longer for life, nowadays they last until Christmas' (Read, 1997). Recent governments have followed a similar strategy of making 'it easier for companies to hire and manage staff' which 'should encourage employers to create new jobs' (Swinson, 2013). With the newly passed Retained EU Law (Revocation and Reform) Act 2023, which gives ministers the power to remove or replace existing EU laws, the likelihood of the labour market being further deregulated is high, with working hours, part-time work and fixed-term contracts most likely being affected (Parker, 2023).

Accompanying the weakening of the trade unions and the deregulation of the labour market was the promotion of self-employment. Self-employment has been portrayed as providing the possibility of becoming a 'wealth creator' who 'leaves the security of employment' and contributes to economic growth, since 'self-employment is the seed corn of the new enterprises' and creates 'jobs of the future' (Thatcher, 1981, 1987b). The subsequent New Labour government further progressed this focus on an entrepreneurial society and wanted to create a 'knowledge-driven economy' to establish 'prosperity for all' based on stimulating 'enterprise' (Blair, 2000). To support businesses, the government introduced flexible business taxes, widening the number of tax-free business, and reduced higher income earners' tax from 83 per cent to 40 per cent. In contrast, the marginal tax rate was only cut from 33 per cent to initially 30 per cent during the Thatcher years and then to 20 per cent. With the argument that when businesses and wealthier people have more income left, this extra money is reinvested, Margaret Thatcher maintained: 'We were told that it would help if people who have a very considerable income were able to use a part of that income and knock it off their assessment for tax if they invested that income in a new business' (Thatcher, 1981).

Indeed, self-employment nearly doubled from 8 per cent in 1975 to 15.3 per cent in 2019,[2] yet this rise in self-employment was not necessarily voluntary but based on a worsening of labour market conditions, as can be seen in fewer people having been able to leave self-employment in the previous two decades despite a fall in real wages compared to employed people (ONS, 2022b; Giupponi and Xu, 2024). Notwithstanding, the focus has continued to fall on neoliberal policies, believing that profits create jobs for which purpose companies need flexibility.

The three key targets of weakening trade unions, labour market deregulation and motivating self-employment have consequently resulted in a highly flexible and less protected job market. The UK has one of the highest risks of unemployment and one of the weakest employment protection systems among OECD countries, ranking fourth after New Zealand, the US and Canada (OECD, 2015). Yet, while the UK has a highly flexible job market, it has experienced declining business investment since the 1990s and real wage decline since the Global Financial Crisis (OECD, 2023). The UK's private investments are now the lowest among OECD countries, with only Luxembourg and Greece performing worse, and living standards lower than in Slovenia (Burn-Murdoch, 2022; Dibb and Murphy, 2023).

Labour market deregulation has thus resulted in labour being disciplined through rising job insecurity and declining wages but has not created new business investments. The question is why these policies have found such great support despite reducing income for consumption, a key profit source, and thus having the potential to harm economic growth. The answer can be found in the growing importance of finance.

Finance as saviour: normalizing the everyday asset manager

The retreat of the welfare state was accompanied by a significant financial deregulation process that enabled the creation of new financial products supporting asset-based welfare and providing profit opportunities. An expansion of retail financial services to the wider public was seen as a key factor in establishing a 'prosperous country' based on the 'liberated energies of a free people' (Thatcher, 1987b), thus a major overhaul of the financial market was initiated with the Financial Services Act 1986 – also called the 'Big Bang'. Restrictions on mortgage provisions, credit card restrictions and banking activities were lifted (Wood, 2017), for instance, building societies are now allowed to offer credit cards, loans and mortgages. Despite having led to declining lending standards,[3] this change was pronounced to be positive as it forced companies to offer more choice ('deregulatory measures help to increase the competitiveness and flexibility' [HM Treasury, 2004]). The desire for competition remains a key driver up until today, introducing profit measures while ignoring risks of financial instability. Referencing the Big Bang and seeking to 'make the UK the world's most innovative and competitive global financial centre', the chancellor of the exchequer, Jeremy Hunt, announced in November 2022 a reduction of the tax on bank profits from 8 per cent to 3 per cent, and the European-introduced capital reserves for insurers was cut to 'unlock billions of pounds for investments' (Hunt, 2022).

The everyday capitalist: a share-dealing, home-owning democracy

To create 'a property-owning democracy' (Thatcher, 1986), discourses and policies have been introduced constructing the everyday capitalist: 'You have to give people something to go for. We give them a ladder of opportunity and invite them to climb as high as they can. The sky is the limit and it's working. More and more people owning their own home, owning shares, having a stake in society' (Thatcher, 1988).

Economic freedom – 'a man's right to work as he will, to spend what he earns to own property' – is declared as the essence of society: 'on that freedom all our other freedoms depend' (Thatcher, 1975). This agency discourse based on the concepts of freedom, choice and control depicts an important correlate of governmentality which, as presented in the conceptual framework outlined in Chapter 2, works through the notions of freedom and autonomy (Grey, 1997) and is continuously picked up in policy discourses. Establishing an agency discourse where everyone can become an asset owner makes asset norms desirable and undermines the collective identity of the worker, replacing it with individual responsibility.

Creating 'popular capitalism' consists of three key elements of asset ownership: share ownership, homeownership and pensions. In the first instance, a large-scale privatization programme of nationalized companies was introduced and company shares were offered to the general public, accompanied by huge media campaigns, as illustrated in the case of British Gas in 1986. The campaign consisted of informative advertisements outlining the profitability of British Gas and of personal stories where it was emphasized that 'everyone can buy a share of the shares' (Gregory, 1998, p 17). A fictitious everyday person named Sid, who could have been the person sitting next to you, and a popular slogan 'If you see Sid, tell him' were created (Warwick-Ching, 2007). The advertisement campaign is estimated to have reached 98 per cent of the population. In addition to advertisement campaigns, incentives were introduced, for example, in the case of British Telecommunications a 10 per cent discount on phone bills when investing at least £250 was offered (Gregory, 1988). As a result, the government was able to raise substantial funds, up to £44.5 billion with the privatization of state companies, by 1992 (Pitelis and Clarke, 1993).

However, since shares were often taken up by employees of the company being privatized (Gregory, 1998), a lot of smaller investors sold off their shares in the aftermath of privatization, leading to a fall in everyday investors holding shares from 20.6 per cent in 1981 to 10.1 per cent in 2012 (ONS, 2015). In the long term, the trend moved towards the majority of shares being directly held by institutional investors and indirectly held by everyday investors supported by subsidized products. Tax beneficial products such as the stocks and shares Individual Savings Account (ISA) which offers a tax-free allowance of up to £20,000 per year and the Lifetime ISA where the government tops up annual savings of up to £4,000 with 25 per cent were introduced. Investments in stocks and shares is portrayed as a means 'for long-term financial savings with tax-free growth' and investment in trusts, individual stocks and shares, exchange-traded funds as well as open-ended investment companies where one can pool money with other investors are offered as additional investments (MoneyHelper, 2023b). Strikingly, due to there not being an upper limit on the number of ISAs that can be held over the years, the tax allowances on those ISAs has been shown to largely benefit the wealthiest households (Ross, 2023).

The second aspect of popular capitalism is allowing 'more people to have the security and satisfaction of owning property' (Thatcher, 1979). In

1980, the Right to Buy programme, where council tenants were given the opportunity to buy their houses at a discounted price of up to one third, was introduced. Through leaving the constraints of the state ('council housing creates its own demand' [Thatcher, 1974]), households, it was argued, were able to take control over their future, since 'homeownership stimulates the attitudes of independence and self-reliance that are the bedrock of a free society' (Moore, 2014). At the same time the local authorities' obligations to hold social housing was abolished in 1989 and financial incentives were implemented. Between 1983 and 2000, a mortgage tax relief system enabled households to receive full relief on interest payments for mortgages of up to £30,000 (HM Treasury, 2013), and rather than challenging the 'changing labour market that requires greater flexibility and mobility of labour' (HoC, 1999, p 16), New Labour worked 'with mortgage providers to encourage greater provision of more flexible mortgages to protect families in a world of increased job insecurity' (LM, 1997). Mortgages were introduced where only a minimum annual payment was determined and which can be paused or larger repayments can be made, enabling people on irregular work contracts to access mortgage finance. These measures were accompanied by a flexibilization of the rental market. Rent controls were removed and new laws implemented which made it easier for landlords to end a tenancy, evict tenants and to shorten tenancy agreements, which in the majority of cases led to agreements of a maximum of six months (Kempson and Collard, 2012). It thus became more secure to own a house than rent a property and as a consequence of the Right to Buy scheme, which is still in place today,[4] the government's social housing stock was reduced as councils were not allowed to deny tenants the right to purchase and the proceeds were not allowed to be used for building new social housing. While public housing constituted 31.7 per cent of dwellings in 1981 it decreased to 16.6 per cent in 2021. Conversely, homeownership has risen from 51 per cent of households owning in 1971 to 70.9 per cent in 2003 (see Figure 3.1).

More recently, disproportionate house price increases in relation to wages have made it more difficult to purchase a house. Proclaiming that 'homeownership is what overwhelmingly people in this country want. It's good for society, great for the economy, it drives jobs' (Johnson, 2022), subsidies have been introduced such as the Help-to-Buy ISA, where the government contributes 25 per cent on savings for the first house, and the Help-to-Buy equity loan, which provides subsidized loans to first-time buyers (MAS, 2017). Yet, despite these measures, homeownership has declined since 2003 (64.9 per cent in 2021) and inequalities have intensified, for instance, predominantly couples with no children buy a house (58.5 per cent of all owner-occupiers), and a lone parent with child(ren) is the least likely to own a house (3.1 per cent of owner-occupiers [DfLHC, 2022]).

Figure 3.1: Share of housing tenure by type – England

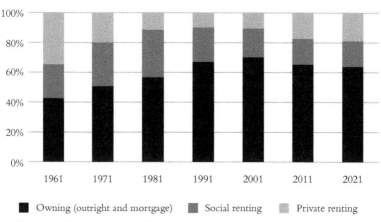

Source: Illustration based on DfLHC (2022)

Finally, to construct a society of 'wealth creators' (Thatcher, 1985), personal involvement in pensions has been emphasized as an aspiring goal, seeking to turn 'passive pension-savers into active investor-capitalists' (Davies et al, 2018, p 486). In 1986, the Personal Pensions Act was introduced, which abolished the right of employers to make being part of the company's pension scheme a condition of being employed, and made it easier to contract out from such schemes by allowing transfers into personal pensions. To motivate personal pensions and involvement in investment decisions, incentives were put in place such as a reduction in national insurance contributions when contracting out from the state-earnings-related pensions (Cutler and Waine, 2001). Besides personal pensions, further investment tools for pensions were set up, including the Self-Invested Personal Pension Scheme (SIPP), providing income tax relief on invested money, and the Personal Equity Plan (PEP). Whereas in SIPPs one self-determines the investments, PEP was a tax incentivized investment tool where households could invest £6,000 per year in a managed investment in exchange for being exempted from income tax on dividends and capital gains tax. While this was abolished in 1999, PEP was a highly successful scheme with 270,000 taking it up in the first year (BBC News, 1999; MoneyHelper, 2023b).

Moreover, defined-contribution (DC) pensions, as discussed by way of introduction in Chapter 1, gained in importance. Until the end of the 1970s, workplace pensions were mainly based on defined-benefit (DB) schemes, which guarantee a pension income determined by accrual rate, salary level and length of working for a company, that is, these schemes are 'divorced from the investment performance of the pension fund' (Cutler and Waine, 2001, p 104). To create active investors and support the flexibility of the labour market, portable pensions were introduced in 1995, allowing the transfer of pensions between companies, which in turn supported the move from DB pensions towards the less generous DC pensions, reflecting a risk shift from companies onto households (Kempson and Collard, 2012). In DC pensions, households are responsible for making decisions with regards to the pension plan, including contribution amount and choice of investment fund. Under New Labour the pension system was further directed towards individual responsibility based on the belief that 'pensioners should share fairly in the increasing prosperity of the nation' (LM, 1997). During the 1990s, the stock market was rising and companies had high pension savings, resulting in the removal of tax relief on dividends which companies were earning when investing pension contributions: 'at present many companies are enjoying pension holidays, so this is the right time to undertake long-needed reform. ... I propose to abolish tax credits paid to pension funds and companies' (Brown, 1997). In its aftermath, companies started to struggle to provide a DB scheme, which further intensified the move towards DC schemes, especially after the dot-com bubble and falling equity values. In 2003 alone 63 per cent of schemes were closed (Langley, 2004).

As a consequence of these changes, a three-tiered pension system was established in the UK, where mandatory pension provisions cover only 29 per cent of previous earnings compared to an average of 63 per cent in OECD countries (OECD, 2017). The first tier, the state pension, is solely aimed at poverty relief while the workplace pension and personal pension investments are intended to provide financial security during retirement. Continuous emphasis is placed on freedom and being able to control the future through choosing investments: 'people's pensions are hard-earned over years of work. It is only right they have the freedom to choose how and when they access them' (HM Treasury, 2014). In the aftermath of the Global Financial Crisis, the government removed the requirement to convert saved pensions into an annuity, introduced flexible drawdowns and reduced taxes for lump sums. By giving autonomy to economic agents, asset norms including stocks and shares investments, property and pensions are made desirable.

The everyday asset manager: from opportunity to compliance

The subject position of the everyday asset manager is not only constructed through an agency discourse but also a discourse of having no choice other than to conform to asset norms, creating an economy in which 'everyone has a stake in society and owes responsibility' (LM, 1997). Similar to the aim of wanting to enable households to become capitalists, New Labour made the pledge to create a society with more entrepreneurs; however, a slight shift can be detected here. Realizing people do not necessarily behave as expected, more focus was put on making sure people complied with taking responsibility over their financial future: 'Everyone needs to plan for their retirement … Putting money aside for your retirement can seem difficult, especially when there are so many other things to pay for. But with a bit of planning, you can help yourself to get ready' (DWP, 2013, p 2). The overall guideline is that 'those who can save have the responsibility to do so' (HoC, 1999, p 17) and need to accumulate assets which can be used to 'meet the cost of living and cover unforeseen expenses' (DoH, 2013, p 7). Even if it is difficult, a nest-egg should be built since 'everyone needs money to live on when they retire' (DWP, 2013, p 6). Saving and investing are normalized to the degree that 'the only time you shouldn't save or invest is if there are more important things you need to do with your money. For example, getting your debts under control' (MAS, 2021). The discourse of hard work is combined here with taking on responsibility over one's financial future: 'The pension system should reward people who work and save. A system in which means-testing plays too great a part can discourage people on modest earnings from making self-provision for retirement' (HoC, 2000). There is an inherent belief, also incorporated in the agency discourse ('citizens have the duty to support themselves' (Thatcher, 1974), that benefits work as a disincentive to providing for oneself.

To 'create a nation of savers and asset-holders', wider access to financial products has been prioritized, particularly focusing on enabling people on low income to save (Blair, 2002). In 2005, a Child Trust Fund was set up that provided families of a new-born child with a tax-financed lump sum of at least £250 to be placed in an account accessible to the child at the age of 18, with £250 extra for low-income households. Furthermore, to incentivize lower income households to save, a Savings Gateway account was suggested by New Labour[5] and then introduced as the Help-to-Save scheme in 2018 under the Conservative government (HoC, 1999; GOV.UK, 2018). This savings account adds 50 pence to each pound saved but is closed after four years and not renewable; it is thus not intended to provide sufficient savings but to change savings patterns among lower income individuals. Besides savings instruments, stakeholder pensions were introduced to give particularly 'those on low and modest incomes and with changing patterns of employment' a chance to access a pension and reduce the reliance on the state (LM, 1997). One of the requirements of the stakeholder pension is that it is a DC scheme, explicitly exempting DB schemes as 'benefits will have to be related to individual contributions plus investment returns on these contributions' (HoC, 1999). Such financial inclusion initiatives are still in place today.

One key area of financial inclusion initiatives is the workplace pension. The deregulation of workplace pension savings led to a fall in pension savings from its peak of 53 per cent of the working age population in 1967 to less than a third in 2012, of whom the majority belonged to public sector pensions (ONS, 2005, 2012). Realizing that people are not making sufficient pension provisions and are not actively engaging with workplace pensions, understandings of bounded rationality have entered the policy discourse. Reasons for people not engaging are proclaimed to relate to present bias and self-control and corrective policy measures have been introduced (Hardcastle, 2012). Following from my initial remarks on workplace pensions in Chapter 1, employees are now automatically enrolled in a workplace pension scheme when earning £10,000 per year in a single place of work, with minimum contributions of 8 per cent, consisting of 3 per cent from the employer, 4 per cent from the employee and 1 per cent from the state as tax relief (DWP, 2011). This is based on the behavioural economic concept of 'nudge', where it has been shown that people are less likely to opt-out when being automatically signed up, with the argument being that 'integrating behavioural and traditional economics measures is probably the best way forward ... rather than ditching one or the other' (Hardcastle, 2012, p 1).

In line with this reasoning, widening access to financial products has been extended with education, with the argument that, even if people have access to financial products, they also need to have the confidence to make financially rational decisions (Prabhakar, 2021). To enable individuals to manage money and save for retirement planning in line with finance rationality, a plethora of financial education programmes and money advice websites has emerged, with even schools offering financial education (FinCap, 2021; MaPS, 2021; Lewis, 2023a). Free advice bodies such as the Money Advice Service (providing advice on debt and money management), Pension Advisory Service (giving advice on the three tiers of the UK pension system) and Pension Wise (providing guidance for over 50 years old) were established and have now been consolidated in the Money and Pensions Service set up by the Department for Work and Pensions and the Treasury in 2019. The service is aimed at providing 'free and impartial debt advice, money guidance and pension guidance to members of the public' to 'improve their financial wellbeing and build a better, more confident future' (MaPS, 2019), and their website calls on individuals to become active in workplace retirement planning ('review the way your pension is invested') and conduct personal pension investments ('the future you will thank you for saving into a pension'). As defined within the concept of finance rationality, pension choices should be made while taking into consideration inflation, risk and 'the period of time you intend to invest for' and the money should be spread 'between different types of investments' and reviewed continuously throughout. That means pension investors should invest in higher risk when they are younger and move to lower risk funds when they are closer to retirement and put any extra savings or income into pensions as it provides tax relief (MoneyHelper, 2023b). Reference is again placed on individual responsibility and hard work: 'planning for retirement is vital for all of us. We are living longer and want to enjoy our well-earned retirement' (DWP, 2019).

Even though automatic enrolment has been successful and led to more people saving in workplace pensions, increasing the level of workplace pension savings by more than double from 7.8 million in 2011 to 17.7 million in 2018, 10 million working people are still excluded due to earnings-related criteria (Morley, 2014; PPI, 2017; DWP, 2018). Workplace pension only apply after earning £10,000 in a single place of work, thus excluding those who are part-time employed and self-employed, which make up over one third of workers in the UK (24.9 per cent worked part-time and 13 per cent were self-employed in 2022 (ONS, 2022b; ONS, 2024)). In particular, women, people from minority ethnic backgrounds, disabled workers and carers are the least likely to meet the eligibility criteria and thus be covered by workplace pensions. Even out of those who do fulfil the eligibility requirements, the majority of these save only the minimum level of contribution, culminating in a pension income of 27.4 per cent of prior average earnings (DWP, 2017; OECD, 2021a), which lies below the replacement of mandatory provisions within OECD countries.

Despite recognizing the limitations of the current asset-based welfare system, accessible asset ownership and behavioural measures continue to dominate the policy discourse. To increase savings for retirement within income-constrained households, a sidecar savings account has been trialled in the UK since early 2019. This account is an instant access savings account with a savings and retirement component (Prabhakar, 2021). Automatic savings would be deducted from an employee's income and once a savings cap is reached, the additional savings would be moved into a workplace pension. Moreover, the following key themes presented within the current financial capability strategy are focused on behavioural changes without challenging external factors which might prohibit responsible financial behaviour: financial foundations (meaningful education for children and young adults), nation of savers (helping income-constrained households to save), credit counts (reducing the number of people using credit), better debt advice and a future focus (create a better understanding how to plan for retirement).[6]

Overall it becomes clear that rather than questioning the structure of the current welfare state when recognizing old age poverty (which was a dominant concern of New Labour) and income constraints, the focus remains on improving individual behaviour, thus implicitly depoliticizing systemic inequalities. When taking into consideration that asset-based welfare has been highly profitable for financial institutions and for the government, the continued focus on individual solutions while ignoring systemic limitations is not surprising. After the deregulation process began, financial assets in relation to national income rose from 162 per cent in 1979 to 211 per cent in 1989 and then made the biggest jump in the following ten years, up to 377 per cent in 1999, compared to an overall net private wealth of 512.7 per cent.[7] A major share of financial assets is taken up by life insurances and pension funds, having risen from 38.1 per cent of national income in 1970 to 102.8 per cent in 1989 with the strongest increase taking place between 1990 and 1999, rising from 102.3 per cent of national income to 210.1 per cent. In absolute terms, pension funds, life insurance and unit trusts investments rose from £181 million in 1982 to £3.4 trillion in 2010 (WID, 2018), of which pension and insurance funds represented 90 per cent, resulting in the UK's 'long-term savings industry' being the 'largest in Europe and the fourth largest in the world' (ABI Analysis, 2017, p 1). With the introduction of automatic enrolment, pension scheme assets have been growing to the extent that they now represent a significant proportion of all institutional financial assets in the UK, amounting to £2.7 trillion held in workplace pensions (ONS, 2022a). Widening access to financial products and financial education are thus highly profitable for financial institutions, while enabling the welfare state to spend less on providing social welfare.

Concluding remarks

Going back to the governmentality framework introduced in Chapter 2, the analysis shown here reveals how the interplay between disciplinary (responsibilization) and regulatory (financialization) mechanisms constructs asset norms and intensifies capital–labour inequalities. Whilst deregulating the labour market and reducing the bargaining power of trade unions weakened labour power, the reduction of direct welfare benefits such as unemployment benefits, sick pay and the state pension has put more costs of social reproduction onto labour. As a consequence, stability in the form of a secure, stable income has been replaced by insecurity, which can be seen in the UK having one of the lowest employment protections (rising job insecurity) and lowest social service provisions among OECD countries (rising money insecurity). This transfer of responsibilities from the employer and state onto households is accompanied with a discursive pattern of hard work and having the responsibility to provide for oneself, depoliticizing social inequalities while reducing costs of welfare provision.

Through offering financial solutions to deal with the rising insecurity, the regulatory mechanism 'does dovetail into it [disciplinary technology], integrate it, modify it to some extent, and above all, use it by sort of infiltrating it' (Foucault, 2003, p 242). In synergy with the disciplinary mechanism, the regulatory mechanism creates an environment which induces households to accumulate assets. The financial market has been deregulated and the subsequent rise in competition has led to a wider access to financial products. At the same time, policies have been introduced which help households to accumulate assets, as in the case of the Right to Buy programme or flexible pension products such as portable pensions. Even when recognizing limitations to asset-based welfare measures, such as the flexibility of the labour market and first-time buyers experiencing difficulties when trying to step onto the property ladder, they are not questioned. Instead, individual solutions such as making financial products more inclusive and financial education are pursued, ignoring factors outside an individual's control and putting pressure on households to accumulate assets despite constraints.

Replacing direct cash transfers with asset-based welfare measures has been accompanied by a dichotomous discourse between agency, portraying asset ownership as the possibility of gaining freedom, and non-agency, arguing that one has no other choice than providing for oneself. Whereas the Thatcher government concentrated more on opportunities and widening asset ownership to the general republic, subsequent governments extended this discussion by emphasizing the need to take over responsibility and save with the help of asset-based welfare measures. Because of the state providing less security in case of income shortfalls, the everyday person is encouraged to accumulate assets and engage with financial markets, for example, through pension funds. Strikingly, this dichotomous discourse between agency and non-agency can still be found in today's government discourses, where tax-free allowances and more freedom of choice is established for well-earning, active investors within the agency discourse and a call for being financially responsible and ensuring long-term investments with the help of more passive financial products such as automatic enrolment is created within the non-agency discourse.

Disciplinary and regulatory power technologies thus establish a regime of truth in which it is seen as normal that households take over responsibility by working hard and accumulating assets which they can draw upon during difficult times. Despite being promoted as an opportunity, the mutually generative relationship between disciplinary and regulatory mechanisms intensifies capital–labour inequalities by putting more pressure on UK households by weakening labour power and placing the costs of reproduction onto households while increasing profit opportunities for financial institutions. The pervasiveness of the new regime of truth can be seen in changing policy regimes adopting the same approach and in some of the recent events, such as the cost-of-living crisis, where the focus of the Bank of England has been on increasing interest rates to tackle inflation and calling on wage restraint by employees, which harms in particular already struggling households due to rising borrowing costs and lower real-time wages while ignoring the unprecedented profits companies have reported (Kim, 2023; Middleton et al, 2024).

4

Becoming an Everyday
Asset Manager

The institutional construction of the UK's asset-based welfare system, outlined in the previous chapter, where direct welfare provisions solely provide poverty relief (disciplinary mechanism) while workplace pensions and personal investments are intended to mitigate future risks (regulatory mechanism) has been accompanied by media discourses constructing norms of asset accumulation. Whereas the disciplinary mechanism influences behaviour through making some activities costlier than others, such as risking old-age poverty when not saving for retirement, norms operate through creating interests and desires individuals seek to adhere to. This chapter therefore unpicks interviewees' discursive interaction with institutional changes and norms constructed in the media. It thus responds to a gap identified in the literature where previous studies have tended to focus either on institutional changes and secondary data (Langley, 2006, 2007; French and Kneale, 2009; Maman and Rosenhek, 2019) or on qualitative research (Coppock, 2013; Lai, 2017; Pellandini-Simanyi and Banai, 2021). Despite depicting individuals as important actors in the financialization of daily life, the Foucauldian-inspired literature has tended to exclude individuals' interaction with the discursive and institutional practices constructing investor subjects. As a result, analyses of the financialization of daily life have resulted in an apparent contradiction, on the one hand suggesting, based on secondary data, that individuals become investors (Martin, 2002; Davis, 2009), and on the other hand arguing, based on empirical data, that 'finance is domesticated' (Pellandini-Simanyi et al, 2015, p 733) – that is, individuals reject the subject position of the everyday investor.

This chapter combines these two approaches, exploring first the construction of asset norms in the media before unveiling how interviewees engage with these norms discursively. The analysis of media discussions uncovers the macro-level discourses which constitute asset norms and how these come into being, 'establishing what subsequently counts as being self-evident, universal, and necessary' (Foucault, 1991, p 76). Within this macro-level discourse analysis, references to financial behaviour and any of its constitutive parts within the texts were identified and examined to identify elements giving meaning to asset norms (Talib and Fitzgerald, 2016). In line with the dichotomous discourse employed in the policy discussion presented in Chapter 3, the everyday asset manager subject is constituted in the media discourse by establishing asset accumulation, on the one hand as a mechanism to gain freedom and prosperity (agency discourse) and, on the other hand, as a necessity (non-agency discourse).

After having seen how asset norms are constructed, the chapter unpacks how UK individuals are transformed into everyday asset managers based on discursive practices and their interaction with non-discursive elements in the form of institutional changes. It thus unveils the transformative effects of discourse. It will be shown that the everyday asset manager subject comes into being by drawing on key elements of the policy and media discourse, albeit differently interpreted. Agency and non-agency discourses are used to express a critical view of finance. Interviewees feel trapped in having to provide financial security for themselves due to rising job and money insecurity while wanting to have freedom when making financial decisions, which originates from their distrust of financial institutions.

The construction of asset norms in the media

Going back to the Foucauldian framework introduced in Chapter 2, this section reveals first how discursive formations represented in the media construct asset norms and then how interviewees engage with these discourses. Discursive formations are understood here as rules of formation 'that systematically form objects of which they speak' rather than linguistic practices 'treating discourses as groups of signs' (Foucault, 1972, p 49), making norms of asset accumulation appear natural: 'Whenever one can describe, between a number of statements, such a system of dispersion, whenever, between objects, types of statement, concepts, or thematic choices, one can define a regularity … we are dealing with a discursive formation' (Foucault, 1972, p 38). In other words, the same kind of discourse based on similar objects, themes or argumentation lines appears in different media texts, establishing in this case asset norms. Three main discursive formations were discovered constructing asset norms: an entrepreneurial discourse, an agency and a non-agency discourse.

The entrepreneurial everyday asset manager

The entrepreneurial discourse emerged in the 1980s, incorporating the finance theoretical concepts introduced in Chapter 2 and calling on households to become everyday asset managers where 'careful planning and saving now would [then] provide a regular stream of tax-free income in the future' (Montagu-Smith, 2001a). An article published by *The Guardian* in 1987 summarizes some key aspects discussed in the media. Referring to the necessity for every form of corporation 'from multinational corporations to village tennis clubs' to produce a balance sheet leads to asking 'why not extend the idea to your own personal finances?' given that 'we all have assets and liabilities'. Listing assets and liabilities in a balance sheet is said to help detect areas 'where further investments are most likely to add to [your] wealth' in line with your current living circumstances. This raises, for example, the following questions:

> Should you extend or improve your house? Will it increase its value by more than the cost of the work? Or is the house too big for you already, now that your children have left home? Perhaps you should sell it and move to a smaller one? How are your investments performing? Should you make any changes? Do you have an insurance policy maturing shortly? Most important, do you have sufficient liquid funds or assets easily transferable into cash to meet foreseeable expenses?

The house value can be determined by 'studying the price of similar properties in your area' or the 'value of stocks and shares, unit trusts and other investments' can be obtained from the companies they are held with (Tidbury, 1987).

Several aspects become clear in the questions previously posed, which are still dominating the personal finance sections of media outlets. First, before any investments in assets is conducted, it is advisable to 'put a little aside for a rainy day' (Richardson, 2008), expressed earlier as 'liquid funds'. A more recent expression used has been creating an 'emergency fund' in case one has unexpected costs or has to take 'unpaid leave from work' (Devine, 2021). Individuals are advised to at least 6 to '12 months' household expenses worth of emergency cash' (Haynes, 2022), short-term savings for holidays or getting married and long-term 'saving for a home, working towards financial freedom or saving money towards the cost of having a family' (Devine, 2021).

Second, the house is portrayed as an investment where one is advised to move up the 'property ladder' from an 'entry-level property' (Pickford, 2017) to a higher priced house ('consider selling up after three years [and you] could then make a substantial profit' (Montagu-Smith, 2001b), and to conduct investments in improving the house only if the costs outweigh the rise in value. The inherent contradiction between being proud to own one's home and the house being an investment (Ronald, 2008) is overcome by connecting emotional values with investment values and creating the desire to own property 'as a way of using property equity to finance future spending' (Vincent, 2007) and establish security ('home sweet secure home' [Dixon, 1987]):

> If you are a homeowner your best option is going to look for some way to realise the huge investment you have made … You can make a straight trade down … But what if you don't want to move? The answer here is to arrange a home income plan. This involves taking out a mortgage on your house and then using the money to buy an annuity. (Hawthorne, 1987)

To realize the equity built up in the house, besides downsizing and losing your home, lifetime mortgages, where mortgages are set up against the equity of the house and repaid when moving into a care home or in the case of death (MAS, 2017), are praised for allowing 'cash-poor but asset-rich pensioners [to tap] into the capital locked up in their home' (Brignall, 2006). Here, equity release is portrayed as helping to finance one's own retirement without having to sacrifice 'a much-loved family home' (Calkin, 2021) and enabling one 'to support your loved ones' (TDG, 2022).

Third, investments into stocks and shares, either directly or indirectly, are portrayed as a viable investment option since 'history shows that equities have always outperformed simple savings accounts over the long term' (FT, 1993). Even in the midst of financial crises such as the Global Financial Crisis equities are portrayed as a good long-term investment ('advisers are confident that equities are still a good long-term bet' [Goff, 2008]) and in the aftermath of the 1987 crash metaphorical strategies were employed to highlight the benefits of share investment: 'When bears prowl in the financial jungle and all hype is abandoned, fun shares[1] provide hope' (Hawthorne, 1987). The widening access to stocks and shares investments is praised in the media, and even described as being similar and as easy as going into a fashion store and choosing clothes, as can be seen in the description of a 'Save and Invest' shop by Buxton (1987):

> It offers a complete range of investment advice, can organise the purchase of shares and unit trusts, and give help on pensions and taxation. The customer can stroll into one of its shops, browse through the displays around the walls which present unit trusts and, if he wishes, discuss his requirements with one of the staff.

Some funds are also promoted to enable smaller investors ('an increasing number of fund management companies are offering hedge funds with much smaller minimum investment' [Thorniley, 2001]) and people who are retired or made redundant to invest ('Unit trusts were offering defensive stock especially for the retired and redundant' [Cannon, 1987]). More recently emphasis has been put on managed funds where one can 'cherry pick funds from three dozen funds' and 'keep money in a balanced portfolio' (Phillips, 2007) and in a stocks and shares Individual Savings Account (ISA) 'where you could select more diversified funds' (Suter, 2017). Interestingly, a distinction is made here between active and passive funds where passive products such as tracker funds which 'follow the movement of an index' or stocks and shares ISAs enable entry into share investments before going into the more actively managed funds where one needs to be 'willing to regularly research and review where [your] money is going' (Hickey, 2021).

Embedded within this entrepreneurial discourse are finance theoretical concepts which are, as stressed in Chapter 2, also employed in financial education programmes (Lusardi, 2010, 2015). Households are conjured to not 'put all their eggs in one basket no matter how strong that basket appears to be' (Worsfold, 1987a) and invest in 'low-risk and high-risk ventures. Relatively low-risk investments include government securities and income bonds from leading UK life assurance companies [and] higher risk investments worth considering are those involving stocks and shares' (Burr, 1984). When investing in stocks and shares directly, understanding risk, rebalancing the portfolio and diversification 'diminishes the risk inherent in equities' (Wright, 2001; Caldwell, 2013). Terms such as 'spreading the risk' have become familiar discursive concepts (Archer, 2006), brought to life by metaphors like 'not having all your eggs in one basket' (Meyer, 2021), which still dominate today's media discourse.

Before investing in riskier assets, one is encouraged to take 'sensible steps to protect [your] finances' if you 'haven't already taken some' (Simon and Farrow, 2008). By referring to this idea, setting up insurances 'which should cover mortgage and loan repayments if you are made redundant', thus reducing the risk of not being able to service the liability related to homeownership, and building up savings cushions before investing in stocks and shares is normalized: 'You want more than a savings account offers. You can face up to bad days on investment markets without worry. You can afford to lock away your spare cash for five years at the least. You are prepared to lose money' (Woodroffe, 2007). The 'rainy-day money isn't supposed to be exposed to any risk' (FT, 1993) and the beneficial role of having an insurance in case of losing a job is emphasized: 'When Harry Hogg was laid off ... just over a year ago, the blow was softened slightly by the fact that he had insurance' (Jones, 2002).

Households are not only motivated to adopt finance rationality, that is financial strategies including diversification and hedging, in the interest of achieving asset ownership, but also to exercise financial self-discipline: 'The UK has a nasty debt habit ... some of today's parents are debt-bingers relying on plastic as a crutch to fuel unsustainable lifestyles. ... While we need to accept that debt used correctly is a powerful enabler, too many still get burnt' (Lewis, 2010). In this message, very strong positive ('powerful enabler') and negative terms ('nasty debt habits') are used as a call for action and provide a rationale for having good debts for asset ownership and for avoiding bad debts for consumption. Since 'affordable debts today may be a burden tomorrow' (Montagu-Smith, 2001c), it is advisable to repay the mortgage earlier if the mortgage terms allow this without punishment ('pay off the loan as soon as you can: It's not the most expensive debt but it's the biggest' (Papworth, 2002). The everyday asset manager is thus constructed as someone who 'insures himself against the risks of the life cycle through financial literacy and self-discipline' (Van der Zwan, 2014, p 113), sacrificing current consumption for future consumption and employing financial strategies to achieve asset ownership.

'We all have dreams about freedom': agency discourse

The financialized subject position of the everyday asset manager is constituted with the help of 'discourses as [are] tactical elements' where there 'exist different and even contradictory discourses within the same strategy' (Foucault, 1978, pp 101–2). In line with the policy discourse introduced in Chapter 3, two overarching, seemingly contradictory discursive formations emerged in the media: an agency and non-agency discourse. The dichotomy between portraying agency and gaining freedom, while outlining the costs of non-complying, results in normalizing asset ownership.

An agency discourse has been constructed which equates asset accumulation with gaining freedom. As expected by the literature discussion introduced in Chapter 2, a reoccurring topic is early retirement, portraying policy changes as the possibility of leaving a job early: 'If work was such a wonderful thing … the rich would keep it to themselves' (Coggan, 1993). Finance is depicted as something which is good for everyone, referring to house equity withdrawals as a 'mid-life joy' (Edwards, 1987) and pensions as something with which one can finance one's dream:

> We all have dreams about freedom from the world of work. My own dream is to travel across the US from East to West by motorbike. Yours could be to see the world on a Swan Hellenic cruise or to just live out your days in comfort and happiness. Whatever your dream you will need an income and this is most likely to be your pension. (Cuthbert, 2006)

Interestingly, an inclusive discourse is used ('we all') assuming a rather homogenous desire for freedom from work. A similar discourse can still be found nowadays, such as in *The Daily Telegraph*, where continual references are made to early retirement ('Can I live my Mamma Mia dreams by retiring early in Greece?', 'How can I be semi-retired by 55?', 'Can I afford to retire at 53?') or in *The Guardian* where the first step to gain freedom is proclaimed to be setting up an emergency fund:

> This fund is so empowering and is the start of your journey to financial freedom and security. ... But this fund is so much more than that – it is going to end up giving you the power to say no to any situation, place, relationship or job you don't want to be in anymore. (Devine, 2021)

'The winning formula for retirement' is combining pensions and ISAs, since 'having both gives you more options and flexibility' (Smith, 2023).

When discussing policy changes in the media, a continuous reference is made to freedom of choice, flexibility and control, for instance, suggestions to move contracted-out pensions into SIPPs due to 'being able to exercise more control over your investments and having more freedom to invest in different things' (Montagu-Smith, 2008). Personal involvement is portrayed here 'as desirable in its own right not just as a means of reducing the dominance of institutions' (FT, 1984). It is argued that 'the only democratic and just position is to give the employee freedom of choice to determine his/her own pension arrangements' (Oppenheim, 1984). Similarly, the new 'pension freedoms' of being able to retrieve a lump sum from the saved pension fund instead of having to buy an annuity, as discussed in the previous chapter, are acclaimed as 'undoubtedly a progressive development – giving people choice and control' (Cumbo, 2015). Connecting financial freedom with freedom of choice is depicted as gaining control and making sure 'that this money is working as hard as it can' (Montagu-Smith, 2008). These discourses imply that people have a 'desire for independence' and demand more 'freedom of choice' (Pauley, 1984).

A similar praise for flexibility can be found with regards to mortgages. Changes to mortgage provisions under New Labour were praised in the media with mortgages being referred to as 'flexible friends', establishing a connection to personal relationships, and as a natural step in line with rising competition and a flexible work environment: 'A booming housing market, rising interest rates and changing patterns of employment have forced banks and building societies to develop a breed of flexible home loans' (Saigol, 1997). People were depicted as having been liberated from too strict financial regulations ('the days of mortgage famine, it seems, are over' [Pauley, 1984]). Even in the current cost-of-living crisis, equity release is discussed as a possibility to tackle rising costs, with *The Daily Telegraph* 'debunk[ing] the six most common myths' (TDG, 2023), portraying equity release as a risk-free income source. The subject position of the everyday asset manager is thus articulated by connecting freedom and control over the future to opportunities.

Yet, since 'power is exercised only over free subjects ... who are faced with a field of possibilities' (Foucault, 1982, p 790), the discourse surrounding freedom does not only empower people to make their own decisions, thereby reducing dependence on institutions, but also functions as an enabler of power. By giving autonomy to individuals and constructing a discourse of freedom and choice, the subject position of the everyday asset manager is made desirable, inducing people to accumulate assets guided by finance rationality.

'You have no choice': non-agency discourse

In contrast to the discourse of freedom and choice, a non-agency discourse of having no choice ('you have no choice' [Worsfold, 1987b]) than to submit to asset accumulation is established since it is 'more difficult to become complacent' (Thorniley, 2001). It functions through relating back to fears and scaremongering, based on outlining what would happen if one does not invest ('Employees wanting a decent income in retirement must make private provision for themselves or through their employer' [Short, 1984]). Questions such as: 'Scared? You're meant to be' (Lewis, 2006) are asked, only to then introduce financial strategies as a solution. By using familiar terms in the form of 'co-op stamps' or 'pot of noodles', the fear of old-age poverty is made relatable and private pensions are promoted:

> But after considering retirement on a state pension last week (a social whirl of Pot Noodle soirees, coupon chic and Co-op stamps), what choice do any of us have? Sweet 16 and street cred is fine. But 65 and on the street is not. Private pensions are now a simple bare necessity. (Langan, 1997)

Retirement planning is being regarded here as an unavoidable truth which one has to tackle, otherwise there is the risk of not being able to retire early, as recently highlighted in the media: 'the cost of living crisis has forced some to reconsider early retirement' (Skopeliti and Otte, 2022).

Even in the face of redundancy and when acknowledging uncertainty, households are advised to take on financial products and prioritize pensions: 'No one can accurately predict which will do best over the next few years. ... It is obviously advisable to try to identify trusts or management companies with a consistent record' (Dickson, 1991); 'If you can afford it, pay some of your redundancy payment into your pension to boost your retirement savings' (O'Neill, 2023). Normalization of asset ownership takes place here by accepting that there are 'problems of the past and uncertainties of the future', 'yet signing up with a company pension scheme if one is on offer is undoubtedly one of the best ways of making provision for the future' (Guardian, 2006). By using words such as 'undoubtedly' and 'obviously', pensions are depicted as the normal solution for dealing with uncertainty, or else one risks being punished with higher costs:

> There's nothing to stop someone eligible for a personal pension plan taking one out now, regardless of all the changes that may be in the pipeline. Every year's delay in taking out a pension plan will cost you money as the premium rises according to your age, and your contributions will have a year less in which to earn an investment return. (Worsfold, 1987b)

Correspondingly, the current discussion concentrates on how the increase of the state pension age from 66 to 68 will further intensify the pressure on pensioners, leaving 'millions to a miserable and impoverished run-up to retirement' (Jones, 2023), as they expected to receive an income from the state at the age of 66.

This discursive formation of non-agency relies on constraints where 'truth isn't the reward of free spirits ... nor the privilege of those who have succeeded in liberating themselves. Truth is a thing of this world: it is produced only by virtue of multiple forms of constraint' (Foucault, 1980, p 131). The financialized subject is constrained by having to take on financial products and accumulate assets or otherwise being punished with higher costs and not having financial security during periods of income shortfalls.

Running through this discursive formation is a distinction between conforming (or desirable) behaviour and non-conforming behaviour. As outlined by Foucault (1972), discursive formations are not only constituted through what unites them but also by the marginalization of others. In line with the policy discourses outlined in Chapter 3, a continuous reference is made to responsible people working hard and saving, and therefore deserving of being helped in difficult situations, and to those people who are irresponsible and cannot expect society to provide for them. The media discourse also develops here a connection to family values, where finance should be taught early on 'to stop this cycle of bad money management and general ignorance about money ... since it's never too early to start learning how to handle money responsibly – children should know about ISAs as well as iPods' (Anstead, 2007). Irresponsible behaviour is defined as being caused by a lack of self-discipline, for example, taking on too much debt or not planning: 'people still make poor choices ... people give up protection before giving up television subscriptions' (Quinn, 2013). Similar to the government discourse, non-compliance is ascribed to the irresponsible behaviour of the individual rather than to systemic inequalities.

The personalization strategy

In constructing regimes of truth, Foucault (1980, p 131) emphasizes not only the importance of 'techniques and procedures' in the form of regulations and discourses, but also the role of experts who claim authority in portraying the truth, which can be seen in the strategies adopted by the media. News outlets have regular as well as invited pension and fund managers who give advice on how to develop an asset strategy. In particular, in light of crisis situations, 'star managers' are asked to suggest 'defensive strategies' (Gammell, 2007). Even though these experts are depicted as knowing the answers, a connection to the everyday person is built by displaying vulnerability ('[they] are also human beings: they can make mistakes' (Waters, 1990). They themselves are in the learning process but are nevertheless able to earn returns, as exemplified in a statement made by an expert: 'Wow said my wife, calculating that the portfolio had increased by 79.48% in only three months. ... I am just a private investor trying to demonstrate that someone can make a profit without specialised information accessible only to professionals' (Goldstein-Jackson, 2000).

In recent years, Martin Lewis has been gaining in importance in the UK as a financial expert with his website moneysavingexpert.co.uk. The site proclaims to adopt a more sceptical view of financial institutions and to 'fight your corner with journalistic research'. The average UK household, Lewis states, is to be able to gain a pay rise of up to 25 per cent based on finding 'tricks to beat the system' and becoming an 'active, savvy customer' (Lewis, 2023a). In the current cost-of-living crisis, personal finance experts have gained even more prominence and appear on daily TV news.

Alongside experts, celebrities are interviewed and asked about their handling of financial affairs to build a connection between people's financial behaviour and the behaviour of their favourite star. To further increase engagement with finance and asset ownership, personalized stories are presented. *The Daily Telegraph*, *Financial Times* and *The Guardian* have sections on personal finance where readers can submit questions and a financial expert gives advice. Because of recognizing that 'people like to personalise their investments' (Burgess, 2002), a connection to everyday life is established by acknowledging that finance is not necessarily an enjoyable topic for everyone. This has been done, for instance, with the help of artificial case studies such as 'The Plowshares' in *Financial Times*:

> John is in his study, perusing the six-monthly interest statement from his wife's building society account. He is appalled to see just how little the return on their rainy-day money has become. Pushing aside piles of papers, he eventually finds a calculator. After a fair amount of cursing and scribbling on the back of an envelope, he discovers that the £22,000 which the couple prudently left in the building society (in Alison's name, for tax purposes) is now getting interest at only half the percentage rate that was applicable when they put the money into the account two years ago. Later that evening, he and Alison are eating supper and discussing life in general. ... Better news on the work front has made him quietly confident that things may be improving generally.

He tells Alison: I've been thinking about our rainy day building society money. We've got over £20,000 which is only earning 6% interest at the moment, while our equity investments through unit trusts made just over 30% last year. I think that we should move some of the savings money over to equities. (Chandler, 1993)

Several aspects are mentioned here which connect to the everyday life and are also picked up in the wider media discourse. First, the discussion surrounding finance is portrayed as a 'normal' activity which households should integrate into their daily routines, for example, discussing finance during supper.

Second, asset accumulation requires active involvement. The statement 'perusing the six-monthly interest payments' shows that it is essential to be active. Even when having set up a pension, 'it is vital to keep an eye on your scheme to check it is performing to target' (Jones, 1997). When experiencing debt problems, one should talk to the bank rather than being 'an ostrich' (Anstead, 2007) and 'sweeping debt problems under the carpet' (Chandler, 1993). Using metaphors establishes a connection to daily discourses and puts emphasis on the severity of inaction. At the same time, one should not make rash decisions. One is advised to be cautious (not to 'invest all your money in the latest whizz scheme ... it is best to be methodical' [Grisp, 1984]) and patient which means 'remaining calm despite the disappointing recent performance' and 'take a long-term view' (Cowie et al, 2008). Here again a reference is made to everyday activities: 'Stock market investment is like growing asparagus: you should have always started five years ago' (Thorniley, 2001).

Third, terms such as 'cursing and scribbling' indicate that finance is not easy, acknowledging the complex character of finance which 'is no longer a matter of stashing away coins under the bed ... because of its complexities and the various changes in the law' (Thorniley, 2001). Articles are started with slogans such as 'Confused?' (Archer, 2006), 'Baffled by the stock market?' (Edwards, 1987) or 'Managing your money in the 21st century is much harder than it should be' (Daley, 2017). Succeeding in managing money does not come naturally but needs to be learned: 'Humans come in two forms, one can manage its money and enjoys budgeting; the other can't and doesn't. Most people belong to the second category' (Dibben, 1984). By acknowledging that it is difficult and not necessarily enjoyable ('there's no way of making this palatable, or amusing. It's both indigestible and dull, but here it goes' [Langan, 1997]), the media establishes a connection to households while pointing out that one must be active, and that this requires self-control and practice:

Frankly, I always find a systematic routine of daily physical exercise difficult to maintain. I know it's good for me, and I always feel a satisfying sense of self-control whenever I carry it out. Yet a thousand and one excuses regularly crowd it out. I suspect that many people's attitude to their personal finances, and I wouldn't exclude myself here, is similar. (Meacher, 1984)

Including oneself in the group of those being less interested in finance while also suggesting ways of overcoming the problem establishes a personal connection to the reader ('it's hard enough to earn, so when you've got some cash it makes no sense to fritter it away. We all do it but there's no reason we shouldn't change' [TG, 2007]). Through being disciplined ('financing a dream retirement takes discipline' [Hunter, 2016]) and accumulating assets, one is rewarded with opportunities: 'Fancy an easy pay rise? Start a pension and you've got one. Not only will the government top up your pension pot, but if you're employed, your employer may also have to help' (Lewis, 2023b).

Asset norms are thus constructed with the help of discursive strategies which personalize the rather abstract, complex financial world and make accumulating assets desirable. The question, however, remains: how do households engage with mechanisms of responsibilization and financialization? This is answered in the next section.

Bringing about the everyday asset manager

Foucault (1977, p 194) understands power as productive instead of restrictive: 'we must cease once and for all to describe the effects of power in negative terms; it 'excludes', it 'represses' … power produces, it produces reality'. This is, however, not understood as a one-dimensional approach; instead one's identity is co-constructed based on power relations and everyday experiences and its concomitant resistances. Indeed, 'there is a plurality of resistances … that are possible, necessary, improbable; others that are spontaneous, savage, solitary, concerted, rampant, or violent; still others that are quick to compromise, interested, or sacrificial' (Foucault, 1978, p 96). For this purpose, it is uncovered here how norms of asset ownership become accepted as routines in everyday life and how everyday practices shape the everyday asset manager subject. Along these lines, the discursive negotiation of asset norms is explored first before presenting asset-accumulation practices and their impact on everyday life in subsequent chapters.

'We all have to do it': rising insecurity as an enabler of asset norms

Reflecting on institutional changes and the accompanying financial insecurity, interviewees doubt that disciplinary mechanisms of responsibilization, namely labour market regulation and the retreat of the welfare state, and regulatory mechanisms of financialization, namely wider access to financial products and asset norms, is for the benefit of the people. They recognize that the rising importance of asset ownership contributes to the decline of public welfare services ("everybody is encouraging you to do it [pension investments]; actually I think it was a way of the government feeling less responsible" [Scarlett]) and identify the privatization of national companies in the 1980s as "a bribe to everyone to invest" while "Thatcher was selling off all the family silver" (James). This trust deficit in government actions is accompanied by a distrust of financial institutions, which are characterized as all-encompassing, profit-seeking institutions ("there's some very greedy people out there" [Robert]). "Finance, big people" are perceived as luring people into disadvantageous contracts which are "valuable to them" (Ruby) and where they solely act in their own interest ("people are out to make their own money" [Baron]), aiming to earn more profits.

Yet, due to rising costs ("people don't have money security anymore" [Ruby]) and job insecurity ("no one's jobs are secure"), both, as suggested in Chapter 2, belonging to the disciplinary mechanism, interviewees are 'quick to compromise' (Foucault, 1978, p 96) and see no alternative than to comply with asset norms ("We all have to do it" [Oscar]). Reminiscent of Foucault's (2003, p 96) elaboration on the role of fear in governing ('sovereignty is always shaped from below, and by those who are afraid') and of the fear of old-age poverty mentioned in the media discourse, the fear of being 'poverty stricken' acts as an enabler here: 'I need to be able to provide for my future, so that I am, I don't like the idea, you know, when you see these things on television of, you know, some little old lady poverty stricken somewhere, I'd hate the thought" (Beatrix).

Since there are no more "jobs for life" (Millie) in an environment of less welfare provision ("your state pension and your private pension will not be enough to look after you when you're older" [Oscar]), security is established through asset accumulation, ensuring "that when I can't work and I don't have, you know, a regular income that I still have a regular income but from a different source" (Pippa). This depicts a difference to the theorized neoliberal investor subject. Rather than being someone who 'embraces, and bears financial market risk' (Langley, 2007, p 70) and welcomes 'the promise of investment returns' (Langley, 2007, p 76), interviewees draw on a discourse of non-agency, emphasizing the need to accumulate assets in order to "have some security and stability" (Fleur). Notions of distrust ("who's gonna get the profits, the directors and the board" [Agnes]) and the consequent justification of asset accumulation based on having no other choice are a common discursive pattern ("It's a necessary evil" [Pippa]) when discussing the three key elements of institutional changes: job security, homeownership and pensions.

Because of the welfare state providing less security in the form of pension provisions and unemployment insurance ("In the olden days … you had a salary, you had a final pension, you had security. It's totally different now" [Clementine]), interviewees emphasize the need to have savings for rainy day funds: "it's important to have a certain amount of flexible cash so in case something crops up" [Tobias]). Rainy day savings create "security that if something were to happen, they can buy some time to make the right decision for the future rather having been forced into snap decisions" (Fern). Strikingly, when discussing rainy day funds, a continual reference is made to how essential it is to be able to provide in case someone in the household becomes unemployed: "We have some kind of savings that put us through a bit, but you only want to do that for a small amount of time I'd rather think. I think my fall back would be to get another job quickly" (Nancy). What this statement shows is the disciplining mechanism of a retreating welfare state where less unemployment protection constructs individual responsibility as a key mechanism to ensure financial security. The interviewees realize that state provision in the form of sickness and unemployment pay would not be sufficient and that employment is less secure ("the whole employment is totally different now. Now you're lucky if you get a two-year contract" [Frank]). Whereas in the "old times ... you could just walk out one job, literally just walk out of one, into another" (Fern), now even public sector jobs are not secure "and those are what I consider the more secure jobs" (Millie). This represents a rather robust understanding of the changes in the labour market, where deregulation has led to higher insecurity due to the threat of unemployment and is reminiscent of the entrepreneurial discourse of emergency savings.

The second element is homeownership, which has been a key element of the change towards an asset-based welfare society, as discussed in Chapter 3, and which was promoted by Margaret Thatcher in the 1980s and deepened by successive governments. Interviewees frame homeownership as the norm ("There is a lot of kind of just preconceived acceptance that buying is the thing to do" [Darcy]) and see renting as losing money ("renting is just, you're throwing money away" [Imogen]). Here, the same metaphors as in the media are used, such as "throwing money down the drain" (Anu [TG, 2007]) to signify that homeownership is a desired form of investing ("I try to think ahead, I wanted to get on the property ladder" [Emily]), leaving no room for choosing to rent ("I could have stayed at home and not moved out" [Layla]). This discourse is supported by non-discursive elements such as the Right to Buy scheme and the deregulated mortgage market. Interviewees who "never thought [they] would own a house" have been able to buy one due to house subsidies ("I actually got this for half the value, which is about £79,000 in the end" [Pippa]) and deregulatory measures: "Thatcher has just altered all the rules for borrowing money and suddenly it became very easy to get a mortgage when I bought a house" (Daniel).

Yet, interviewees recognize that widening access to homeownership has been accompanied by an increasingly insecure rental market: "there is less security you know, the person who owns it might decide to sell it and then what do you do you're paying a lot of money for something that you're not guaranteed" (Darcy). A deregulated rental market where it has been made easier for landlords to end a tenancy and raise prices has forced some of the interviewees to step onto the property ladder:

> 'Our rent was £750 a month for this one bedroom flat and then we get a notice and they want to be up to £1,260 a month , which is something like nearly a 50 per cent or 40 per cent increase ... it's a £500 increase which was not feasible for such crappy accommodation. We started to look around ... We got our house that way ... and it was more expensive if we had been paying rent but it was cheaper than what we were going to be paying rent.' (Oscar)

At times this even led to lower mortgage costs than rent: "the rent was more expensive than my mortgage repayment" (Akio). The discourse of non-agency is employed here through repeating the commanding verb 'have to', which denotes an obligation to conform to asset norms even when resenting these:

> 'You sort of feel like you have to play the game that's the thing for me, well, but I've got on it because otherwise I won't be able to and everyone else is doing it ... I sort of resent that. I am having to buy a house, but everyone says it's the right thing to do and you sort of go, is it? ... well other countries don't and why you sort of feel like you've been sucked into this perspective. Well, you've got to have this because that's what's going to give you security in the future.' (John)

When having a family, this is further deepened because of being "locked in the rat race" (Millie) – for example, by setting up insurances because of wanting to provide for the family: "You buy into one financial package, that means you have to buy into these other financial packages, and all that probably does is increase your reliance on those financial packages" (John).

The third element where the interplay between responsibilization and financialization emerges goes back to the privatization of pensions, which involved reducing the state pension and promoting private pensions. The replacement of defined-benefit (DB) workplace pensions (also referred to as final salary schemes) with defined-contribution (DC) schemes (also referred to as money purchase schemes), as outlined in Chapter 3, is foregrounded in interviewees' discourses: "gradual backing out from the final salary scheme, so everything became money purchase" (Alfred). Interviewees deconstruct the understanding of pensions as universally beneficial by highlighting the uncertainty inherent in workplace pensions ("not as good as they used to be, they used to be final salary pensions" [Amy]). A particular reference is made to the numerous pension scandals where continuous changes and less protection led to people losing their pension investments: "pension schemes although supposedly ring-fenced had actually been raided by the company and pensioners are left without their money" (Alfred). This is a quite rational understanding of the ambiguity inherent in pensions where pension income is reliant on the performance of the funds without having a guarantee for generating sufficient value for retirement (Langley and Leaver, 2012; Webber, 2018): "there had been cases where people consolidated their pensions into one big pension system and that system either failed or its investment hasn't worked very well" (Edward). In spite of this negative view, due to having less security through the state ("pension is important for everyone because the state pension is not gonna be enough" [Agnes]), interviewees articulate the necessity to develop a "safety net" (Nancy).

The disciplinary mechanism, that is, the 'activity of conducting', thus works in tandem with the regulatory mechanism ('the way in which one conducts oneself' [Foucault, 2004, p 258]) in constructing asset norms. Despite negatively reflecting on asset norms, interviewees pursue asset ownership to be financially secure: "financial products aren't necessarily set up to do you a massive favour but sometimes you just have to have them" (Oscar). Feeling trapped in the treadmill of asset ownership results in being relieved when the pressure to accumulate assets disappears at retirement: "hunting the house, buying the house, selling, the job changing and things like that and thank goodness, it's over really" (Hattie). "Now the only time I get on a treadmill is at the gym. I am not on the treadmill of life anymore. The house is bought and paid for … I've got another four pensions" (Charles).

The coexistence of antagonistic modes within the same subject position reflects a 'sacrificial' form of counter-conduct where individuals express an unwillingness to submit to asset norms but are 'quick to compromise' in action (Foucault, 1978, p 96). Using metaphorical expressions such as being "sucked into this perspective", "locked in the rat race", "play their game" (Ruby) and not wanting to have the "wheels fall off the cart" (Isabella) position households as passive subjects that are trapped on the treadmill of asset ownership. By expressing dissatisfaction with having to accumulate assets ("the private sector pension industry, a money-making industry for the private sector" [Nadeem]), they smooth the contradiction between conforming to asset norms and having a critical view of it. Resistances are thus 'possible, necessary' (Foucault, 1978, p 96) in normalizing asset ownership.

'I wanted to be free': positioning as an everyday asset manager

The everyday asset manager subject comes into being by not only drawing on a non-agency discourse, but also by having internalized an agency discourse, albeit differently interpreted than the government and media discourse. As in the case of the non-agency discourse, the agency discourse is found to be reconstructed to represent a critical view of finance and not seeing finance as unequivocally beneficial.

Within the agency discourse, asset accumulation is framed as a key factor in gaining freedom ("gives you freedoms and it gives you choices, you wouldn't otherwise have" [Habib]), and freedom of choice is depicted as essential in pursuing asset ownership by employing discursive practices in the form of value terms ('fortunately') and metaphors: "Thank God that they got rid of the obligations to taking an annuity because that would have been complete suicide" (Alfred). Interestingly, a parallel can be drawn to the policy discourse provided in the previous chapter where, rather than solving underlying inequalities, further deregulation of financial products is seen as beneficial. Feeling constrained in their mortgage choice, arguments for competition are put forward in the interest of increasing flexibility ("more flexibility and freedom for some of the products" [Millie]), and having more mortgage providers is equated with beneficial rates: "there was only one mortgage provider ... and of course, that meant that their rates were not terribly competitive" (Theodore). The concept of competition is enacted with the help of a comparison to other countries ("we have no rule variety") and assigning strong adjectives to the term, for instance, "real competition" (Oscar).

However, while the discourse drawing on freedom ("it's giving me financial freedom now" [Millie]) and choice can be found here, financial institutions are viewed critically ("I never really trusted financial institutions" [Alfred]). Freedom is not seen as gaining the possibility to be a 'wealth creator' and to fulfil 'dreams' by climbing up the social ladder (see media discourse), but as being able to gain control and be independent ("financially independent no matter what happens" [Isabella]). Because of distrusting financial institutions and wanting to achieve financial security, the discourse of independence is foregrounded here: "I wanted some financial security ... My mom wasn't an independent person and I really wanted to have financial independence, and not rely on anybody ... so as soon as I could I bought a property" (Millie). Not having "to ask anybody's approval" (Scarlett) when not having sufficient assets to provide financial security, thus having to take out debt in case of income shortfalls, is depicted as essential in pursuing asset ownership ("I wanted to be free to decide what I want to do" [Fleur]). Agency and non-agency discourse are used to express a critical view of finance, showing among the 'plurality of resistances' (Foucault, 1978, p 95) that households 'can never be ensnared by power, they [we] can always modify its grips' (Foucault, 2003, p 280).

The coexistence of antagonistic discourses within the agency discourse where, on the one hand, financial products are depicted as helping to deal with institutional changes ("you are expected to have the house, for this you need a mortgage" [Layla]) and, on the other hand, as disadvantageous for the everyday person ("they can speculate with our money on the stock market and make themselves big bonuses" [Richard]) has led to distancing oneself from investments. When being asked directly how they would define investments, interviewees appear to equate them with stocks and shares: "I don't really have any investments, you know, I don't really have stocks and shares and all of those kind of things" (John). In contrast to an asset which is "something solid", which you are able to see ("It's something you can see and it exists" [Millie]), investments are established as being distant ("something externally managed" [John]) and incorporating risk ("investment is risk" [Agnes]). Distancing oneself from investments, the declaration of "not [being] a financially investment-oriented sort of person" (Alfred) is made and emphasis is placed on not taking on risk by means of investing in stocks and shares ("I wouldn't want to take this risk" [Rita]).

Power is argued to be specifically strong if it operates 'on a much more minute and everyday level' (Foucault, 1980, p 60), in particular in the case when asset norms enter one's own desires without necessarily being aware of it. Despite rejecting investments when being asked directly, the discourse of investments is all-encompassing in interviewees' discourses when not being questioned directly about them. The house is described as an investment rather than a home ("That's why I invested in my house" [Bethany]) where improvements such as "putting new double glazers" is perceived as "an investment in the home really more than anything" (Beatrix) and a house seen when driving to lunch is identified as a potential buy-to-let purchase: "I mean this conversation literally just came up because the house went on sale over the weekend and we went out for lunch on a Sunday and as we're driving past, you know, we were saying: gosh, we should maybe think about another future investment" (Emily).

Not only is the house constructed as an investment but also savings ("last investment I took out was the savings account with HSBC" [Fleur]) and pensions ("you need your pension as an investment" [Millie]). A recurring figure of speech used here is "something that appreciates and puts money in my pocket" (Vibha). By employing metaphors, such as "it has the potential to sort of wash its face" (Eva), the normalization of an appreciating value ("anything that increases in value" [Ida]) for the future becomes clear.

Perhaps more importantly, the pervasiveness of the new regime of truth becomes evident by having adopted the underlying reasoning for establishing asset-based welfare. Interviewees recycle the political discourse of self-reliance without being necessarily aware of it, illuminating the 'masked' character of discursive formations such as self-reliance (Foucault, 1972, p 12).

'There are some people that don't own their houses and they are burdens to the state, so to speak, and those people will never have anything. They might get a little bit of money, every single week to do something with ... then you've got people that ... work really hard to have what they've got, but no one cuts them a break.' (Oscar)

Through the criticism that hard-working people do not receive sufficient support, people who rely on the state are victimized, echoing the discourse of 'workfare' where only the ones who actively seek jobs deserve to receive help (White and Lakey, 1992). A dichotomy between the ones who deserve it, namely hard-working people, and the ones who don't deserve it is constructed: "actual English grannies, old people, sat on the street with a begging bowl. I am not talking about junk derelicts, drug abusers, I am talking about genuine people who've worked hard all their life" (Daniel).

Normalization of asset ownership thus has a 'massifying' effect on households ("it was just sort of what everybody did" [Tobias]). Interviewees coming from different family backgrounds and belonging to different income brackets stressed the need to accumulate assets in order "to have some security and stability", since "there is always that fear that you sort of think, yeah, you could lose everything and you just wanna hedge" (Fleur). Asset norms are discursively resisted but households are 'quick to compromise' in action (Foucault, 1978, p 96).

Having seen the transformative effects of institutional changes and discourses, the question remains how financial concepts enter interviewees' discourses, for which reason, 'the status of those who are charged with saying what counts as true' (Foucault, 1980, p 131), that means the rules of evidence have been investigated. As highlighted in the personalization strategies discussed in the previous section, interviewees assign authority to experts presented in newspapers: "I used to be an addict of *The Daily Telegraph* Saturday financial thing. Because you would have people there, so I'd read that" (Harriet). Yet, these experts need to be relatable and not "city slickers" (Theodore), developing a clear demarcation between the greedy financial person and the everyday person. A key expert mentioned here is Martin Lewis ("I do like to listen to Martin Lewis" [Tobias]):

'[Choosing ISAs] always for me and, you know, if you'd ask for something like, Martin Lewis he would always go, you know, you go for the, the, the best ones first, which are the ISAs because they're safe, your money is, you always, well, cash ISA you're gonna get money back. Share ISAs you might lose but, you know, the chances are because of the tax advantage, you'll do ok anyway.' (Fern)

By establishing him as a 'guru' ("Martin Lewis is the guru now" [Rita]) and a really 'tight guy' ("Martin Lewis is a celebrity, the really tight guy" [Akio]), distance to the normal person is created and authority assigned. The website of Martin Lewis is used as a source when looking for something specific ("I think that the approach he has is quite interesting … I'd go and have a look at it if he's talking about something" [Ida]) or people sign up for its newsletter: "it caught my attention a couple weeks ago" [Ruby]).

Concluding remarks

While Chapter 3 has shown how the interplay between regulatory mechanism, in the form of asset-based welfare measures, and disciplinary mechanism, in the form of rising insecurity, constructs norms of asset ownership, this chapter has sought to reveal the transformative effects of discourses and institutional changes, being one of the first studies to show how macro-level discourses constructed in the media (rather than policy discourses [Gurney, 1999]) are incorporated in households' discourses.

Replacing direct cash transfers with asset-based welfare measures has been accompanied by three discursive formations constructing asset norms (see Figure 4.1). The entrepreneurial discourse calls on households to accumulate financial and non-financial assets (including bonds, stocks and shares and unit trusts), avoid debt except for asset-accumulation purposes and integrate finance rationality (including diversification and hedging). This subjectification of households depicts a difference to the theorized everyday investor subject (Langley, 2006). Rather than property investment being a deviation from an envisioned investor subject who develops a portfolio based on financial market assets, it is part of the everyday asset manager constituted in the governmental and media discourse. Realizing that people do not necessarily behave as theoretically expected and wanting to ensure they still conform to asset norms, the media discourse has more recently focused on managed investments where the first step is to invest in, for instance, stocks and shares ISAs before directly investing in stocks and shares.

Figure 4.1: Construction of the everyday asset manager

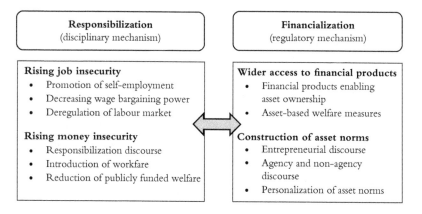

In line with the policy discourse, asset norms are made desirable by employing a dichotomous discourse of agency and non-agency. Whereas the agency discourse focuses on creating opportunities where everyone can become an entrepreneur, that is, adopt the characteristics of capitalists, the non-agency discourse puts emphasis on having no other choice than to adopt asset norms or otherwise risk old-age poverty. By employing personalization strategies, a connection to everyday life is built. These personalization strategies, including the views of experts, are also reflected in interviewees' rules of evidence, that is, the identification of perceived trustworthy sources.

Through these mechanisms individuals engage with the subject position of the everyday asset manager, revealing the transformative power of institutional changes and discourses as assumed by the Foucauldian-inspired everyday financialization literature. The dominance of the media discourse can be seen, among others, by employing the 'same play of metaphors' (Foucault, 1972, p 33) when putting forward arguments for accumulating assets. Yet, the governmental construction of conduct brings with it not only the freedom to adhere to norms of conduct but also the possibility of counter-conduct. Interviewees engage critically with notions of asset accumulation due to financial institutions being perceived as profit-seeking. While having internalized the dichotomous discourse between agency and non-agency when discussing institutional changes, these discourses are used to express a critical view of finance, showing the 'plurality of resistances' (Foucault, 1978, p 95). Freedom of choice is not seen as the opportunity to climb up the social ladder but a way of gaining control (agency discourse), and reflecting on institutional changes in the form of less social welfare provisions (disciplinary mechanism) is given as underlying reasoning for feeling trapped in having to provide financial security for themselves. Less security originating from decreasing state provisions and rising job insecurity has resulted in the need to establish a safety net through accumulating financial and non-financial assets.

Given that households draw on notions of insecurity to justify asset accumulation, it is argued here that while investment choices might be limited by contradictions incorporated in adopting a financialized subjectivity, these do not lead to a rejection of asset accumulation, as suggested by the literature (Munro, 2000; Langley, 2008; Lai, 2017). Instead, the disciplinary technology of power and its concomitant insecurity acts as an enabler in normalizing asset norms (regulatory mechanism). Despite viewing institutional changes critically, interviewees state that they have no choice but to accumulate assets in order to mitigate future risks. Metaphorical expressions and discursive strategies are used to smoothen this contradiction between viewing financial institutions critically while having to use them to accumulate assets. Interviewees distance themselves from investments. A clear differentiation is made between investments which are equated with stocks and shares and accumulating assets to provide for oneself during retirement.

PART III

Being an Everyday Asset Manager

The Conduct of the Everyday
Asset Manager

After having established the mutually generative relationship between disciplinary and regulatory mechanisms in constructing asset norms and interviewees' discursive engagement with these, this section will reveal how discourses are translated into everyday financial practices. The goal is to discover if and how households adopt norms of conduct – defined as developing a diversified asset portfolio guided by finance rationality (Pellandini-Simanyi and Banai, 2021) – and thus impersonate characteristics of capitalists and non-capitalists at the same time (Weiss, 2015).

If workers have moved closer to becoming capitalists by being investors, it should be reflected in accruing capital income from a highly diversified asset portfolio (Martin, 2002; Allon, 2014). Consequently, and as constructed in the political and media discourse, everyday investors should not predominantly rely on 'passive' financial products (Lai, 2016b, p 38) and instead should actively engage with riskier investments such as bonds, stocks and shares and investment portfolios. To achieve financial growth, they embrace risk as an opportunity and adopt financial strategies similar to companies, such as diversification and hedging, thus internalizing finance rationality (see Chapter 2). In contrast, the characteristics of labour can be seen when interviewees do not enjoy the same investment possibilities available to capitalists and adopt self-disciplining mechanisms to achieve asset accumulation. This is the case when households overly rely on low-yielding, illiquid forms of wealth, that is, if they do not diversify their asset portfolio, do not hedge against future income losses and restrict their everyday life to achieve asset ownership. For this reason, this chapter will first uncover interviewees' asset strategy before highlighting in the next chapter its impact on everyday life.

In this context, examination of households' asset composition, combined with the analysis of the semi-structured interviews, gauges the extent to which households have actually been empowered and how far they have adopted a financial calculus into their financial practices. Taking data from the Wealth and Assets Survey (WAS), and incorporating insights from semi-structured interviews, provides an overview of households' balance sheets while simultaneously disclosing the motives behind financial decisions. The asset composition will reveal whether private asset accumulation has resulted in an engagement with riskier assets within all income groups, and this will be followed by an exploration of finance rationality which will uncover the financial strategies employed or rejected. Even though the survey offers interesting insights, it is not seen as generalization but as part of the qualitative research. The chapter positions interviewees' statements and balance sheets within the asset composition of UK households and discusses how interviewees situate themselves with regards to asset norms and how this is reflected in their asset ownership and strategies employed. This approach not only demonstrates motives behind financial practices but also reveals that interviewees respond to forces of responsibilization and financialization as proactive and discerning actors.

Composition of the asset portfolio

Based on a restructuring of the welfare state into an asset-based welfare system, policy and media discourses, as outlined in the previous two chapters, have called upon people to take on financial responsibility by accumulating assets and using financial markets to hedge against future risks. Deviating behaviour such as overly relying on one asset group, for example property or investing mainly in liquid assets, is identified as counter-conduct which needs to be corrected. This chapter explores the 'regimes of practices' (Dean, 1999, p 23) within asset accumulation, making it possible to depict a nuanced picture of counter-conduct. Here it is acknowledged that due to there being 'a plurality of resistances' (Foucault, 1978, p 96), those resistances which 'are quick to compromise' (Foucault, 1978, p 96) can also form part of a financialized subject position, enabling a welfare system which responsibilizes its citizens for their financial welfare. To unpick financial practices, a snapshot of UK households' balance sheets will be combined with interviewees' underlying rationalities.

'Gaining control': the three-pronged asset-accumulation strategy

According to norms of asset accumulation, a financially rational household should not only accumulate assets but also integrate a balanced overall risk level in their asset portfolio, including clearly safe (transaction and savings accounts, government products), fairly safe (housing assets, life insurance policies, managed bonds and shares, pensions, unit and investment trusts), and risky assets (stocks and shares, undiversified bonds, business assets, main residence with underlying mortgage, other real estate [Guiso et al, 2002; Lowe, 2010, 2023]). Yet, besides a substantial growth of financial and non-financial assets since the deregulation and dismantling of the welfare state, the two components growing the most were housing and pension wealth (WID, 2018). This has resulted in them representing the two biggest components of UK households' balance sheets (see Table 5.1), only switching in relative importance from property to pensions in the more recent versions of the survey, which can be explained by the introduction of auto-enrolment in 2012.

While 68 per cent of employees are currently contributing to a workplace pension (ABI Analysis, 2017), the majority of new savers have a defined-contribution (DC) scheme and save less than what is needed for income replacement during retirement, often only making minimum contributions (Cribb et al, 2023). This could be levelled out with investments in financial assets; however, while around one third of UK households own bonds and shares, they comprise only 4.6 per cent of the overall wealth (see Table 5.2). A similar distribution can be found in interviewees' balance sheets, where property and pensions dominate (see Table 5.3), but with a higher focus on property than on pensions and an even lower relative importance assigned to bonds and shares (comprising 1.8 per cent of the overall assets). This has been represented in the literature as a rejection of the investor subjectivity, with the argument being that property is used in a non-strategic manner (Langley, 2007; Mitchell and Lusardi, 2012; Clark, 2014) by overly relying on property instead of developing a 'portfolio of financial market assets'

Table 5.1: Composition of household wealth in the UK

Years	2006–2008	2008–2010	2010–2012	2012–2014	2014–2016*	2016–2018
Total assets (net) in £billion (nominal)	8,426	8,946	9,448	10,886	12,934	14,628
Property wealth (net)	42%	38%	37%	35%	35%	35%
Financial wealth (net)	12%	12%	14%	14%	14%	15%
Pension wealth	34%	39%	37%	40%	41%	42%
Physical wealth	11%	11%	11%	10%	10%	9%

* Up until Wave 5 the survey period covered July to June, but starting in 2014 it switched to April to March.

Source: Author's own presentation based on ONS (2018)

Table 5.2: Proportion of UK households holding assets and liabilities

Share of total assets	Assets	Ownership rates	Asset share	Ownership rates	Liability share	Liabilities	Share of total liabilities
Property wealth 40.8%	Main residence (FS–R)	66%	34.66%	33%	73.00%	Main residence	Property debt 89.5%
	Other houses (second houses FS–R)	4%	1.60%	1.6%	3.00%	Other houses (second houses)	
	Buy-to-let (R)	5%	3.17%	3.2%	11.4%	Buy-to-let	
	Other property (R)	5%	1.41%	0.7%	1.47%	Other property	
Transaction accounts 1%	Current accounts in credit (CS)	93%	1.05%	0.1%	0.60%	Equity release	
Savings products 4.3%	Savings accounts (CS)	57%	2.64%	16%	3.17%	Formal loans	Financial liabilities 10.5%
	Cash ISA (CS)	41%	1.56%	1%	0.27%	Informal loans	
	Other children's savings (CS)	13%	0.08%	6%	2.32%	Student loans	
Bonds 1.4%	National Savings Certificates and bonds (CS)	19%	0.45%	15%	1.62%	Hire purchase	
	UK and overseas bonds/gilts (FS–R)	1%	0.09%	24%	1.69%	Credit and charge cards	
	Fixed term bonds (FS)	8%	0.85%	13%	0.38%	Overdrafts (in use)	
Shares 3.2%	UK shares (R)	11%	1.20%	4%	0.04%	Store cards and charge accounts	
	Stocks and shares ISAs (FS)	12%	1.26%	5%	0.08%	Mail order accounts	
	Employee shares and options (R)	6%	0.58%	5%	0.11%	All household arrears (excl. mortgage arrears)	
	Overseas shares (R)	2%	0.17%				
Other financial assets 1.7%	Investment trusts, unit trusts etc. (FS)	5%	0.79%	2.4%	0.77%	New loans (formal and informal)	
	Child's trust funds (FS)	17%	0.06%				
	Insurance products* (FS)	4%	0.38%				
	All endowments (FS)	1%	0.11%				
	Other financial assets (FS)	1%	0.34%				

Table 5.2: Proportion of UK households holding assets and liabilities (continued)

Share of total assets	Assets	Ownership rates	Asset share	Ownership rates	Liability share	Liabilities	Share of total liabilities
Pension wealth (FS) 38.5%	Current defined-benefit plans (FS)	29%	12.47%				
	Current defined-contribution plans (FS–R)	22%	1.46%				
	Personal pension (FS–R)	12%	1.25%				
	AVCs (FS)	1%	0.06%				
	Retained rights in defined-benefit pensions	14%	3.60%				
	Retained rights in defined-contribution plans (FS–R)	17%	1.30%				
	Rights retained in personal pensions (FS–R)	1%	0.08%				
	Pensions expected from spouse/partner (FS–R)	1%	0.15%				
	Pensions in Payment (FS)	30%	18.17%				
Physical wealth (FS) 9%	Home contents (CS)	79%	7.14%				
	Collectables and valuables (CS)	12%	0.35%				
	Vehicles (CS)	17%	1.54%				

Note: Data based on cross-sectional household weight; CS = clearly safe; FS = fairly safe; R = risky; ★ insurance products are insurance products which include an investment component, solely life insurances are not included in the WAS. Other financial assets include other investments, informal assets, ISAs (type unknown). Other property includes overseas property, land UK, buildings. Other houses include second houses/flats in the UK to live rather than rent out as in the case of buy-to-lets.

Source: Author's calculation based on ONS (2018)

Table 5.3: Balance sheet composition of interviewed households

Assets		Value in £	Ownership rates	Asset share	Ownership rates	Liability share	Value in £	Liabilities	
Property wealth 58.4%	Main residence (FS–R)	13,260,995	77.80%	37.09%	40.0%	59.78%	2,512,040	Main residence	Property debt 94.7%
	Buy-to-let (R)	5,232,900	24.40%	14.64%	6.7%	21.35%	897,000	Buy-to-let	
	Other property (R)	2,385,000	13.30%	6.67%	6.7%	13.61%	572,000	Other property	
Transaction accounts 0.2%	Current accounts in credit (CS)	75,704	NA	0.21%	11.1%	1.12%	47,000	Formal loans	Financial liabilities 5.3%
Savings products 4.5%	Savings accounts (CS)	1,298,197	73.33%	3.63%	15.6%	3.17%	133,009	Loans from the Student Loans Company and bank	
	Cash ISA (CS)	300,350	22.20%	0.84%					
Bonds 1.3%	Premium bonds (CS)	115,000	6.70%	0.32%	11.1%	0.11%	4,618	Credit and charge cards	
	Other bonds (FS)	350,700	15.60%	0.98%	13.3%	0.39%	16,250	Other liabilities (dentist fees, phones)	
Shares 0.5%	Stocks and shares (R)	79,760	11.10%	0.22%					
	Stocks and shares ISAs (FS)	83,300	8.80%	0.23%	6.7%	0.47%	19,876	Car loans	
Other financial assets 1%	Insurance products (FS)	15,500	2.20%	0.04%					
	Other financial assets (awaiting inheritance sell)	335,000	4.40%	0.94%					
Pension wealth 31.9%	Defined-benefit plans (FS)	750,073	15.60%	2.10%					
	Defined-contribution plans (FS–R)	4,096,367	46.70%	11.46%					
	Pensions expected from spouse/partner (FS–R)	127,938	2.20%	0.36%					
	Pensions in Payment (FS)	6,436,143	24.40%	18.00%					
	Pensions in Payment (DB)	5,726,143	13.30%	16.02%					

Table 5.3: Balance sheet composition of interviewed households (continued)

Assets		Value in £	Ownership rates	Asset share	Ownership rates	Liability share	Value in £	Liabilities
	Pensions in Payment (DC)	710,000	11.10%	1.99%				
Physical wealth 0.7%	Home contents	55,600	0.13%	0.16%				
	Collectables and valuables	20,500	0.05%	0.06%				
	Vehicles	164,000	0.38%	0.46%				
Business assets 1.6%	Business assets	566,000	13.00%	1.59%				
Total assets		35,749,027					4,201,793	**Total liabilities**
							31,547,234	**Net worth**

Source: Author's calculation and illustration based on the provided balance sheets by interview participants (n = 45)

(Langley, 2007, p 74). Having explored the underlying reasoning for this asset composition has, however, revealed that these distributions should not be seen as financially irrational but as logical reactions to the contradictions inherent in asset norms, forming part of a financialized subject position.

Contrary to not investing because of the uncertainty involved in financial investments and recognizing that one needs to have sufficient money to invest according to asset norms ("I don't have a shit load of money to invest" [Ida]), interviewees amend asset norms according to their own possibilities and "avoid risks that jeopardizes [their] family's security" (Nancy). Instead of embracing risk, interviewees make sure to "risk a little bit, but only what [they] can afford to lose" (Pippa). Whereas the everyday asset manager presented in the media is someone who invests in stocks and shares, interviewees clearly distinguish themselves from this kind of investment. Comparing shares to gambling is used as a justification to exclude direct share ownership ("I'd never play the stock market or anything like that ... I think of it as gambling actually" [Imogen]). They proclaim that one would need to have sufficient money to invest in riskier assets ("I don't think we're at the financial stage to be doing things like that" [Adhira]), emphasizing that not every income level is compatible with these investments: "me taking 200 quid would be nothing" (Isaac). In contrast to shares, which have been fluctuating substantially, and with one interviewee even equating them to betting on horses ("I don't ever go to a casino, no I never bet on horses" [Bethany]), property is referred to as the "gold standard" (Richard) due to its giving a guaranteed return: "regardless of what the economy seems to do historically, property, if you can ride it out, doubles in value every ten years" (Isabella). Yet, while everyday asset managers invest, among other reasons, in property, it is not the sole investment. Instead, the everyday asset manager relies on an asset strategy consisting of, as suggested in Chapter 4, savings, homeownership and pensions.

The first step of the three-pronged asset-accumulation strategy is to save: "I think I am somebody who believes you do have to save for the future" (Eloise). The average savings of interviewed households, at around £16,302 (excluding an outlier with savings of £532,000), is in line with average savings reported in the WAS. As expected from the entrepreneurial discourse, interviewees define two categories of savings. On the one hand, savings are accumulated for rainy day funds "because you never know what's around the corner" (Baron). These funds are set aside for the purpose of avoiding debt ("rainy day funds really so and I never liked to borrow" [Fleur]) and being able to keep assets in case of unexpected expenses ("I wanted to maintain a level playing field" [Ida]). On the other hand, since "money devalues over time" (Vibha), the main goal of savings lies in using them as a means to generate income: "As long as you got enough to live on then anything extra is obviously going towards your future ... I am trying to save enough money ... that I can put in an OK, you know, percentage as deposit down" (Anu). Hence, once the rainy day funds are covered, savings are invested, either through investment in a house ("buy a house or something that could be used as a means to generate some money" [Nancy]) or through further investments when having already invested in a house ("I've got some savings, I want to do something with it" [Aditi]). Savings thus provide short-term security (rainy day funds) and long-term security (asset accumulation), emanating from the interaction between the disciplinary mechanism of less state provisions creating a preference for liquidity in case of emergencies and the regulatory mechanism of asset norms creating the desire to invest. As a result, and similar to the figure for UK households overall, 73 per cent of households have savings, comprising only 4.5 per cent of assets.

Second, when accumulated savings are sufficient for a house deposit, the everyday asset manager steps onto the "property ladder" (Theo). The importance of property can be seen in the property wealth of interviewed households, comprising 58.4 per cent of overall assets (see Table 5.2).[1] Similar to UK households overall, property wealth is mainly comprised of the value of the main residence. Whereas the focus on homeownership is not a new phenomenon (Gurney, 1999), its perception has changed. Because of it being considered a more trustworthy asset than financial investments ("never seemed to get the returns they were promised" [Ethan]), and in line with the entrepreneurial discourse, the home has become an investment object ("our house is an investment" [Agnes]). Underlined by metaphors ("money is safe in bricks and mortar" [Scarlett]), interviewees justify the aspiration of owning a house not with wanting a home for life but with financial arguments: "We can afford to buy a place and it made sense ... with the UK housing market as it is to invest some money ... that would help us long-term" (John). The first house is often a starter house which is used for five or ten years and then one moves up the property ladder with the goal of making financial gains ("I would have it for a few years, thinking maybe it's the first house" [Saskia]): "[talk between a couple] We wanted to move up the ladder ... the other house was only ever sort of a five-year house" (Amy). "So moving to this [the new house] would be a bit longer term" (Isaac). "Yeah so it's like a ten year house" (Amy).

Also, it is noticeable that households know the current value of their investment and can estimate the future value, as expected by the entrepreneurial media discourse outlined in Chapter 4:

'our aim really is, as I mentioned earlier our house was 414 when we bought it, looking at recent estimates, it's already 445 or something like that. In just nine months it's gone up £30,000 in value but actually by the time we come to sell, it hopefully, it's worth half a million and we might buy a house worth £300,000 … so we then have £200,000 worth of cash.' (Tobias)

This interviewee plans to use the anticipated return as pension income, which illustrates the third pillar of households' asset-accumulation strategy: pensions (Table 5.4).

After having stepped onto the property ladder, interviewees articulate a desire to take advantage of rising property values for the purpose of generating pension income in the future (through downsizing rather than equity withdrawals – "we're going to realize our investment" [Hattie]). For interviewees, it is essential to build sufficient pension provisions ("if you want to have a pension, you gotta do something" [Nadeem]), either in the form of moving up the property ladder, conducting further investments ("some kind of asset that would bring a revenue stream for me" [Akio]) and/ or by contributing to a pension scheme. There is a view that purchasing a house and not being able to put money aside for a pension during that time means that one needs to catch up on pension contributions: "I'm catching up because you should start a pension as soon as you can, so 28, you

Table 5.4: The three-pronged asset-accumulation strategy

Theme	Illustrative quotations
Savings	'When we bought the house, I didn't have anything after that for a while but then after a while we, I, started to save up again, build a pot, I always got a pot.' (Aditi) 'We were starting to accumulate savings so what were we going to do with them? Well we've decided then to buy another house, sold the one we were in and moved into a larger house.' (Scarlett) 'I said we could buy that … it was a better, better return than having the money in the bank, we're getting.' (Rita)
House	'Well I would have it for a few years, thinking maybe it's the first house.' (Saskia) 'It's still in the same area but we did buy again. We had a mortgage on that but that one rose quite considerably in value so we used the money that we got for that to buy this, the bigger house.' (Joseph) 'We would want to get to a point where we own the whole house and then we could sell it, downsize, live off the profit.' (Amy)
Pension	'It was the highest return but it was also the highest risk. My view was because I haven't been able to pay into pension perhaps during my mid-twenties that being able to do it now was a way of catching up in a way.' (John) 'I have an occupational pension, yes I do, and that will start actually when I am 60. And I also bought AVCs [additional voluntary contributions] quite, quite heavily to make sure that absolutely everything has been thought of.' (Eva) '[speaking about moving jobs] My highest priority was looking after my pension rights.' (Baxter)

Source: Author's illustration of the interview data

should have started earlier, so I wanted to gain money as quickly as I can" (Saskia). Becoming clear in this and the following statement is the normal behaviour of making pension provisions, as expressed with 'should have started earlier' and stating a discomfort when not being able to put money aside for a pension: "this is the first time in my life when I have not paid a pension (just realizing it). It does feel quite odd ... I know that's where the brunt's being felt" (Ida). Despite these financial practices, the shift between strong pension provision for the older generation compared to less pension provision for the younger generation, as discussed in the previous chapter, can be seen in interviewed households' balance sheets. Only 28.6 per cent of interviewees contributed to defined-benefit (DB) pensions, which was mainly due to belonging to the older age group or being employed by the government. Despite the higher risk, when compared to a DB pension, interviewees having access to a DC workplace pension contribute to them as they would otherwise lose out on the employer's contribution: "I just thought it made sense financially because I'd get an extra 4 per cent paid in by the company" (Isabella). As a result, similar to UK households overall, the interviewees' biggest asset after property is pension wealth, comprising one-third of their gross wealth.

By amending asset norms to one's own needs, the disciplinary mechanism, that is, the 'activity of conducting', works in tandem with the self-conduct incorporated in the regulatory mechanism (Foucault, 2004, p 258), enabling the asset-based welfare state. Rather than not accumulating assets due to the inherent uncertainty and income constraints in contrast to high-income earners, interviewees emphasize the need to provide financial security for themselves in an environment of less welfare provision, and choose investments which appear to be more safe:

'[It] feels like a start towards a little bit of security in the background. I pay into a mortgage, I pay into a pension 5 per cent and my company puts 5 per cent as well, but I am pretty much aware that that's not going to be enough for how I'd like to live when I retire, so putting money into that is thinking it's definitely going to be some kind of security for the future.' (Saskia)

This focus on pensions and property instead of establishing a diversified asset portfolio including clearly safe, fairly safe and risky assets is arguably a responsible strategy when taking into consideration that interviewees do not want to risk their own home base. The paradox, however, is that despite seeking safety, the strong focus on property and pension wealth has created fragile balance sheets. The share of liquid assets in the form of transaction and savings accounts is low, while half of UK households who own a main residence hold a risky asset, according to finance theory

(Lowe, 2010), due to it being mortgaged. If the interest rates become too high, the costs of mortgages can increase and they cannot easily sell their house and perhaps have to go further into debt since the house is their living base, as seen during the cost–of–living crisis (Peachey, 2023b). This is particularly risky in an environment where mortgages are usually fixed only for 2 or 5 years instead of 25 to 30 years as in other countries. At the same time, pensions are long-term, inaccessible investments which cannot be easily cancelled. In the majority of the cases it is only possible to cancel them in the short-term with a substantial loss. Accumulating assets thus becomes an extension to previously held risks by households, which is intensified when experiencing income constraints, as discussed in the next section.

Unequal wealth distribution

The processes of financialization have played a crucial role in the distribution of income and the types of wealth accumulated by different households. From 1995 to 2009 the top 1 per cent income earners share increased by nearly 5 percentage points from 10.75 per cent to 15.42 per cent. By comparison, over a similar time span in the years prior to the financial deregulation, starting in 1984, the top 1 per cent income earners share increased by only 0.12 per cent (1970–1984 [WID, 2018]). This in turn has an impact on the possibility to accumulate assets. Data from the WAS reveals that wealth is more unequally distributed than income, with a Gini coefficient[2] for asset wealth of 0.60, far exceeding the Gini index of 0.36 for household annual income (ONS, 2022c). Perhaps more importantly, household asset composition reveals a distinct structure of social stratification.[3] We can detect an upper income group of diversified asset portfolio owners earning high rates of return on diverse financial asset holdings (see Figure 5.1), a lower

Figure 5.1: Breakdown of aggregate total wealth per income deciles

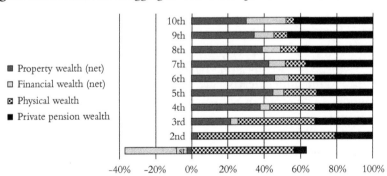

Source: Author's calculations based on ONS (2018)

Figure 5.2: Share of selected financial assets per income deciles

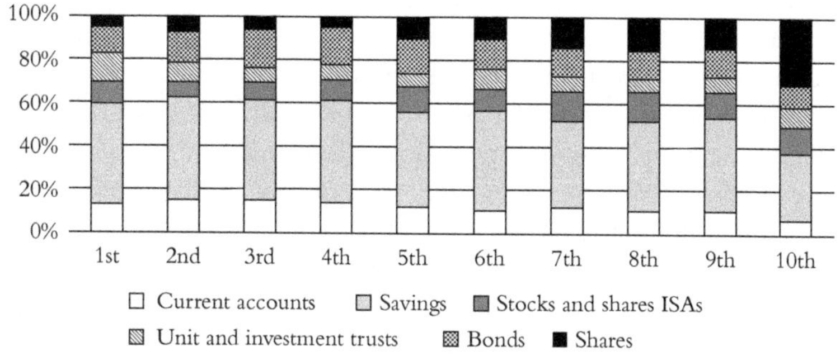

Note: Categorization is taken over from the Wealth and Assets Survey (WAS).

Source: Author's calculation based on ONS (2018)

income group of households renting their accommodation and relying on physical wealth, and a middle-income group characterized by relying on housing and pension assets. The wealth inequality is even more striking when considering the generational gap driven by 'a number of factors, including a growing and ageing population, and the rates of return on different forms of wealth' (ONS, 2018). Whilst older households have increased their property and pension wealth and are now more likely to own their house outright, having benefitted from rising house prices, younger households struggle to buy a house.

The most unequal distribution can be found in net financial wealth where 77.2 per cent is owned by the top 20 per cent income earners and the Gini index increased from 0.81 in Wave 1 (2006–2008) to 0.91 in Wave 5 (2014–2016), culminating in the top 1 per cent income earners holding more financial wealth than the bottom 80 per cent earners (ONS, 2022a). Shares are mainly held by the 10th income earners (30.9 per cent of financial assets pertain to shares here) and direct share ownership becomes relatively more important in the 7th income decile (see Figure 5.2). In contrast, the biggest share in the middle-income group comprises savings accounts. There is, however, a stronger focus on managed investments, specifically in the form of stocks and shares Individual Savings Accounts (ISAs) (13.5 per cent in the 7th decile) and bonds (on average 16.9 per cent between the 3rd and 5th deciles compared to 11.8 per cent in high-income deciles). The interviews have revealed that once households have stepped onto the property ladder and are contributing to a workplace pension, they conduct fairly safe investments when having accumulated savings. Since bonds "are not gonna go crazy but just perhaps the next step out of cash" (Eloise) and one does not risk too much: "I get every month an income … I am not going *oh my god, I am losing money* whereas with shares I probably would be" (Eleanor), they are considered a viable option for investment. Moreover, wider access to stocks and shares by means of managed

ISAs has made it easier to engage with share investments, and the tax allowance has incentivized UK households to contribute to these: "moving all into the stocks and shares ISA each year because it's tax-free … I wouldn't dare to invest directly in stocks and shares" (Harriet).

Even though lower income deciles also include bonds, unit and investment trusts (enabling people to pool their money to invest) and stocks and shares ISAs, net financial wealth is negative or very low in absolute terms and they represent only a small percentage of the overall value in these income categories, ranging from 1.98 per cent for stocks and shares ISAs to 2.67 per cent for unit trusts and 2.94 per cent for bonds out of the overall volume of these assets. The interviews have shown that bonds are often related here to premium bonds, which are government-sponsored, tax-free bonds where the interest is based on a monthly draw (MAS, 2017) and which have often been inherited or bought by the parents ("my Dad bought me some premium bonds" [Robert]). Yet, premium bonds have been shown to generate substantially lower returns than savings accounts (Lewis, 2023c), which in turn results in their real value declining. Employing these products can be a logical reaction to experiencing constraints due to their accessibility, yet it also reinforces wealth inequalities with higher income households being able to rely on financial products which generate higher yields and lower income households predominantly relying on low-yielding premium bonds or risking relatively more of their income by investing in ISAs and unit trusts.

A similar picture can be seen in the case of pension wealth, which is the second most unequal asset category. Out of the four components, it was, however, the only category which experienced a decline in its Gini coefficient from 0.77 in Wave 1 (2006–2008) to 0.72 in Wave 5 (2014–2016) which can be partly explained by the introduction of auto-enrolment workplace pensions in 2012. Overall, the average pension values of the 9th and 10th deciles amount up to £394,756 and £606,305 respectively. In contrast, the average pension wealth in the medium-income group ranges from £74,195 in the 3rd income decile to £185,116 in the 6th decile, reaching £284,895 in the 8th decile. This is a continuing trend as seen in the most recent wave (2018–2020) where it has been revealed that the top income decile holds 64 per cent of all private pension wealth, with a median pension wealth of £637,500 and income deciles 1 through 5 holding less than 1 per cent (ONS, 2022a). When comparing the share of pension contributions, excluding pensions in payments, higher income earners tend to have access to DB pensions whereas middle-income earners rely on retained rights in DB pensions rather than current DB pensions. DB pensions provide more security and households are then able to take on risks in other areas of investments, for example, investing in shares. Higher income households thus not only have higher workplace pension provisions but also less risky pensions. Moreover, while all income deciles contribute to personal pensions, the large majority of these can be found in the 10th income decile, comprising 43.2 per cent of the overall value of personal pensions, with the figure less than 5 per cent up until the 6th income decile.

The third group of assets is property wealth. Here, the Gini coefficient has increased from 0.62 in Wave 1 to 0.67 in Wave 5 with homeownership rates increasing with the income deciles. Fifty per cent of households in the 3rd income decile own their house compared to 67 per cent in the 5th and 85 per cent in the 8th decile. Other types of real estate, including buy-to-let properties, second houses (houses/flats in the UK to live in rather than to rent out as in the case of buy-to-lets) and other property (overseas property, land in the UK, buildings) constitute on average around 10 per cent of property wealth for middle-income households in deciles 5 to 8, compared to 25 per cent for high-income earners. Perhaps most importantly to note here is that property wealth is underpinned by high levels of mortgage debt: 91 per cent of UK household debt consists of property debt, including mortgages and equity release, and half of the households who own their main residence have an underlying mortgage on it (ONS, 2018, 2019). Whilst the secured debt level is also high for high-income earners, this is mainly related to investment properties aside from the main residence which generate regular income and can be easily sold in a crisis situation due to not being the home base. Finally, lower income deciles rely on unsecured debt which is costly and does not build asset ownership.

The internalization of the need to provide financial security has resulted in fragile balance sheets for the majority of households because they are diversifying less and rely on debt-financed homeownership. Low-income households' wealth is primarily comprised of physical wealth and low-yielding financial assets; middle-income households depend on debt-financed housing and pension wealth; and high-income households rely on diversified asset portfolios including high-yielding financial assets, buy-to-let properties and secure DB pensions. Rather than promoting social upward mobility, the increase in asset ownership, associated with the process of financialization, based on rising house prices and future capital income through private pension wealth, has only seemingly boosted the capitalist status of labour,. While the access to pension wealth does translate into future capital income, these funds are managed by institutional investors with no direct influence over how investments are conducted and debt-financed homeownership has made households dependent on house prices and interest rates.

Finance rationality: managing everyday risks

After having seen how the asset composition of UK households does not correspond to adopting characteristics of capitalists but instead reinforces capital–labour inequalities, this section looks at the second component of asset norms – finance rationality. According to finance theory (see Chapter 2) and the entrepreneurial discourse presented in the media (see Chapter 4), the everyday asset manager is expected to embrace risk and calculate an optimal composition of assets with regards to their future retirement needs. This would mean taking into consideration the impact of inflation, interest rates and risk/return relationships when composing their asset portfolio and hedging against future income losses. Instead of embracing risk, the previous sections have shown that interviewees feel trapped in having to accumulate assets and adjust the risk levels of their asset-accumulation strategy to their own needs. The following two sections now look at the other element of finance rationality: adopting financial strategies such as diversification and hedging to achieve asset ownership.

Elementary form of diversification

Diversification has been a key topic in the media and financial education outlets (see, for example, Lowe, 2010, 2023), emphasizing that assets in a portfolio should not be correlated or only weakly correlated, which means if one product or sector is affected, it can be balanced out by another sector. Whilst this has been originally established in the case of direct share ownership, it has been extended to asset classes such as cash, bonds, property and equities, where it is argued that 'a relatively low-risk portfolio' can be constructed 'by combining assets that have a low correlation' even if these include higher risk investments (Lowe, 2010, p 301). Due to risk being perceived as omnipresent in investment ("everything's got a risk in it" [Oscar]), interviewees seek to make sure not to lose money that they worked hard for ("I suppose more so when you're parting with money that you have earned" [Layla]), resulting in an elementary rather than sophisticated form of diversification. Instead of calculating the optimal composition of assets according to their risk preferences, interviewees' discourses reflect the logic of the concept, yet they apply it in an unsophisticated way.

First, interviewees apply a wider form of diversification in the case of bank accounts to ensure and maximize savings. A discourse of keeping control is interweaved with a discourse of distrust, resulting in having several bank accounts:

'I generally keep eggs in different baskets ... I don't like to have it all in one place ... keeping your savings in a different bank account to where you have your current account because if you go overdrawn, you don't want them stealing the money from your savings account.' (Alfred)

Suggesting that a bank requesting one to pay back debt is stealing money shows the categorization of financial institutions as not trustworthy. This form of diversification had been reinforced by the previous low interest rate environment. With the aim of earning the most amount of interest rate on existing savings, some interviewees diversify their saving accounts and shop around ("it's a very small amount of money but you just scrabble the interest where you can" [Fleur]). As shown in the following statement, this can result in a quite extensive system of moving money between accounts to make sure of receiving the highest possible interest payments:

'My salary goes into Barclays, as soon as it goes into Barclays, £500 goes into Nationwide because with Barclays if my salary goes in there I get paid £5 a month for it just going in there. And then I get a small percentage of interest and then £500 goes to Nationwide a month and for that going in there I get 5 per cent interest up to £2,000. Another £1,000 goes into Santander and that's what pays our mortgage, but also because I am putting it in there I get 3 per cent ... several bank accounts because one feeds the other automatically.' (Tobias)

Second, in trying to reduce risk in pension provisions, interviewees invest in managed, diversified products ("There's no point in you're going like specific companies as such, you get like a mixed fund" [Aditi]). This means that in case of a downturn of one asset value, it can be balanced out with the increase of another asset: "If you've got something going down a bit over here, it's not everything. It's probably going up over there" (Harriet). The dominance of the finance discourse can be seen here by employing the 'same play of metaphors' (Foucault, 1972, p 33) as incorporated in the media discourse outlined in Chapter 4. A typical expression used by interviewees to describe diversification is: "keep eggs in different baskets" (Vibha). Because of investing mainly through managed funds, the risk of home bias, that is, the tendency to mainly invest in domestic equities, is reduced (Bekaert et al, 2017), while at the same time it reflects 'naïve diversification' (Benartzi and Thaler, 2007, p 87) where the choice offered by the provider determines the extent of diversification. Households decide on an asset mix according to their desired risk level, with the provider then investing in various countries ("60 per cent of it was invested in the Far East and 40 per cent in Europe" [Ida]) and products:

'It was set so that the investment goes something like 20 per cent shares, 20 per cent savings, 60 per cent property, you know, you set out these things and what I've got, it's probably around there. So, I took a very middle ground low risk which is low reward but if you're gonna piss about and give lumps of money every month then I'd rather not just go and put it all on black. I'm not a gambler, I don't find enjoyment in that.' (Harry)

Interestingly, as expected from the entrepreneurial media discourse, a recurring statement was made that one should invest in high-risk investments when younger and switch to lower ones later on: "it's gonna be thirty years until I retire, so I will probably move it in maybe 10 or 15 years, maybe make it to a lower risk" (Saskia).

Third, because of the inherent uncertainty of financial investments and wanting to achieve financial security, everyday asset managers do not solely rely on one form of investment but conduct several pension investments – for instance, setting up a private pension in addition to the workplace pension ("not just stick with the [workplace] pension, get another" [Anu]) or diversifying pension income sources ("We've got rental income. We've got state pension. I've got my civil service pension" [Theodore]). Emphasis is placed on wanting to establish a buffer if the pension does not perform well and making sure one is prepared in case there are regulation changes: "[It] feels a bit safer to have it than not have it [a buy-to-let property] because lots of pensions and the terms of pensions has changed, doesn't it?" (Nancy). "I currently pay into a pension with work … but I would like to set up a private pension to pay into, just so, that I've got just a little bit of a buffer" (Layla). As a result, 24.4 per cent[4] of interviewed households who provided a balance sheet and 29.1 per cent of overall interviewed households have a buy-to-let property which they rent out ("this house we've bought is a pension" [Rita]) and over one third of interviewed households compared to 12 per cent of UK households have set up a private pension because of wanting to mitigate a potential fall in the value of their pension. Moreover, when moving jobs, pensions are kept separate: "I had different jobs and each job gave me a pension and I left them separate. This is the case of don't put all your eggs in one basket" (Charles).

Despite being critical of financial investments, interviewees drawing on this subjectivity still take the necessary steps and accumulate assets to keep "[their] head above the water" [Darcy]), yet they do not take on higher risk assets and adopt an elementary form of diversification. Emphasis is placed throughout on financial security and not risking too much since "there is the potential that you won't get anything" (Layla). Resistances such as amending asset norms to one's own needs and realizing that investments are uncertain thus not only represent 'ruptures' but also 'innovation' (Hardt and Negri, 2009, p 59) and are taken as reasoning to establish an elementary form of diversification to mitigate the potential fall in the value of one's investment.

Elementary form of hedging

Besides accumulating assets, the entrepreneurial media discourse calls upon the everyday asset manager to take measures to hedge against future income losses and protect the accumulated assets reliant on this income.

Advertisements for insurances have grown substantially in the UK, ranging from life insurance to funeral cost insurance. A reoccurring statement which is employed in the media is the rather absolute discursive statement of 'Unless you're immortal, you need life insurance!' which has been used by several insurance companies and has resurfaced on social media such as Instagram, Pinterest and YouTube (Crafts, 2023). This has resulted in even lower income interviewees being influenced by these advertisements, as shown in the following example. Amidah, a single mother, living on a low-income, part-time job, picked up the phone after seeing an advert for a life insurance ("it just came, honestly, just came on the TV") and was particularly enticed by the possibility to take it up as a protection for her son. Interestingly, because of being income-constrained, she reflected on the information given after the initial phone call and decided against it:

> 'Honestly, I tried one time, but then I realized there's something dodgy to me. Why dodgy? ... It's like you're paying for 20 years. If nothing happens, that's it. You won't get your money back. You won't get anything. ... I was like *If that's the case, why can't I just open one of my account and put my own money in?* It's like you're just gambling with your own life.'

Given her tight, unpredictable monthly budget and because of being tied down to a minimum number of years without a guarantee of payment, it is arguably a logical reaction not to contribute to a life insurance. Again, comparing it to 'gambling', as was done in the case of stocks and shares, is employed as a discursive justification.

Notwithstanding, life insurance is reinforced by financial institutions who suggest taking one out when having a mortgage, even offering incentives such as receiving a £100 gift card (Legal and General, 2023). Not surprisingly, interviewees who had a mortgage had a life insurance policy to offset the risk of family members losing the house when becoming ill ("if I've become severely ill or, I think, when I think it's terminally ill then I've got that, so that would cover my family for the mortgage" [Aditi]) and wanting to make sure the partner can maintain the property: "We also have both a life insurance because we were getting a mortgage and we were getting a house, it just made sense for that" (Bethany). Besides the mortgage, becoming married or having a family acts as a trigger for life insurance because of wanting to ensure financial security for family members: "I have one insurance which is the life insurance for in case something happens to me where, you know, to look after my children" (Namono). These two triggers of life insurance show the mutual relationship between economic and social relationships (Zelizer, 2012), where asset ownership leads to wanting to provide more security for family members.

Another key insurance outlined in the entrepreneurial discourse in the media and adopted by interviewees is critical illness insurance. This is set up to counterbalance the potential value loss in future income as a result of being sick: "The critical illness cover, again something could happen that could stop me from working and I want to make sure I don't end up in a financially bad situation" (Darcy). Critical illness cover also has two triggers, the first one being again wanting to secure mortgage payments:

'So I sort of know I got an income for the next three months that's all I can guarantee, I can't really guarantee anything beyond that, hence, the sort of you know life insurance, critical illness insurance, redundancy insurance, those kind of things that I felt were necessary … hopefully they will provide us with the security that if something were to happen we can buy some time to make the right decision for our future rather having been forced into snap decisions … some of the financial products now is about longer-term security but I still see them as expensive and long-term but then … I sort of resent the British housing market.' (John)

An interplay between agency and non-agency discourse can be detected here where a desire for long-term security and not having to make a quick decision forces this interviewee to take on financial products which are expensive, culminating in even resenting having to do that when owning a house. Second, it is triggered by ill health: "[I] had cancer actually along the way, that was painful, painful financially because I didn't have insurance, so basically I just had my savings, so my savings just got completely absorbed by a year and a half being ill" (Isabella). This interviewee then emphasizes that she would advise her friends to get critical illness cover ("I definitely agree with critical illness cover"). Despite being sceptical of insurances, an illness has led to trusting critical illness insurance.

Both life and critical illness insurance show that in addition to adopting an elementary form of diversification, hedging in the wider sense is employed by incorporating insurances into interviewees' financial strategies. As noted in the earlier discourses, a unifying reasoning for getting insurance, despite a general distrust of financial products, is the disciplinary technology of power. Interviewees unpick the disadvantageous relationship between insurance customers and insurance providers but feel they have no choice other than to purchase one as a homeowner, reflecting the dichotomous relationship between agency and non-agency. A key element of norms of asset accumulation, namely homeownership, thus works as a reinforcing mechanism for everyday financialization, tying UK households closer to financial markets by means of mortgages and insurances, consequently creating further income sources. Similarly, it becomes clear here that having the lowest amount of sick pay among OECD countries works as a disciplining mechanism, incentivizing UK households to take on financial products to provide financial security for themselves in case of becoming sick. Bringing the previous sections together, we can see that by trying to provide security in an insecure future and reduce risk levels, interviewees translate asset norms into a three-pronged asset-accumulation strategy: interviewees set aside savings, acquire a house and secure pension provisions. At the same time, an elementary form of diversification and hedging is employed, reflected in diversifying bank accounts and pension income sources in addition to investing in managed financial products and employing life and critical illness insurance to hedge against future income losses.

Concluding remarks

With regard to debates in the literature over whether households internalize financial subjectivities and through this become capitalists and non-capitalists at the same time (see Chapter 2), the findings presented here suggest that households do adopt a financialized subject position, albeit differently than expected. The characteristics of financial products in connection with a discourse of wanting to establish financial security shape the asset-accumulation strategy. Instead of embracing risk (Lai, 2017; Pellandini-Simanyi and Banai, 2021), assets are chosen which are perceived as safe. Due to stocks and shares fluctuating too much they are excluded, but property is included in the strategy, representing an adjustment to the governmental and media discourse. While the media calls on households to include stocks and shares, bonds, unit trusts and managed investments in the asset strategy, interviewees' asset strategy consists of savings, homeownership and pensions. Further, managed investments are only conducted when having fulfilled this three-pronged asset strategy. As a consequence, both UK household balance sheets as well as interviewees' balance sheets are dominated by savings, property and pensions instead of depicting a diversified asset portfolio. With interviewees prioritizing homeownership before pensions, the adopted three-pronged asset strategy also deviates from recent calls to first invest in pensions and set up emergency cash before investing in property and further financial assets (Lowe, 2023). This three-pronged asset-accumulation strategy is guided by an elementary form of diversification and hedging. Rather than calculating an optimum level of risk and return and constructing the relationship between assets accordingly, the everyday asset manager chooses managed funds, diversifies pension investments and savings accounts, and employs insurance to hedge against potential future income losses.

Far from being irrational in not taking on higher risk investments (Clark, 2010; Lusardi, 2015), financial discourses and practices of the everyday asset manager represent logical responses to limitations of asset norms. Realizing the uncertainty of financial investments and the need to have sufficient income and wealth to adopt sophisticated diversification constitutes a fairly robust understanding of the inherent contradictions of the investor subject. Counter-conduct, or the unwillingness to engage with the investor subjectivity and its notions of risk and investments, helps them to cope with these contradictions while nevertheless accumulating assets in order to provide long-term security. The amendment of asset norms thus not only gives agency to individuals but is also necessary for everyday financialization to take place, mitigating its inherent contradictive forces. This highlights the mutually constitutive relationship between conduct and counter-conduct where counter-conduct enables conduct, reproducing a welfare system based on individual responsibility.

Even though counter-conduct in the form of transfiguring the subject position they are called upon to adopt to one's own needs enables asset accumulation, it reinforces capital–labour inequalities instead of labour adopting capitalist characteristics (Bryan et al, 2009; Weiss, 2015). As a consequence of access to different financial means, lower to medium-income households tend to focus on clearly safe or fairly safe financial assets while incorporating riskier investments in their balance sheets by means of a mortgage-financed main residence. Only after having contributed to a mortgage and a workplace pension are investments in managed products such as bonds conducted. The majority of people thus rely on low-yielding, illiquid forms of wealth and not on a diversified financial asset portfolio, with clearly safe, fairly safe and risky assets, as higher income earners do. Imperfections of asset norms, on the one hand, thus enable financialized subject positions, albeit differently interpreted than expected, and on the other hand, reinforce capital–labour wealth inequalities and enable the dismantling of the welfare state.

6

The Disciplining Effect
of Asset Norms

Due to the retreat of the welfare state, everyday asset managers feel forced into the social practices of asset accumulation despite being critical of them due to their immanent contradictions (Langley and Leaver, 2012; Huber et al, 2020). Being able to transfigure the subject position they are called upon to adopt to their own needs enables individuals to give meaning to asset accumulation and overcomes the contradiction between the inherent uncertainty of financial investments and having to have sufficient income to diversify investments and accumulate assets to provide financial security. Whilst the previous chapter has shown how this has resulted in financialized subjects, albeit differently than expected, and has intensified capital–labour wealth inequalities, this chapter moves on to exploring the impact of asset norms on everyday practices within consumption, work and relationships, and its empowering or disciplining characteristics.

Going back to the understanding of governmental reasoning outlined in the conceptual framework in Chapter 2, where power is not only repressive but productive of subjectivities based on interests and desires, Foucault (1980, p 39) understands the regulatory mechanism as operating through the transformation of norms into everyday practices and discourses where 'power reaches into the very grain of individuals, touches their bodies and inserts itself into their actions and attitudes, their discourses, learning processes and everyday lives'. Put differently, constructed norms would not be seen as oppressive but as desirable, even if there were concerns with regards to their benefits. Strikingly, this can be seen in interviewees' statements where asset norms are not only adapted but determine one's own success as a person. Despite being critical of financial institutions, being an effective everyday asset manager, who accumulates assets to provide financial security in the future, has become a way of being – 'a means for the acquisition of the self' (Martin, 2002, p 3) – even going as far as connecting self-confidence to it: "If I'd had no savings and had an overdraft, I would feel like I was failing a little bit as a person, so it's a little bit self-confidence linked to that" (Saskia). "If I haven't made enough money to retire on when I'm 65 then I failed and I don't deserve a pension" (Akio). Generating savings and buying a house has come to define one's personality, denoted as 'failing as a person' if one is unable to continue saving after buying a house or is unable to set aside enough money to provide a sufficient income in retirement.

This chapter therefore seeks to bring attention to the intersection between norms of asset accumulation and everyday practices. Of specific interest here is whether interviewees through the process of asset accumulation also adopt – as proclaimed within the governmental discourse – the characteristics of capitalists by gaining more control over their everyday life and financial future or whether these forces instead discipline labour. For this purpose, the impact of having internalized asset norms on everyday life is explored, that is, the practices interviewees adopt when seeking to become an effective everyday asset manager and how these interplay with everyday rationalities in the spaces of consumption, work and relationships.

Self-governing measures

The regulatory power technology works through constructions of interests and desires such as wanting to accumulate assets even when being limited. To adhere to norms, individuals are argued to employ mechanisms which regulate their behaviour according to what they have learned is desirable by reflecting on their actions, evaluating them and adjusting them accordingly, that is, they self-improve their behaviour by employing 'technologies of the self' (Foucault, 1997, p 177), which are: 'techniques that permit individuals to effect, by their own means, a certain number of operations on their own bodies, their own souls, their own thoughts, their own conduct, and this in a manner so as to transform themselves, modify themselves.' This section thus reveals the 'technologies of the self' or self-governing measures interviewees adopt in an effort to achieve saving goals and be able to invest.

The dichotomy between 'spoken-for' and 'guilt-free' money

As shown in the previous chapter, the everyday asset manager justifies not investing in riskier investments such as stocks and shares due to lacking sufficient money that one can put at risk. Realizing that one needs to take on some risks to accumulate ("I should become a little more risky in order to gain something" [Namono]) but wanting to avoid risks that "affect your everyday life" (Layla) results in interviewees categorizing money into "*spoken-for*" asset category (Edward), that is, fulfilling the three-pronged asset-accumulation strategy consisting of savings, property and pensions, and "*guilt-free*" asset category (Oscar), that is, investing in riskier investments once the elements of the three-pronged asset strategy are fulfilled ("If you have spare cash that you don't need to spend, it's in your interest to invest it" [Clementine]). Riskier investments are only undertaken if there is sufficient *guilt-free* money available which one "can afford to lose" (Harriet). Oscar's admission is illustrative of this distinction where he quite rationally unpicks the differing degrees to which one can take on risk dependent on income, emphasizing that not every income level is compatible with investing in riskier assets:

> 'The risk if you've got the money, it doesn't matter so much. But if you don't have the money then that might be the difference between you keeping or losing your house ... if I was on £50,000, £60,000 a year, and we had everything paid for and you've got this money burning a hole in your pocket, you speculate, don't you? And you have a bit of fun doing it and it's like a hobby. But I don't think I could do it to make money, no. I think of it as just too unpredictable.' (Oscar)

The distinction between *spoken-for* and *guilt-free* assets seems to be reminiscent of mental accounting where households develop a system of accounting that makes a distinction between spending accounts and asset accounts in order to restrict their spending (Thaler, 1990). One could argue that this is simply a further division of the asset account into different asset strategies. Yet, interviewees' statements make it clear that this is not solely about individual self-control issues but also about social meanings and relations (Zelizer, 1994; Murdoch, 2017). Oscar goes on to discuss how he would assign money to the *guilt-free* category. Money associated with work is categorized as essential money which needs to be used to pay for continuous costs and contribute to providing financial security (*spoken-for*), whereas money earned through an investment which is not part of the three-pronged asset-accumulation strategy can be used on frivolous spending or speculative investments (*guilt-free*):

> 'A little bit of speculating, so you can feel like you're making your own money, can't you? It's guilt-free money that, isn't it? ... Guilt-free money. You can blow it if you want. You don't have to. You can say *I made that money myself from an asset, so I don't need to put that into the running of the house or vet's bills* or whatever. I can actually just say, *Right, that's it. I'm going to go out and buy something to eat* or something, and not feel bad about it, if that makes sense?'

A difference is made here between your own money and money which is pre-assigned to provide financial security, indicating a perception of having no other choice than to use work income to provide financial security.

This is a reoccurring theme where money is earmarked according to how it was earned, with emphasis placed on needing to protect "money that you've worked really hard for" (Claudia). As a consequence, money which has been gained through working is unlikely to be invested in risky assets ("what I earned, hard earned, I couldn't bear the idea of putting any at risk" [Habib]), while money made from an investment can be invested in riskier assets.

A second social meaning which in interplay with income shapes investment possibilities is inheritance. Higher income earners earmark inheritance from family members as additional money which is not needed for the *spoken-for* asset category. They can thus either leave the inheritance in the riskier asset category and/or use it as a starting point to try out actively trading in stocks and shares investments: "I've got a few BT shares at the moment which my grandfather left me. He worked for BT. I went through a period of not actively trading but buying and selling relatively quickly – didn't really make any money on it I have to say" (Charlie). Yet, this at times can result in feeling guilty when losing the value of the inherited money. Being part of a higher income household that owns assets and has savings, Beatrix decided to invest her father's inheritance directly in shares. However, she now expresses regret, as it "immediately lost its value" and "only now kind of seems to be getting back to a sort of level that it was originally". She struggles with having violated the social norms of protecting the hard-earned money of her father:

'I suppose I got a bit of a shock that you know he saved all his life, you know, he didn't have a lot of money and I kinda felt that I've been left a bit of money and I put it somewhere that I thought was you know a wise investment and it kind of all it just was lost and you know that just seemed, I felt a bit guilty in a way I suppose.'

In contrast, income-constrained interviewees earmark inheritance for the *spoken-for* asset category and emphasize the need not to waste it on everyday expenses or risk losing its value through riskier investments ("the money my granddad gives me to put into something that loses all of the money. I would feel awful" [Bethany]). Instead, inheritance money is used to save for a house deposit or to reduce a mortgage, for example when there is only one household member working full time in a three-member household: "The inheritance last year that came through which was about £16,000 from, from an uncle of mine who died and so we basically used that towards the costs of the house to bridge the gap to make the mortgage" (Tobias).

This is intensified when having experienced a difficult situation, as shown in the following case where the husband made sure not to waste the inheritance on spending due to having grown up in an income-constrained household: "I think that because his dad died young, he had from the age of 16, he found he had his inheritance in a savings account, I suppose. Then he decided not to spend" (Ai).

The origins of money based on social relations in interplay with income constraints determine the asset category, for which reason, 'earmarking' – which acknowledges the impact of 'a variety of social relations rather than individuals' (Zelizer, 1994, p 25) when assigning money – as a concept is more suitable to explain these decisions. Money assigned to the different asset strategies is not perceived as fungible or interchangeable between the different categories as assumed by the concept of mental accounting, but emphasis is placed on achieving the three-pronged asset-accumulation strategy. This reinforces the need to move beyond concepts of mental accounting based on individual self-control and towards relational meanings.

'Trying to be a responsible adult': self-restrictive savings measures

'Earmarking' based on social relationships has an impact in two respects, where relational meanings not only emerge before a decision is taken, shaping investment decisions, but also impact decisions after having categorized money, thus disciplining spending decisions (Zelizer, 1994; Murdoch, 2017). Social meanings are drawn upon to highlight the morally acceptable behaviour of accumulating assets: "You have to grow up. You should be able to discipline yourself … You should think about more than tomorrow for your family's sake, for your children, your wife, or whatever, your husband" (Isaac). What is striking here is the resonance with the media discourse which recontextualizes the financial discourse within family relationships, where owning a house and saving in a pension scheme is presented in the same light as getting married and having children, that is, a natural step when getting older: 'At my age, I should be thinking about getting a mortgage, a pension, a wife, a Volvo, two kids of my own and a Labrador' (Langan, 1997). Working hard and disciplining oneself are seen as key success factors to be rewarded with financial security.

In line with the two meanings of savings outlined in the previous two chapters, the kind of accounts employed for savings is determined by their purpose, either rainy day savings or long-term savings. To access money in case of an emergency, such as having to pay a house repair ("even though I am not renting anymore, I'd have to repair what goes wrong" [Pippa]), while at the same time not wasting it on frivolous spending, semi-accessible savings accounts are usually chosen ("it's a bit more fluid, so you're able to access it a little bit easier" [John]) to separate rainy day funds "from the current account, so just keeping it separate" (Imogen). To save long-term, interviewees transfer money automatically into a fixed, non-accessible savings product where it can be "actually a bit of a pain in the arse to get to", due to having to "send an email request off for the money and it might take five days for them to enact it" (Harry) and/or savings products where you would lose money when taking out part of the savings earlier than the agreed time period ("I can pull it out if I have to but if I do it now, it would have been at a loss" [Pippa]). By taking out fixed savings products, interviewees make sure that this money is distinguished from everyday money, even leading them to forget about it: "I didn't really think about the money for five years, because that was the whole point" (Florence). The two functions of savings have thus led to a dichotomy between wanting to be liquid in case of emergencies and locking away money.

To achieve savings goals for the *spoken-for* category, besides transferring money automatically into less accessible savings products, consumption is restricted by means of budgeting because "if you don't spend money, it accumulates" (Florence). Criticizing the financialized consumer society: "after the deregulation of financial services in the 80s if you were a fool to be in debt before but after that you were a fool not to have credit" (Nadeem), interviewees reject the neoliberal consumer subject put forward in advertising, described by Langley (2007, p 84) as someone who 'communicates their freedom, aspirations, and individuality through commodity ownership'. "Trying to be a responsible adult" (Isabella), almost all interviewees give priority to amassing property and financial wealth and avoid taking on debt for "flashy technology", hence, "live cost-effectively rather than spend money on unnecessary brands" (Agnes). Similar to the media discourse, interviewees distinguish between good debt (asset-driven) and bad debt (consumption-driven). Only debt which can be used to build up the *spoken-for* category and "to provide for family" (Nancy) is seen as acceptable, while consumption debt is seen as bad because of "not really getting ahead" (Layla):

'I have a nice car, but I wouldn't spend thirty thousand on it. You know it's that kind of, why would you do that rather than buying a house … it will not earn you money back on it, so sort of almost limit how much you spend on it.' (John)

As a consequence, mortgages are depicted not as debt per se ("I don't think of those as debts") but acceptable borrowings ("I think of those as very measured risks" [Scarlett]). Some interviewees even expressed their bewilderment at them being seen as negative within a credit score ("so they put having mortgages down as negative" [Isabella]). To reduce non-essential spending, the spending account is divided into an essential ('bills account') and non-essential spending ('fun account'):

'I have my main account that my wages come into and all my bills go out of and then I have another account which I call like my fun account, so some of my wages I got a standing order. So I transfer a set amount of money into the social account and I know if I wanna go out for dinner with my friends or, you know, whatever it has to come out of that account and if I get to the end of the month and there is no money in that account, I can't go out. I can't do the fun things.' (Layla)

While some use accounts to limit their spending, others develop annual budgets to discipline their consumption as shown in the case of Nancy:

'We would budget to see if we could buy a house or something that could be used as a means to generate some money ... look at everything that we spend in a year and then allocate what we think is there like the bare minimum that you can spend but also give yourself a bit of a buffer because sometimes, you know, you do so well, sometimes you might think, or I don't know, that jumper is really nice but I've allocated myself this amount of money and if I buy that I'm going over a little bit. But sometimes it's nice to be able to do that rather than thinking constantly I can't.'

This statement exemplifies two things: (a) the self-governing measure in the form of budgeting enters one's own reasoning, resulting in one being proud for having restricted oneself, (b) reward systems are set up to motivate oneself, for instance through buying something that is not needed or being generous to others: "I just like to blow loads of money on them [her nephews]" (Emily).

Strikingly, the intersection between social meanings related to inheritance and being income-constrained can result in employing 'bad debt' where credit cards are used for consumption spending, as shown on the case of Imogen:

'My credit card is essentially what functions as a savings account ... I have the money that I inherited in my savings account. I don't intend to add stuff from my wages in there because simply there is not enough, you know, I'm always tight on cash ... I think every, every time I'm spending my savings to live is a slightly worse house that I could buy ... it's best for me not to touch it at all than to, you know, touch a little bit because then, then it opens, opens the floodgate.'

Whilst this practice appears to echo a mental accounting practice (Thaler and Sunstein, 2021), where individuals irrationally use expensive credit cards instead of employing their savings when experiencing constraints, it is a quite rational reaction when taking into consideration social meanings attached to inheritance and asset norms. On the one hand, the interviewee does not pay interest on the credit if it is paid within a month, which she does every month, and she earns interest on her savings, so enabling her to build up more for her house deposit and contribute to the *spoken-for* category. Being aware that it is not morally acceptable to use debt for consumption purposes, she equates the credit card with a savings account, justifying using debt by means of asset accumulation. On the other hand, the social meaning attached to the inheritance results in not wanting to waste the inherited money on everyday expenses but instead employing it for long-term financial security. Besides deviating from theoretical expectations of finance rationality, where credit should not be used if one still has access to liquid money, it is arguably a logical reaction to avoid decumulating the inheritance of £60,000 on everyday spending and accumulating interest on those savings while employing an interest-free credit card for everyday expenses.

What these discussions have shown is that asset norms exert 'power over life' (Hardt and Negri, 2009, p 57) by impacting consumption behaviour. Contrary to 'privileging current consumption over future consumption' (Clark, 2012, p 1192), interviewees emphasize the need to "defer the sort of richness today to look for the future" (Eloise). By means of earmarking assets into *spoken-for* and *guilt-free* asset categories and spending into essential and non-essential spending categories, they force themselves to save and restrict their consumption. Consumption is thus not only reduced by debt commitments, their respective level of interest rates and the resulting wage residual (Bryan et al, 2009), but is also limited due to norms of asset ownership.

The disciplinary technology of labour

Extending previous insights into power inequalities with a focus on debt (Schwartz, 2012; Karacimen, 2015), this section reveals how asset norms not only exert power over everyday life in the form of consumption practices but also intensify the disciplining mechanism of labour. Previous research has shown that rising job insecurity within an environment of less social provision by the state constructs 'indebted subjects' (Karagaac, 2020, p 8), strengthening the unequal relationship between capital and labour. Debt results in labour not only being tied to capital in the present but also in the future, by the need to generate income to service debt, thereby reducing labour's bargaining power (Bonefeld and Holloway, 1996; Di Feliciantonio, 2016; Karacimen, 2015). In the following two sections, I extend these insights by bringing attention to the interplay between asset norms and work relationships.

Money people vs hard work

In line with the media discourse, the subject position of the everyday asset manager draws on notions of hard work and discipline, which will lead to financial reward in contrast to making fast money ("I would still probably prefer to work harder with a few risks rather than take loads of risks" [Tobias]). Yet, contrary to the policy discourse, which depicts being a hard-working citizen as someone who conducts investments and takes the opportunity to become an everyday capitalist, an alignment with labour takes place. Not only are understandings of labour employed when assigning work income to the *spoken-for* asset category and distancing oneself from capital income by assigning it to the *guilt-free* asset category (as discussed in the previous section), but the social construction of money people as greedy and wasteful culminates in distancing oneself from the investor subjectivity. Running through the discussion presented in the last two chapters is the omnipresent view of seeing finance people as gambling with the money of those who have worked hard for their income: "the big managers and the college people, they can speculate with our money on the stock market and make themselves big bonuses" (Richard). Feelings of distrust extend also to those in government who have not sufficiently safeguarded pension investments ("Equitable Life, which was rated to be one of the best pension companies ... but in fact they went spectacularly bust" [Nathan]) and are wasting taxpayers' money:

> 'There's no money in the support system, so it's important to have your own pension but then you are paying a lot of tax actually ... you think, you know where is all our money going, is it all going to feed all these people dinners, you know, the meeting and the flying private jets ... there is so much waste.' (Agnes)

Taking into consideration the numerous pension and investments scandals and the retreat of the welfare state which has taken place in the UK, this is a rather robust understanding of the profit-seeking character of financial institutions. As a consequence, rather than being ambitious and seeking to climb the social ladder, as expected of the everyday investor (Pellandini-Simanyi and Banai, 2021), interviewees distance themselves from finance people with the help of metaphorical expressions such as "money people" who "produce magical income": "money people keep coming with wonderful schemes somehow which are gonna produce magical income and millions of pounds, just like that, without me doing anything at all and we know damn well nothing comes without hard work" (Charles). They ("from our point of view as lay persons" [Eloise]) position themselves as everyday asset managers for whom accumulating assets is essential to sustain oneself in an environment of less welfare protection but it does not bring happiness in itself ("In an end itself, it doesn't serve purpose" [Habib]). Instead of embracing asset accumulation ("We're not enthusiast about making more money" [Hattie]), the underlying relationship between asset norms and a retreating welfare state is foregrounded, and seeking richness is disregarded ("we're not really striving to be multimillionaires" [Agnes]). Hence, investments should be for providing safety ("We are not wealthy but we are safe. We feel safe" [Ai]) and achieved through hard work.

The dichotomy between the finance person and the hard-working, non-financial person results in a conflict when being successful in asset accumulation. In the case of not having earned the wealth "through any hard work of my own" (Florence), it does not feel right ("more comfortable than we've ever been, it doesn't seem right" [Charles]), and asset ownership is assigned to luck ("I have to say I'm well off ... I've been lucky to have been able to accumulate money" [Florence]). Being a landlord to earn a pension income can therefore lead to a conflict in which the subject position of the everyday asset manager needs to be justified by emphasizing that one worked hard for it ("I am embarrassed, almost embarrassed by the fact that I am okay ... but I did work quite hard for it in the past" [Millie]).

As discussed earlier, interviewees position themselves as passive subjects who have no choice other than to start to invest ("there were no council houses left, Thatcher sold them all" [Daniel]), for example, by taking in a lodger because of not being able to finance a mortgage: "We are hard-working people, we can pay a mortgage, there is no doubt about it, what we did, we took in a lodger ... taken someone else they're pay off your mortgage ... we didn't have any choice" (Ruby). Interestingly, what can be witnessed here is an asset amnesia, extending Soaita and Searle's (2016) concept of debt amnesia, where one's own wealth is downplayed, for example, referring to oneself as poor despite having a net wealth of £182,000 at 34: "I'm quite poor" (Akio), and when exceeding the *spoken-for* category, further investments are de-emphasized, classifying stocks and shares investments as minor: "it wasn't very much money" (Beatrix). The sum identified as not very much amounts to £60,000 and makes up half of the participant's net financial wealth.

Feelings of hostility towards elites in the form of financial and governmental organizations are an integral element of understanding why everyday asset managers become proactive over their pension planning by amending norms of asset accumulation and distancing themselves from the norms constructed in the media and governmental discourse. If through the process of asset accumulation they accumulate wealth beyond the three-pronged asset-accumulation strategy, that is, the *spoken-for* asset category, a conflict emerges resulting in discursive justification of the wealth.

The intensification of labour discipline

The realignment with labour while accumulating assets binds the everyday asset manager closer to work when seeking to comply with asset norms in three different ways. First, work hours are increased with the goal of accumulating assets. Young households want to get through university as fast as possible, find a job and then increase work hours to secure savings: "I'd rather just be working and earning the most amount of money so that I can prepare for the future now" (Anu). In some cases, this has led to locking away too much money and, as a result, having to work more hours: "I probably shouldn't have locked away that much money at the time because obviously we were still in a flat at the time. We weren't struggling in like we couldn't feed ourselves but I just had to pick up a lot more hours" (Isaac).

To finance a house is the second guiding principle ("I work to pay the mortgage, so if I didn't have to pay the mortgage then I would not need to work so much" [Ida]). Since "there are no secure jobs anymore" (Millie), interviewees put pressure on themselves to pay off its finance as fast as possible ("so that if we were to find ourselves unemployed, our monthly burden would be lighter" [Oscar]) and praise their father's ability to do so by having increased work hours:

'He's been able to pay off his mortgage because he's produced his hours of work. So, he's got more time at home now whereas he didn't have that luxury when he was in his twenties and thirties, probably a bit like me now. I don't really have the luxury of fewer hours, you know, I can't, I can't.' (John)

A similar aspect can be seen in the case of pensions, where work hours are increased with the goal of setting aside sufficient pension provisions: "We just work loads of hours, lots of weekends ... basically anything extra we can pick up [to] be able to retire in normal age" (Amy). The rise in work hours is accomplished with either the main job or a side job ("our savings are jumping quite quick because ... had a part-time job" [Ruby]).

Second, to mitigate the impact of uncertain work contracts on the ability to conduct investments (Langley, 2007; Huber et al, 2020), everyday asset managers seek to establish stability by diversifying income sources ("it's good to have separate sources of income" [Akio]). For instance, in the quest to secure an income at all times, they might set up a business alongside their main job as a backup, thus, increasing their workload: "There were some changes happening in my job and I thought I knew there was going to be a restructure and although I didn't think that my post would be made redundant I thought it could be, you know, so what can I do to make some money" (Nancy). Moreover, part-time jobs are taken on because "if you can have even very small streams of income in different places that's really positive" (Akio) and "if anything happens you're never just left without a penny":

'I write pantomimes, comedy sketches and things. So that's not large income streams but I get performance rights for that from my publisher,

I think it's a couple of hundred pounds a month just coming in from that, which is nice. And also I have a small side business training elves for Christmas grottos. It's what I do for the past six years and that's on top to the full-time work, running a business.' (Harry)

When taking on additional work commitments, they are often not connected to the main job, for example setting up a "street food business" when being a "government officer" (Amy). The interviewees thus adopt an elementary form of diversification with regards to their work income due to rising job insecurity. In case of difficulties, they will take on any job to secure an income flow and keep their assets, independent of whether they like the job or not: "I don't feel like we're in danger of losing the house or anything like that, and I feel like even if, even if I had to change jobs, if one of my jobs stopped or something, I feel like I could get another job, you know I'd do anything" (Darcy).

Third, less interesting jobs are chosen because they offer more work hours and are better paid, which helps to build up pension savings and provide for the family: "really interesting but such a low pay ... They were desperate for me to stay but again I just couldn't afford [to]" (Pippa). Work is selected based on higher income, even leading some to change from studying to become a photographer, for example, to training as a teacher ("I would have loved to have gotten a job in doing something creative but I knew I wanted to obviously move out and have a house" [Layla]), or based on the possibility of being promoted and having a higher income in the future: "Something else which was on my mind ... it was very few people that got to move up" (Oscar). Even though households earn higher incomes through being promoted or choosing a job based on income, the higher income levels are connected to working hard: "you have to earn the money that they're paying" (Saskia) since "nothing comes without hard work" (Charles). It is used as a hedge against potential redundancy by helping the company succeed and ensuring one keeps the job: "Well work as much as I can, I guess, I just have to make sure I keep working hard and I still have my job because nothing's guaranteed, so I wouldn't wanna get sacked" (Aditi).

This analysis adds a new dimension to the discussion surrounding the interaction between labour relations and asset norms. Asset accumulation in itself, rather than debt commitment (Karacimen, 2015), intensifies the discipline of labour. Going back to the argument that households show similarities to capitalists through accumulating assets (Bryan et al, 2009; Weiss, 2015), asset norms should rather be understood as a power technology, strengthening the existing power relationships embodied in capital–labour inequalities. "Trying to make an additional security for the future" (Tobias), interviewees employ technologies of the self in the form of increasing work hours, choosing a job solely based on income and making sure that they work hard. The interaction between the regulatory and disciplinary mechanisms thus constructs the everyday asset manager and the resultant asset norms intensify the disciplinary technology of labour. An everyday asset manager lives the paradox of being called upon to incorporate characteristics of capitalists while at the same time being disciplined through asset accumulation.

Emotions and finance

After having seen the self-governing measures adopted within consumption and work practices, this section unveils the interplay between asset norms, consisting of asset accumulation and finance rationality, and relationships drawing on Zelizer's (1994) conceptualization of social relations within economic aspects. Whilst emotions are perceived as a disturbance in theorizations of finance rational behaviour (see Chapter 2), Zelizer has argued that emotions are immanent in financial decisions, challenging the possibility of money being a neutral, objective medium of exchange and introducing the notion that emotions and relationships enter monetary transactions: 'money used for rational instrumental exchanges is not "free" from social constraints but is another type of socially created currency, subject to particular networks of social relations and its own set of values and norms' (Zelizer, 1994, p 19).

Feeling vs unfeeling

Accompanying the creation of asset norms, the media discourse has also established finance rationality and its return-maximizing and cost-minimizing approach within the domain of family relationships. Norms are constructed that households should use business principles and set up contracts in dealing with family affairs, for instance, in the case of giving mortgage money to newlyweds who might later on split up: 'It may seem unfeeling to use business principles when dealing with your own family but in the casual climate of today's relationships ought you to do otherwise?' (Cannon, 1985). A contrast is built between co-habiting and married couples, emphasizing that staying unmarried is costlier ('the system for co-habiting couples is a real hotch-potch' [Phillips, 2006]). The costs of a wedding are compared to the costs of not getting married with regards to inheritance, tax implications and pensions. At the same time, the implications of a separation on asset ownership are outlined ('a pension, too, is an asset accumulated during a marriage, and that both parties have a claim on it' [FT, 1993]) and people are called upon not to 'remarry in haste' when having divorced before because of the costs involved: 'one divorce is bad: two could mean financial ruin' (MacErlean and Insley, 2007). Additionally, a clear emphasis is placed on the financial implications of death in the family and jokes are employed to encourage households to think about sad events which they might naturally avoid: 'All my wife and I need now is a protection policy that provides for bodyguards to appear whenever our children consider putting soap on the stairs or crushed foxglove leaves in our tea in the hope of benefitting financially from all our insurance policies' (Goldstein-Jackson, 1987). In this way, a family discourse, including children, partnerships and divorce, becomes intertwined with the financial discourse, coined here as 'unfeeling', which calls on people to adopt a rational approach when dealing with relational questions (Cannon, 1985).

Strikingly, interviewees appear to pick up these terms and negotiate the interaction between the normative script of families ridden with emotions and the non-emotional, business-like approach of finance where "emotions don't count, family don't count" (Adhira), as shown in the following case. Due to not being married, and as expected by finance rationality, an interviewee and her partner had set up contracts defining a potential split of assets in case of separation. The interviewee describes the emotional stress in having the discussion about these contracts but emphasizes that it is essential to determine them despite moving together being a "happy incidence":

'It's a risk not only financially with the house but also with our relationship ... where this is us coming together to spend the rest of our lives together in this house before we even started, we've had to have the conversation what's gonna happen if it goes wrong ... you know people don't stay together forever but I think it was the amount of times we had to go over it and deal with these various different things and it almost felt like we're broken up already, like we almost saying: *oh when we break up, this is how we're gonna split it up.* So, yeah, it was quite, for me it was a testing time and I didn't particularly enjoy it but we've done that now.' (Layla)

The discourses involved in the negotiations had transformative power, leading to a changing perception of the relationship itself. After numerous discussions surrounding the contract, it no longer felt as if this was a case of 'if' they broke up, but that it was only a matter of time when this would happen. Because of violating normative understandings of a love relationship, Layla draws on a discourse of necessity to justify having adopted this approach, since if there is a break up "it's almost a cleaner, cleaner break because you've agreed it and you signed it".

Seeking to provide financial security for the partner can, besides changing the perception, also result in changing the relationship itself, where, like the media discourse suggests, a wedding is planned to ensure that the partner is:

'entitled to my pensions and all the life insurances ... it's less about romance, it's more about security, if I'm honest. So as unromantic as that sounds, but that's the truth ... this is gonna show how unromantic I am. We were having a conversation on Valentine's day ... I just said: *Look there is nothing stopping us now, so why don't we actually get married?* Mainly because I was thinking if I died, if I got, you know, in a car crash or something like that, I just didn't want it to be difficult for her to access the financial benefits.' (John)

By continuously referring back to being "unromantic" and having this conversation on "Valentine's day", it becomes clear that social norms come into conflict with asset norms. Whereas getting married might have been the natural next step in the relationship ("we've got engaged 'cause we've been together for a few years"), the financial concerns led to them getting married, which is justified by drawing on a discourse of security and honesty ("that's the truth" [John]). The dichotomy between feeling and unfeeling thus reshapes relational discourses and practices.

At the same time, as also seen in the newspapers, jokes are employed when expressing the need to establish provisions for one's partner in case of death. Eloise, for instance, feels the need to provide for her husband in case something happens to her:

'We have life insurance in place, my fear has previously, had always been up to this point, should the worst to happen and I passed away and I die, David would be left in a situation where he would have to sell the home ... So that wouldn't be really a fear now. I think the way we've sorted our personal finances out now, it would leave him able to cope in the house whether he wanted to stay there or not or whatever would happen. He'd probably have a life insurance sum, he could go on a world cruise with his girlfriend.'

Extending Polillo's discussion on how 'the spread of capitalization legitimizes people's orientation toward their intimate lives as capitalized assets' (Polillo, 2017, p 101), the pressure to accumulate assets due to a decline in social welfare provision justifies the insertion of finance rationality in relationship decisions. The conflict between financial concerns and relationships is overcome by rationalizing the situation by means of wanting to provide financial security for their loved ones, thus employing the social relationship to justify the assimilation of economic concerns within the relationship.

In addition to economic concerns entering relational meanings, and as expected by the literature introduced in Chapter 2 (Pellandini-Simanyi et al, 2015), feelings and relationships also domesticate asset norms, for instance, houses are bought at a higher price than budgeted for because of their being close to family and friends:

'I love the area, all my friends are there ... Mum who isn't in the best of health was in South Manchester and the area is kind of in between ... Everybody was kinda against me, you can't afford it but you know it meant that I got to live where I wanted to live, so when the house prices have rocketed, absolutely rocketed there, and a tram stop has been built right outside it, so the prices really have gone up.'

Emily found herself prioritizing family relationships over solely monetary aspects. Interestingly, by pursuing this strategy and financing the increase in price by having a lodger, Emily invested in a house which saw substantial price increases. Similarly, seeking to avoid family conflicts, one interviewee chose not to invest money with the father-in-law due to it potentially causing issues in the future if they needed access to it or the investment lost its value: "it's always a bit messy when family members are involved and the last thing what I want for us to do is for something to happen that we're falling out over" (Charlie). Compromises are similarly found when investing to keep "matrimonial loveliness": "I was trying to convince my wife, we should buy a second house as an investment ... we sort of compromised on moving to the larger house, hoping that if things got 10 per cent up, the bigger the house is an increase in value" (Tobias).

As these discussions show, finance rationality interacts with social relationships, resulting in a mutually generative relationship rather than 'unfeeling' overriding emotions. Concerns of asset accumulation manifest themselves in relationships while also being shaped by these.

Caring in times of asset-based welfare

Besides economic relationships being productive in shaping and being reshaped by social relationships, personal relationships also operate within the frame of caring. Caring is understood here in a wider sense: that is, using relationships in connection with return-maximizing strategies to enable asset ownership. There is a strong awareness of institutional changes, with the older generation feeling "very privileged" (Eleanor), having benefitted from house price increases, better pensions and stable jobs (as discussed in Chapter 4): "It's like young people who are going to struggle and I think it's people like me that have had these gilt-edged pensions, a final year salary scheme, I mean I couldn't have hoped for better" (Chris). As a consequence, those of the interviewees who are able to help their children to conform to asset norms do so. Whereas the bequest motive in the form of wanting to give to the children is not a new phenomenon (Zelizer, 2011), the scope and purpose of the traditional bequest motive has been modified. The traditional bequest motive relied on affluent families passing on their assets, deepening existing wealth and income inequalities. In contrast, 'inheritance is now relevant to the majority of families' (Finch and Mason, 2000, p 2) based on less stable jobs, stagnating wages and rising property prices ("in the early 1990s, the houses were 40, 50, 60,000 pounds ... my son is looking at £180,000" [Tobias]), representing an additional form of 'a continuation of parental care' (Singh, 2017, p 192). Interviewees provide help for their children with regards to the three main aspects of the asset strategy.

First, parents take over a carer role by helping their children to save for a house deposit. Several younger interviewees mentioned moving back with their parents with the purpose of saving enough for a house deposit ("so we decided that we wanted to buy, we moved home again for six months with our respective parents" [Amy]). Even in the case of asking children to pay rent, the rent is decreased so that they are able to save:

'had the conversation with my Mum and Dad: *You know, I wanna move out, I wanna have my own place, I need to save up for it.* So there I was paying them rent anyway, so they say: *Well you pay us like less than you would do if you were gonna go and rent somewhere and then you save the rest of your wages and stuff.*' (Layla)

Two aspects emerge from this statement. On the one hand, moving out is seen as synonymous with buying a place rather than renting, depicting the normalization of asset norms. On the other hand, the dichotomy between feeling and unfeeling is evident where children, despite saving for a house deposit, are asked to pay rent.

Second, parents help children directly through gifting ("obviously from gifting from our parents, and then we took out a mortgage with our salaries" [Aditi]) or lending money ("we'd saved a bit of money for a mortgage anyway and we borrowed some money, my Mum gave us some" [Oscar]). This has also been recognized by previous studies, where it has been shown that an increasing number of first-time buyers have to rely on family support to put up a house deposit since 2009 (Heath and Calvert, 2013). This situation has only worsened, with rising house prices and rising interest rates following the COVID-19 pandemic. In some cases, interviewees utilized their own inheritance to help:

'I had inheritance from my mother, as well. I got half her estate, but then two thirds of that I actually gave away – topped up my two daughters and gave £10,000 each to each of my grandchildren, purely to use towards deposit for the house and they would with the strings it came attached to.' (Harriet)

Interestingly, in this case the gifted money is simultaneously used as a 'medium of control' (Singh, 2017, p 185) and a way of caring, where Harriet wants to ensure that the grandchildren use it in line with her expectations. In particular since three of the five grandchildren are seen as wasting money ("the oldest one, you give him money and it's got to be spent"), she wants to ensure that they spend it on asset accumulation. The social meaning of inheritance thus comes into play, with helping family members to conduct investments reinforcing the *spoken-for* asset category.

Third, higher income or wealthier parents do not only help with savings and house purchase but also plan tax efficient inheritance with the purpose of increasing children's investments and pension pots: "[father speaking directly to daughter] I remember when I was in Ireland and you made a statement that you never have a pension and my reply to you was I provide you a pension. Do you remember? Well you have a pension now" (Richard). This includes strategies for maximizing inheritance income, for example, by setting up a company ("effectively they own them now so there will be no inheritance tax issues … they own the company outright" [Peter]), gifting children during the life time ("they want us to have the money and use the money now and see where it goes, rather than giving us the money when they passed away" [Bethany]) and investing money to help children with pension provisions ("I've made several investments for children and grandchildren in a variety of things" [Baron]). This intensifies the wealth inequalities depicted in the previous chapter, where wealthier households are able to transfer better pension provisions and financial investments to family members.

Interestingly, instead of feeling uncomfortable about receiving help from family and wanting to pay it back, as shown by Heath and Calvert (2013) or Durat and Ronald (2017), children also indicate an expectation of receiving an inheritance ("my grandparents are still alive … so you sort of know at some point we may end up with another 50, 60, 70,000 pounds" [John]). The daughter who is referred to in the earlier statement from Richard calculates the future inheritance into her pension income. Belonging to a medium-income household (£36,000 for a two-person household), having a low amount saved in pensions for a 58-year-old (£47,000) and a net financial wealth of £55,500 results in her relying on the parents' inheritance as future pension income, mirroring the father's discourse: "I'd be totally brutal my parents have a few quid" (Ruby). Similarly, an interviewee who had been struggling to invest according to the norms of asset accumulation is calculating a future inheritance:

> 'My parents have assets and they don't really have a mortgage and their house is probably worth 400, 500,000 and there is only me and my sister. So my hope would be when they shuffle off the old coil that that will almost be a partial of my retirement. … you don't wish for it but the reality is probably sometime in the next 20 years when I'm thinking about getting to retirement age.' (Harry)

Interviewees negotiate the dichotomy between feeling and unfeeling within the frame of inheritance. Whilst the finance approach is to calculate a future inheritance into pension income, it stands in conflict with moral norms where the normative script of the family dictates the wish for family members to live as long as possible. To overcome this contradiction, interviewees continuously maintain that they do not wish for this to happen and hope that it will be a long time in the future, realizing it is, as expressed in an earlier statement, 'brutal' to think about that. The inherited money is then earmarked for the *spoken-for* asset category.

Social relationships are thus productive in transforming financial relationships while financial relationships are productive in transforming social relationships by changing the perception of inheritance, extending previous arguments that everyday financial practices of individuals should be seen as generated by relationships and their meanings (see Chapter 2). Rather, we can see here the mutually generative relationship between economic and social relations.

Concluding remarks

In the UK's asset-based welfare system, labour is called upon to internalize the everyday asset manager subjectivity, accumulating assets with the goal of providing adequate income during retirement. By accumulating assets and receiving income from their investments while being workers, it is argued that individuals become capitalists and non-capitalists at the same time (see Chapter 2). While Chapter 4 has shown how asset norms are constructed through the interplay between responsibilization (disciplinary mechanism) and financialization (regulatory mechanism), where asset norms also enter the disciplinary mechanism, for instance by offering financial products in line with the flexibility of the job market (see Figure 6.1), Chapter 5 has revealed that instead of moving towards adopting capitalist characteristics, inequalities between capital and labour are intensified within an asset-based welfare society. Trust deficits in government and financial institutions are integral in motivating the proactivity of individuals in amending asset norms. Due to being critical of institutions but feeling trapped because of less job and money security, the everyday asset manager translates asset norms into a three-pronged strategy consisting of savings, homeownership and pension provisions guided by an elementary form of finance rationality. These practices of the everyday asset manager do not help labour to adopt more capitalist characteristics but instead reinforce existing inequalities by overly relying on low-return, liquid financial assets and high-risk, illiquid non-financial assets.

While 'investment as a technology of the self does not take the form envisaged' (Langley, 2007, p 81) by finance theory, where households develop

Figure 6.1: The normalizing society and asset norms

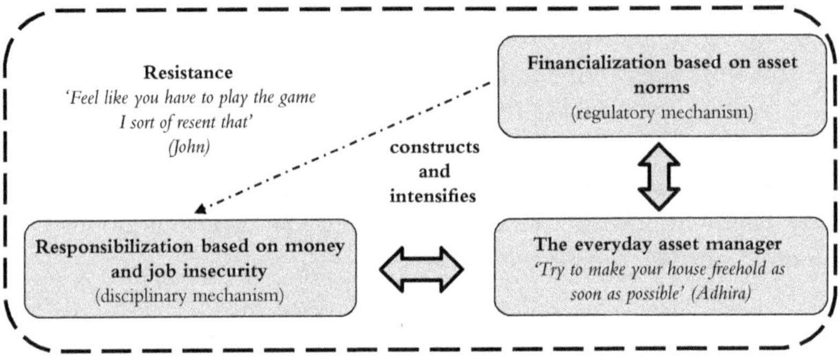

Source: Depiction developed based on conducted interviews in connection with Foucault (2004) and Sotiropoulos et al (2013, p 166)

a 'portfolio of financial market assets' (Langley, 2007, p 74), incorporating the everyday asset manager subjectivity culminates in individualized solutions by adopting practices of 'self-mastery' (Foucault, 1984, p 84) in a quest to fulfil the three-pronged asset-accumulation strategy (see Figure 6.1). In a first step, relational meanings are employed to earmark money into *spoken-for* (three-pronged asset strategy) and *guilt-free* asset categories (further investments) where the origin of money not only determines how it is spent (Zelizer, 1994) but also how it is employed for achieving financial security. Whilst some of the practices presented seem to be reminiscent of the mental accounting techniques introduced by behavioural economists (Thaler, 1990), that is, measures to implement individual self-control, it has been shown here that they should instead be understood as social practices, not solely shaped by individual, monetary goals but by social meanings and relationships. As a result of these categorizations, interviewees employ non-accessible savings accounts and adopt a non-materialistic lifestyle. Second, by employing technologies of the self in the form of increasing work hours, choosing a job based solely on income and making sure that they work hard, everyday asset managers bind themselves closer to work. At the same time, they increase their own workload when diversifying income sources. Third, the non-emotional, business approach incorporated in finance rationality intersects with relationships, culminating in a mutually generative relationship between asset norms and relationships. This again challenges the behavioural economic insights outlined in Chapter 2 which seek to reduce the employment of emotions by means of financial education and simplified financial products, assuming 'emotions drive economically irrational decisions' (Bandelj et al, 2017, p 43). Instead, it reveals that personal relationships help to achieve asset ownership and economic relationships are productive in transforming social relationships.

These self-governing measures reveal how the 'real subsumption of society within capital' takes place through incorporating social life itself rather than 'solely' labour in the capitalist accumulation (Hardt and Negri, 2009, p 142). Despite proclaiming that asset-based welfare would lead to prosperity for all, the mutually generative relationship between norms of conduct and self-conduct intensifies the existing power relationships embodied in capital–labour inequalities. Self-governing measures work as a disciplining mechanism in everyday life, including everyday spaces of consumption, relationships and work, and create reliable financial subjects who meet their financial commitments. By 'routinely perform[ing] new and changed forms of financial self-discipline' (Langley, 2008, p 243), interviewees become financialized subjects and inadvertently strengthen the unequal relationship between capital and labour by means of enabling the dismantling of the welfare state, widening the use of financial products and restricting everyday practices. Individuals are thus governed and govern themselves based on becoming an everyday asset manager – resulting in an iterative relationship between power relationships and everyday practices.

PART IV

Variegated Financial
Subjectivities in the UK

7

Coping with Constraints

The discussions provided in the previous chapters suggested an unequal wealth composition, reinforcing inequalities inherent in a capitalist society between high-income earners and medium- to low-income earners. This chapter extends these insights and unveils how structural and normative constraints contribute to counter-conduct, that is, 'the will not to be governed, thusly, like that' (Foucault, 2007, p 75). In addition to the contradictions identified in the previous chapters, namely inherent uncertainty and income limitations, constraints built into the existing asset-based welfare system shape variegated financial subjectivities and practices.

Policy makers have increasingly realized that individuals do not invest as expected by asset norms. Even though the vast majority of eligible workers save in workplace pensions (84 per cent [DWP, 2018]), they do not actively engage with pensions, often saving only the minimum contributions (see Chapter 5), and when excluded from workplace pensions due to earning a low income or being self-employed, they do not conduct voluntary contributions (DWP, 2017, 2018). Not actively engaging with financial products has been identified in behavioural economic and financial literacy campaigns as 'irrational' (Altman, 2012, p 680) and intensified the utilization of measures to nudge people into behaving as expected. Following financial literacy and behavioural economic insights (see Chapter 2), a plethora of financial education and money advice services have emerged, including a government-sponsored financial advice website (FinCap, 2021; MoneyHelper, 2023b). These initiatives reinforce individual responsibility, seeking to make behavioural changes without recognizing the impact of factors outside an individual's control, such as structural and normative constraints. Women in the UK, for instance, are on average paid 19.9 per cent less than men (Eurostat, 2022) and normative assumptions of task divisions within the household impact the time they can offer to the labour market, both ultimately impacting the ability to sufficiently contribute to pensions (Loretto and Vickerstaff, 2013).

While asset-based welfare has been criticized for its lack of attention to the context of financial decisions, too often the focus lies on either identifying deviations from assumptions of financially rational behaviour as irresponsible or non-strategic (Clark, 2010, 2014) or on highlighting how structural and normative constraints determine behaviour, thus, marginalizing everyday practices (Grady, 2015; Hamilton and Darity Jr, 2017). Both of these explanations construct counter-conduct as a passive construct, simply emerging from the context. Yet, little is known about how people make decisions within existing constraints or why they choose a retirement strategy which is deemed less beneficial. This chapter thus explores the active meaning-making processes when experiencing constraints, understanding counter-conduct as forming part of a financialized subject. It will be shown that disengagement from pension investments is not irresponsible and needing to be corrected, but is a logical reaction to constraints. We shall get back to these insights in Chapter 8 when introducing variegated financial subjects originating from the contradictions and constraints inherent in asset-based welfare.

Reacting to structural constraints

The current asset-based welfare system assumes that one works in a full-time job with an increasing salary throughout one's lifetime. As outlined in Chapter 3, the full state pension is based on 35 years of national insurance contributions independent of the partner's contributions, and workplace pensions only apply after earning £10,000 in one place of work (Morley, 2014; DWP, 2018). Being self-employed, part-time employed or working across multiple employment contracts as well as earning less thus impacts the ability to accumulate pension investments (Clark, 2014). Strikingly, predominantly women and people belonging to minority ethnic groups are affected by these differential work trajectories, inhibiting them from benefitting from the full contribution to a workplace pension made by an employer (ONS, 2021b, 2022d). Women are 20 per cent less likely to contribute to a pension than men and minority ethnic pensioners' income is almost a quarter lower than the pension income of white pensioners, which is even worse (51 per cent lower) for women with a minority ethnic background (Vlachantoni et al, 2014; Gardner, 2020; Palmer, 2020; ONS, 2021a). The following sections therefore elucidate the experiences of these sub-groups of interviewees.

'Non-traditional' work trajectories and pensions

Behavioural economic and financial literacy studies operate within an understanding of pensions being universally beneficial, creating tax-efficient retirement income, provided one actively engages with them (Storper, 2014; Prabhakar, 2021). Deviating behaviour, such as not choosing an investment package in line with one's own retirement needs and adjusting its asset composition throughout one's lifetime, is perceived as financially irresponsible, which needs corrective policy measures (see Chapter 2). Countering this position, everyday financialization literature argues that the context of fundamental uncertainty in financial investments and less job protection 'undercut[s] workers' [their] capacity to perform the subject position of the investor' (Langley, 2007, p 83; Erturk et al, 2007). Yet there is little empirical knowledge of how being self-employed, working part-time or experiencing a patchy work history shapes the extent to which people perform the financial subject. This section thus sheds light on the interplay between uncertainty and occupational constraints.

Where experiences of work differ from the immanent assumption of stable, continuous employment throughout one's lifetime, the very character of pension saving can cause self-employed people to question the suitability of pensions, as illustrated in the case of Fleur. Fleur had been self-employed on an irregular, uncertain income for the majority of her working life, which first started with the desire for flexibility and was later reinforced by seeking to fit her schedule around childcare duties ("I had my son so it fitted well around his school and everything else so I could fit around child care" [Fleur]). Her experience of earning income in irregular sums rather than as a regular monthly salary culminates in a pension being not seen as a viable investment. In particular, the inaccessibility and long-term character of pensions seem to militate against the need for flexibility when being self-employed:

'I've got very little pension provision because when you're self-employed, it's the last thing you tend to put money by for ... you earn only in lumps, so it's easier to actually save a chunk of that then putting it away as if you're on a monthly salary ... So most of my money, we're not talking about large sums here, is within ISAs [Individual Savings Accounts] or interest-bearing accounts ... there were little pots [of workplace pensions] and since I never made regular amounts to put by, so you have to sort of let them stand there and didn't top them up, so I tried to consolidate these. It's through Hargreaves Lansdown, so they sort of manage the portfolios ... we didn't have certainly the flexibility in previous years to do anything with those pensions, yeah, you put them in and then you couldn't access them.'

Not engaging with a pension is arguably a logical reaction to the constraints of self-employment. When being self-employed, one would need to put more aside to achieve the same pension income as someone who has contributed continuously to pensions and had access to employers' contributions, so they would be risking more of their income by investing in pensions. Yet, this disinclination to pay money into a pension does not entail a rejection of asset accumulation altogether. Fleur tries to save as much as possible and has consolidated small pension pots she had built up in prior jobs. She thus actively tries to prepare for retirement, but the current construction of workplace pensions – based on a presumption of stable and continuous employment – prevents her from benefitting from these.

Lack of access to workplace pensions, caused by eligibility criteria for automatic enrolment, directly inhibits many people from saving in pensions and leads them to consider other forms of long-term savings, which do not have the same tax benefits. Not having access to a workplace pension results in needing to actively decide to set up a personal pension, a decision which employees with automatic enrolment pensions would not need to undertake, as illustrated in the following case. Agnes works as a part-time debt consultant at a church and lies below the income threshold to be eligible for automatic enrolment. She realizes that both state and workplace pensions would not be sufficient to provide for sufficient retirement income and that she needs to save more for later life, yet because of her exclusion from automatic enrolment, she considers what the best route for her is:

'I mean I have money in the bank, I don't really see that as investment … you have your state pension possibly coming in when you retire but in my case it's not gonna be much because I haven't worked full time. … when I worked in the local government I had some extra pension. I had tiny blocks of pension but not really, it's not gonna make anybody, maybe buy a pint of milk with it possibly or two, if you're lucky you get one week of shopping maybe but, no, that is something I need to look into, I know in the moment I have no extra pension but I need to somehow put aside money but I guess then the question is, is it better to have a pension or do you put the money aside into a Cash ISA? … for me investment is risk … you don't know, what happens, the financial world we live in it fluctuates really.'

When weighing up her need to invest for the future, she suggests that a Cash ISA may be a better form of investment for her, rather than a pension. Agnes distances herself from pensions by equating its investments with risk ("it's better to have your money under your pillow") while classifying savings not as an investment, echoing classifications put forward in finance theory, where savings are categorized as the safest financial asset and investments are considered medium to higher risk, including defined-contribution (DC) pensions where one is 'directly exposed to the risks of fluctuating stock markets' (Lowe, 2010, p 197).

Third, interviewees with a 'non-traditional' work history, who had experienced many different pension saving options, were often sceptical of the pensions they were offered. This was not an unsubstantiated opinion: interviewees quite rationally questioned the effectiveness of DC pensions, for example, that the high charges and fees associated with DC pensions ("the fees that you're charged are quite hidden" [Fleur]) can result in poor value for money in contrast to the guaranteed income from defined-benefit (DB) pensions (Ayres and Curtis, 2015; Webber, 2018).[1] Declining asset values since 2008 have even resulted in DC pensions being at risk of underperforming with regards to retirement provision (Cribb and Karjalainen, 2023). To illustrate this, Nadeem has worked in several lower paid jobs throughout his lifetime ("I have sort of chequered work history really"), including teaching, sales and importing goods from India. Despite some of them having provided workplace pensions, Nadeem does not engage with these and only contributed to them because it was set up by the workplace. He does not feel that DC pensions generally are reliable and effective in contrast to DB pensions:

'I got a private pension, it's not a great private pension and I think you know private pensions, all the money goes out in charges and fees and so on, so I never bothered with that I had it years ago I never bothered topping it up or doing anything with it because I felt it wasn't worth it. And there's, you know, choices between pensions and property and British pensions are rubbish, they are rubbish and the private sector the way they deal with pensions I think is daylight robbery, so I don't feel confident with private pensions ... So I think you know if you want to have a pension, you gotta to do something you've got to have a business going, carry on working until you retire unless you've got a really good final salary pension scheme or something like that you know they were really useful or public sector pension.'

Because of his opinion that DC pensions are not reliable, Nadeem highlights the need to look towards other forms of provision for later life, such as property, business investments or continuing to work. While these sorts of provisions are not unique to groups who have experienced non-traditional employment trajectories, the greater emphasis on them compared to workplace pensions in their plans for the future was a recurrent theme among interviewees with a patchy and more uncertain work history.

Far from representing a lower level of financial literacy (Clark et al, 2021), the disengagement from pensions either by not actively engaging with them and/or not contributing to one is arguably a logical reaction to the occupational constraints faced by individuals within the context of uncertainty, constraints which are not accommodated for in a pension system based on the assumption of steady and continuous employment (Strauss, 2014; Grady, 2015). Someone who does not have access to a workplace pension would not benefit from an employer's contributions and would need to risk relatively more than someone who has access to employers' pension contributions. Interviewees who are excluded from or marginalized within the current pension system appear to realize that being self-employed, experiencing a patchy work history and having less continuous income will most likely lead to an inadequate pension income in later life and adjust their financial practices accordingly. In particular, the inflexibility of pensions is foregrounded here: "a flexible pension scheme whereby ... depending on what stage of your life you're at and how you felt you could need the money or not, you know, you could put more into your pension for later on or less" (Charles).

In addition to occupational constraints, interviewees who had experienced a 'non-traditional' work history were sceptical of the pensions they were offered due to the high fees charged. This, however, does not entail a rejection of asset norms altogether – rather, investments are used strategically, including tax-efficient savings and property, and are employed to overcome obstacles incorporated in the current pension system. While these may ultimately be investments which are considered less beneficial than pensions within the theoretical understanding of finance rationality (Guiso et al, 2002; Clark, 2010), meaning such behaviours could be interpreted as irrational, they are considered appropriate strategies within the frame of occupational constraints and uncertainty of financial investments.

Impact of caring work on pension savings

Besides 'non-traditional' work arrangements impacting everyday pension practices, being a carer prevents women from continuously contributing to pension provisions throughout their lifetime. As shown in Chapter 3, the UK has one of the lowest maternity pay benefit systems and ranks among the highest for childcare costs among OECD countries, resulting in inequalities around the burden of care, where those who can pay leave care work to the market (Fraser, 2017; Bargawi et al, 2021). Also, and crucially, for many women the ability to commit to regular pension payments is reduced.

Given the lack of support, either by government ("daycare ... it's very expensive in this country" [Daiyu]) or by family members ("my parents and Jack's parents didn't live near us" [Ai]), women are often limited in the time they can offer to the job market, culminating in prolonged periods of leave from work and breaks in employment: "Each time I had a baby or childcare needs I had to drop a job and deal with my children first and then return to jobs" (Namono). A similar picture can be found in elderly care, where some interviewees were limited in the time they could offer to the job market because of caring for a family member:

'She wears an alarm that if she falls it goes off. Because it goes – and 2:00 in the morning last week I had a phone call. So I'm always on call. So, it's very difficult for me to look for a job ... I'm not bothering because I just can't.' (Haima)

Income and time constraints are intensified when there is an "above and below happening" (Zara), where interviewees need to take care of children and elderly parents.

Even when being able to finance the caring costs, prevalent gender norms around caring result in childcare costs not being considered as equally shared between parents, and are only taken into consideration by women when deciding to continue or to leave work: "I got pregnant and decided, ok, I take a little break because basically whatever I earned would have gone to childcare, so we felt it wasn't, it just didn't feel right to have all my earnings going to nursery fees" (Agnes). It is notable that the interviewee switches to the plural pronoun when discussing the justification for not working, this representing her partnership, yet the childcare costs are not considered to be equally shared, suggesting an underlying assumption that the woman should undertake the caring work. The comparison of childcare costs to earnings is a deciding factor in preventing women from returning to work before the age where free childcare hours start (three years) – precluding any workplace pension saving:

'It was a workplace pension but I have stopped contributing because I don't have any form of revenue [in my self-employment]. It's more or less put into savings. ... I'm not earning as a salary because I could be working and all that and my services to the family, plus the lack of savings and the fact that I do not save for my retirement, I've got. Because I used to put money aside when I was in paid employment, not self-employed.' (Ai)

Given that a two-earner household with two children would have needed to earn at least £20,400 each before tax to cover childcare costs and to have a minimum acceptable living standard in 2017 (the year of the interview [Padley and Hirsch, 2017]), it is a meaningful decision for one of the partners to not use their income for childcare when household members earn less than that. Yet, since Ai's income was on a similar level to her husband's, the husband could have taken on the caring work; however, gendered understandings of caring led Ai to quit her job and take on self-employment, culminating in a lower ability to save for retirement. This not only demonstrates that stereotypes about 'appropriate' female behaviour continue to determine the burden of unpaid labour within the household, even when earnings are equal or greater than a partner's (McMunn et al, 2020), but because women undertake the main caring work such stereotypes also result in their pension savings being compromised.

After returning to work, caring duties often lead to women following non-typical employment paths, creating the occupational constraints discussed in the previous section. They work in part-time positions, which translates into a declining income and being unsure what they will earn in the future, or become self-employed with lower income possibilities due to its flexibility (as shown in the case of Fleur): "I went on maternity leave and then came back part-time … Before I had children, I had a happy salary … and then when I stopped working and then I had a really, tiny part-time job, I had a lot less" (Nancy). "To juggle everything on my own, I needed to look at something where I had that much more flexibility, ok, it wasn't a guaranteed income but … it gave me that flexibility that I needed" (Claudia). As a consequence, taking care of children culminates in lower earnings possibilities, impacting one's ability to save for retirement:

'It wasn't a career trajectory that if you said somebody did a degree, they did an MBA, you know. It's not a trajectory a man would necessarily have taken up or non-parent, you know, it was defined by having the kids … I reduced my workload or wasn't doing a career type of job.' (Scarlett)

This interviewee, who is on a low income, negotiates the experience of having taken time off for children and not being able to go back to a 'typical' career path. Being a mother, therefore, adds a further layer of uncertainty to the rising job insecurity within financialized societies (Erturk et al, 2007; Langley, 2007), suggesting that it may be unlikely that mothers will return to full-time work and be able to continuously contribute to pensions ("never let it be said this stopping work for children doesn't make any difference because financially it makes a massive difference" [Scarlett]).

In dealing with these structural constraints due to caring duties, some interviewees aim to increase pension contributions before starting a family. Reference is made to the fear of being constrained in saving for retirement when having children: "I also wanna do it before I have children, so I am trying to save enough money" (Anu). They also employ more flexible investment products which allow them to maintain savings when their circumstances change ("I didn't want anything that, that I couldn't access …, I needed to access it whenever I needed to" [Layla]). Being able to react to changing circumstances and accessibility when needed are key factors in deciding on financial products ("I have an online ISA which I can from time to time I put money in but it's also a very flexible ISA, if I need money I can take it out" [Namono]). As in the case of experiencing occupational constraints, the inflexibility of pensions prevents carers from contributing to them. Not being able to reduce pension contributions during maternity leave or prolonged periods of reduced work hours is a key disadvantage of pensions.

After having children, if money allows, female interviewees try to go back to contributing to workplace pensions and to conduct additional "investment and stuff and paying for the pension that was the thing, you know, after finally getting around of doing a pension really" (Pippa). However, due to lower earning possibilities, their contributions to workplace pensions are low in comparison to someone who works full time and therefore unlikely to provide adequate income during retirement: "they take some each month out of my wage, it's about £80 a month roughly" (Claudia).

The structural constraints limiting women's accumulation of pension wealth, such as the burden of caring work, curtailed career progression and high childcare costs (Loretto and Vickerstaff, 2013; Ghodsee, 2019), leads to a position of frustration where interviewees feel they have to prioritize their current situation even though they want to save for the future ("I would love to have savings ... I would love to invest in something. I would love to see my money grow" [Namono]). Women are thus not less inclined to conduct long-term financial planning, as suggested by the literature introduced in Chapter 2 (Grace et al, 2010; Lusardi, 2015), but the constraints they experience prevent them from contributing to pensions in a sustained way. Consequently, inequalities arising from gendered social reproduction (Fraser, 2017; Bargawi et al, 2021) are intensified because women have to opt out of the workplace pension or reduce their contributions because of the inflexibility of pension schemes and their lower earnings due to childcare duties, which disadvantages them in comparison to men. These circumstances could be changed by implementing a system which does not assume a typical male life trajectory, and yet the UK government has not tackled this. Instead, a discourse of individual responsibility has been intensified and financial literacy programmes advanced which target mothers and troubled families (Nunn and Montgomerie, 2017; Montgomerie and Tepe-Belfrage, 2019).

Experiencing normative constraints

Structural constraints inherent in the current pension system interact with normative constraints, as shown earlier in the case of caring duties where gender-normative assumptions of caring result in predominantly women taking a break from work, inhibiting them from saving into workplace pensions. Besides caring duties impacting asset accumulation, norms concerning finance have been found to interact with investments. While financial literacy campaigns and their underlying research have pointed to behavioural differences where women are identified as less financially inclined and more risk averse than men (see Chapter 2), others have instead highlighted the impact of gender norms on financial decisions (Booth and Nolen, 2012; Eswaran, 2014). Having internalized the stereotypes embodied in policy initiatives and media (Joseph, 2013; Hasler and Lusardi, 2017), women often are less confident when conducting investments (Bucher-Koenen et al, 2016) and adopt lower risk levels (Booth and Nolen, 2012). There has been, however, little empirical attention given to how women make decisions within normative constraints when being part of a household.

Management of household finances

Extending insights on earmarking spending money within the household, where it has been unveiled that 'money earned by husbands is often demarcated from money earned by wives, with different sets of expectations, obligations, and restrictions around how much money is spent' (Murdoch, 2017, p 25), the interviews have revealed that gender-normative roles also influence how assets are earmarked. Two different approaches to financial planning within the household emerge here.

In the first instance, which was also the dominant approach in the interview data, household members seem to have adopted gender-normative roles within the management of household finances. Supporting statements for the separation of financial chores, where women manage short-term financial decisions such as shopping and men manage the long-term retirement planning, were found: "the deal is Amy organizes life and then I make sure we save properly for it" (Isaac). Interestingly, even when a discourse of equality is employed ("we've got some very core and common values" [Tobias]), it is often one partner making the long-term financial decisions:

> 'I do most of the spreadsheet, every new thing I bounce off her and say look I am thinking about doing this, what do you think? So she often has some very good questions which makes me then dig a little bit further, and then we decide jointly really but she, she, she relies a lot on my advice. She asks the questions and if I satisfy myself, she's ok with it.' (Baron)

Despite 'bouncing' everything off her and mentioning that they make decisions jointly, he closes the statement with saying that she relies a lot on him and, if he is satisfied, the investment is made. Although he consults with her, he is the one conducting the research and ultimately in charge of the strategy. Hence, in spite of not legitimizing gender-normative roles in dividing the financial management of the household discursively, they often emerge in financial practices. Budgeting is left to women ("I don't know, I left it to my wife" [Joseph]) and men take on the responsibility for determining future household finances, independent of the income of household members: "he sort of watches things what's going on ... and things, I just leave that to him because he does it. So not one of my jobs really ... I do the day-to-day accounts, he does the forecasting" (Fern). Interestingly, although both earn a similar annual income, the interviewee uses the term 'jobs' when declaring that long-term financial planning is not part of her tasks within the household, reinforcing a clear task division between husband and wife. Arguably, this approach results in women reacting to, but not acting within, long-term financial decisions, intensifying the inequalities created by caring duties.

Strikingly, members of households who conform to this task division have not only internalized gender-normative roles of financial responsibilities but also developed differential financial practices. Men who are responsible for the household's long-term financial strategy seem to have internalized norms of being financially inclined ("I would consider myself financially literate" [Baron]) and are confident in investing ("I'm quite confident, in my own judgement, on what I do" [James]). They focus on amassing monetary profits ("I want capital growth" [Baron]), resulting in setting more ambitious savings goals than their partners ("I'm probably a bit more ambitious in terms of investing and trying to make more, my wife is more cautious in terms of making sure we've got enough" [Tobias]). These ambitions do not just relate to the individual but comprise the whole household, as shown in the following statement made by a husband to his wife: "I don't think you have to work all your life either" (Isaac). Having internalized the gender-normative role of the breadwinner thus tends to result in men setting more ambitious savings goals when part of a couple (Agunsoye et al, 2022), since gender norms dictate that their role is to ensure the provision of resources for the household.

Women who are mainly responsible for the day-to-day budgeting within the household instead appear to have internalized norms of being less financially inclined ("I left it to him because I'm not a numbers person anyway" [Vibha]), reflected in expressing being less confident in making financial decisions and concentrating on the occurrence of adverse events ("I always felt the world ahead could be much, much harsher" [Eloise]). Interestingly, this has a twofold effect on their approach to savings and investments. On the one hand, they refrain from taking on too much risk ("for me to do something, it would have to feel like it's stable" [Emily]) and emphasis is placed on having the security that the money will not be lost ("I want to have some sort of peace of mind that this lump sum is kind of still there" [Claudia]). On the other hand, since they anticipate experiencing financial constraints in the future, they focus on being able to access the money ("I need some sort of security there to make sure if things, if something awful went wrong, I got money to be able to rely on" [Beatrix]). A recurrent reference is made to the possibility of losing money:

'It's the possibility it could go wrong as well and the risk involved in, you know, yes it could make you some money but equally you could lose everything as well … I wouldn't be prepared to take that risk … if there would be a guarantee, it was gonna be some long-term investment and there was guarantees and assurances there then I would consider it but I don't think there's anything that's guaranteed.' (Claudia)

In contrast to men, who have developed an optimistic view of long-term investments, women see these as problematic due to the "possibility of failure outweigh[ing] the possibility of success" (Imogen). This fear of adverse events results in preferring a savings target which they are certain to reach without risking too much, culminating in, as previous quantitative data has shown (Agunsoye et al, 2022), gender attitudinal differences in savings goals that are not dependent on difficulties in meeting financial plans due to income and/or wealth but are connected to marital status.

In the second instance, the organization of household financial management deviates from gender-normative roles which expect the man to be responsible for long-term financial planning. Instead, women are assigned the task of managing the investments of the household: "Edward is incredibly disorganized … so I am trying to get the pensions together" (Darcy). Even when earning substantially more than the women in the partnership, men leave the long-term financial planning to their wives:

'He earns much more than I do. … In our family I am the one that knows about our finances, so you know, I produce our investment spreadsheet, I do our budgeting for our house renovation … sometimes we buy bonds or something like that, just if I've got money that I think *oh we're not doing or haven't got a project on.*' (Scarlett)

What is striking here is that despite women taking over the financial management they are still responsible for the main caring duties within the household. This then entails being responsible for the day-to-day budgeting ("I sat down and I itemized everything in a spreadsheet from all the cards, just everything, just so I can see" [Pippa]) in addition to the long-term planning.

These two dynamics contribute to women's savings goals not increasing even when they have internalized a male-normative finance role. While they understand the need to take on risk in order to accumulate financial wealth, they focus on reaching a comfortable lifestyle ("I'm quite comfortable" [Harriet]). By repetitively using the term 'comfortable' and viewing an aim to grow financially as being greedy, women put emphasis on the fact that they want to have stability for them and their family:

'I just want enough money to be comfortable. I think for most part of it and then, you know, have enough money to then eventually be able to have children and have – my children and let my children be comfortable. … I think money is just a way of keeping you – you shouldn't be greedy for it, do you know what I mean? I don't think it's the be all and end all. I think as long as you have enough to be comfortable, I think that's good.' (Bethany)

According to this perspective, women would find no reason to try to make more of their savings if the latter allowed them to reach their goal of living a comfortable life. Moreover, even in those cases where women make the main financial decisions, either by making investment decisions themselves or suggesting the investment products, they concentrate on accessibility ("you have children … you need to have access to some money" [Rita]). It appears that being responsible for the day-to-day budgeting and the concomitant need to ensure financial security in the short-term influences the kind of financial products used, focusing on accessibility in case of adverse events. The stress that women put on the accessibility of savings would explain why they refrain from investing in a self-invested personal pension scheme if they can afford to do so (Agunsoye et al, 2022), which, in contrast to ISAs, are investment vehicles with limited accessibility and higher risk, but which are also associated with higher savings goals.

These insights reveal the contribution of gender-normative roles in the shaping of counter-conduct. Gender-normative roles interact with asset norms, constructing variegated forms of everyday financialization where women amend the three-pronged asset-accumulation strategy to the constraints they are experiencing, reflected in contributing less to pensions, setting lower savings goals and prioritizing accessible financial products rather than personal pension products. The discourse of the everyday asset manager of not being enthusiastic about making money and distancing themselves from the investor subject is intensified here to justify this decision, emphasizing instead the goal to provide a comfortable life for themselves and their children rather than being greedy.

Employing the normative context to disengage

After having seen how women are excluded from workplace pensions due to caring duties and their underlying reasonings for not setting up personal pensions, this section highlights what happens when they have access to workplace pensions. Realizing the importance of pensions, the women interviewed contribute to workplace pensions when these are offered but they do not engage with them; they recognize that pensions are necessary to "give you some security for the future" (Saskia), but feel constrained because of having no control over the investments: "You're putting your money into their hands essentially and hoping that they're gonna do something with it and return with more, but I guess as soon as you put it into their hands the onus is on them really, isn't it? And it's, it's out of your control" (Layla). In particular, the locked-away design of pension products, with long-term investments managed by the pension fund on behalf of the members, seems to be of concern for women. Because of expecting the occurrence of adverse events ("it's always worrying that I might need money" [Rita]), emanating from the gender-normative roles of being responsible for childcare, the daily chores and day-to-day budgeting within the household, women want to be able to access the money they have saved: "I like to know where my money is and that I can get a hold of it when I need to get a hold of it" (Claudia). The desire to remain flexible in case of short-term financial needs stands in contrast to the lack of accessibility and flexibility of workplace pensions.

Grasping, nevertheless, the importance of pensions, which "give you some kind of security for the future" (Saskia), and realizing that they would lose out on the contributions of the employer, those who have access to workplace pensions sign up for them despite their lack of accessibility and flexibility:

'You'd pay 4 per cent and they would match you with 4 per cent, but if you wanted to pay more in and you did pay more in, the company would increase their amount that they'd pay in ... so I basically paid in the maximum which I think was 12 per cent, and then they would pay 8 per cent of my salary. ... But that was okay if you could afford to do it, if you had financial responsibilities, like kids and other things, then you're less likely to do that.' (Millie)

Some women even make additional voluntary contributions ("I bought additional voluntary contributions as soon as I could" [Fern]) or choose the higher contribution amount to not lose out on the extra payments made by the employer ("I wanted to get as much out as I could" [Millie]). Consequently, an income increase results in additional pension contributions: "it made sense because ... we continue living on what we're living on and I can at least put that there" (Adhira). Yet, women who increased their contributions tended to be predominantly those who did not have caring responsibilities, further demonstrating the restrictive role of structural constraints on women's financial decisions.

The conflict between wanting to remain flexible in case of unexpected events and contributing to an inaccessible pension is overcome by representing pension contributions as largely driven by social norms. It is implied that it is the "right thing to do", reinforced by a prevalent media discourse surrounding pensions ("they talk about it more, don't they, it's generally more out there" [Pippa]). Using generic pronouns such as 'they' and posing a rhetorical question ('don't they') indicates a social obligation to take out a pension, accepted as a particular course of action rather than being specific to one's situation. Strikingly, while participants contribute to pensions, they disengage from them, drawing on gender-normative assumptions of being less financially inclined (Joseph, 2013; Roberts, 2015) to justify a strategy of reduced time investment in the perceived inaccessible and inflexible workplace pension: "I suppose, I'm a bit jaded ... I didn't look, you know, at the different options because I thought, well I don't really understand" (Millie). Rather than calculating their financial needs during retirement and choosing an investment package with the appropriate risk level, as expected by finance rationality, interviewees often choose the default option: "It's always with the employer, whatever the employer suggests ... It's always the company that the employer suggests I've taken and they take it off my salary, maybe 5 per cent or something" (Namono). Claiming not to be a person to whom finance comes naturally ("I'm not an economically minded person" [Imogen]) results in less confidence in dealing with pensions ("it was a little confusing for me ... I wouldn't know how to make the right decision about a pension" [Isabella]). Since "it is quite complex" (Ida), the investment package offered by the company is selected with no consideration of alternative options.

Even though participants worry about pension choices ("I worry that I don't know enough about it. And I'm paying into something and I don't really know what it means" [Emily]), drawing discursively on gender norms constructs an image where it would appear to take substantial effort to inform oneself about pensions:

'If you haven't got the natural, you know, gifting in finance, which I haven't, it's even less incentive to, I want to do it ... I am frightened by finance and I don't feel confident about finance and because I know, I am not very organized with finance, I would take the, you know, the easiest option ... it's really important thing, pensions are important. I just gotta be a good girl and get down to it [sort out the pension] but then, you know, we do lots of other stuff besides the work and so it's really difficult, there's always something else that needs doing, it's difficult to sort of get down doing the stuff that I really should do.' (Darcy)

The interviewee draws on the media personalization strategy introduced in Chapter 4, where finance is connected to personal traits, to justify her disengagement. Because of not having the personal traits necessary to deal with finance, it is seen as too complex, resulting in less confidence in dealing with it. Moreover, gender norms with regards to finance interact with normative assumptions of caring duties, where women are expected to undertake the daily chores, amplifying the constraints women experience in actively engaging with pensions.

The normative context of caring and financial behaviour thus culminates in a reluctant acceptance of workplace pensions, where many women save if they can, but the details are largely ignored. Constraints emanating from caring duties lead to perceiving pensions as inappropriate due to their inaccessibility, and gendered roles of financial behaviour are employed to justify the disengagement from pensions. This disengagement should not be considered irresponsible behaviour or the result of being less financially literate (Bucher-Koenen et al, 2016; Hasler and Lusardi, 2017), but instead reflects a 'necessary' form of counter-conduct (Foucault, 1978, p 96); it is a coping mechanism to deal with the ways the system does not fit with women's experiences, and, having internalized normative constraints of being less financially inclined, reinforces the perception that it would require too much time investment when having to manage the daily chores. However, this counter-conduct means that some women, especially those who face income constraints, miss out on additional contributions from their employer and potentially higher returns on their pensions due to paying minimum contributions and choosing the default option. A simple solution could be to implement a system where contributions from the employer and government do not rely on one's own circumstances. Instead, the discourse of individual responsibility and financial literacy, which ignores the normative context, prevails in the UK.

Multiple dimensions of constraints

The previous two sections have revealed that people experiencing a non-traditional work trajectory and women with caring duties are not passive victims of an unequal welfare system or less financially responsible due to their disengaging from pensions, but that the actions taken are logical and aptly negotiated responses to an unequal welfare system. Counter-conduct, that is, 'the will not to be governed, thusly, like that' (Foucault, 2007, p 75), should therefore not be seen as irrational but as emerging from the contradictions and constraints immanent in the current asset-based welfare system. As suggested at the beginning of this chapter, these constraints are worsened across intersections, for example, women from minority ethnic backgrounds tend to have the lowest pension outcomes. A pertinent question is thus how do interviewees who experience multiple constraints navigate overlapping points of disadvantages? For this purpose, three case studies where interviewees have encountered multiple constraints are discussed.

In the first case study, which concerns Vibha, whose parents are from India, structural constraints intersect with relationship dynamics and inhibit pension savings. After marrying her English husband, Vibha moved with him on a spousal visa abroad, where she was not allowed to work. As a result of this, and despite having a law degree, she has an inconsistent employment record which includes periods of childcare and part-time work, meaning she does not have access to a workplace pension. Her husband, however, has been able to contribute to one throughout his working life and this is now part of divorce proceedings: "I've not been able to work. I won't get a government pension or a very, very small one ... whereas my husband kept his going and that's part of the big divorce thing". The UK is one of the few countries in the OECD which does not have an automatic legal regulation for the splitting of pensions in the case of divorce (OECD, 2021b), for which reason she has had to fight for a divorce settlement of £12,000 per year in pensions. Yet, this will not be sufficient to sustain herself due to her age (59 years old) and her lack of workplace or state pensions. Notwithstanding, she actively seeks to plan for retirement, informing herself about her options, for instance, the possibility to top up her state pension:

'I worked for British Telecom for six years, and then we went abroad. I had a little pension there, so apparently I'm going to get £50 a week from my state pension. ... So apparently I can go back and pay something like £3,000 to top me up, to bring me back up, but I don't know if it would give me the full pension. So I might do that after the divorce.'

This interplay between occupational constraints due to unpaid care and relationship dynamics is intensified when not being able to divorce. Amidah, a single mother on a low income, who moved to the UK 20 years ago, has struggled to gain access to a higher paying job due to childcare duties, and she has not received child maintenance support in line with being a single mother. Because of the UK partner arguing that "the separation is very expensive" and that they "don't have the money to pay for it, not now, maybe later", Amidah is separated but not divorced. With no support from family, Amidah's access to full-time employment has been significantly limited and has restricted long-term financial planning, a situation which she struggles with:

'I try to save as much as I can ... My main aim, one day I'll go for a full-time job and life will be even better ... if he grows up more and then maybe things will get even better, then I can work more, that's one of my big dreams ... with the amount I'm having, I cannot save much, but I'm trying my best.'

Rather than opting to prioritize current needs over long-term needs (Thaler and Shefrin, 1981; Grace et al, 2010), Amidah, and other interviewees like her, still seek to conform to the norms of financial self-governance by adapting practices to the constraints they are faced with. Despite not qualifying for automatic enrolment in a workplace pension, due to her income being below the threshold, she has signed up for a workplace pension, even though her contributions reduce her current available income and the pension will not provide a sufficient income during retirement ("I'm paying pension automatically at work. They advised it two years ago … They're taking I think about £2 something every week").

Besides relationship dynamics intervening in pension savings, having experienced different life trajectories from those expected by the UK pension system culminates in additional pressures on constrained pension savers, as shown in the case of Kojo. Throughout his lifetime Kojo has lived in different countries, moving from Ghana to the Netherlands in his late twenties before coming to the UK in 2006:

> 'At work I pay pension and I made a pension for myself [a health insurance plan with a pension element]. I think that one I pay £40 every month … here let's say if you are not working, the government will help you but in Africa is not like that, so sometimes it will come to a point that you have to struggle. In Africa our family depends on us, you see, so the family will look after you and after 15 to 20 years the family expecting something from you. So the family wants you to go and work so that you can look back and take care of them … That's why I can say my country people who are living here, most of them they don't want to stay at home, they want to work because if you are here you still have to look for your family back home, so if you're not working how are you going to look for them? And the government can't help you to look for them … so it's good if you save and the pension can help you … I decided to buy a house instead of renting because if … I stay here 20/30 years and I pay it [a mortgage] I can get maybe £1,000 from it that is the profit at least £1,000 from it, profit from it but if I rent it I don't get nothing from it, you lose.'

Two elements transpire from this statement, indicating the disciplining rather than the empowering mechanism of everyday finance in interplay with 'moralities and value judgements' (Lai, 2017, p 923). First, reflecting 'moral expectations of reciprocity in parent–child relationships' (Singh, 2017, p 185), Kojo articulates that his background has instilled in him a moral obligation to look after his family ("sometimes you have to send money home to your family in Africa"), which he contrasts with the situation in the UK where the state offers, even if it is limited, financial support to individuals. To help meet this moral obligation, he has migrated in order to work and seeks not to be reliant on the welfare state. He works hard and is even thinking about taking another part-time job ("I'm a security officer at Asda and all those things and I want to try taxi driver to do as part-time, so I've got the license … just try, keep on trying" [Kojo]), hence intensifying the disciplinary technology of labour identified as a self-governing measure in Chapter 6. Even on a lower income (£21,600 per year, which is below the average income within his age range and below the UK's median earnings [HMRC, 2022]), Kojo is actively adopting financial solutions to further this goal of conforming to asset norms, such as contributing to a workplace pension (which he gained access to two years prior to the interview), investing in homeownership (shared ownership – 20 per cent, equal to £95,000) and even setting up his own pension insurance arrangements. It is noteworthy that this active pursuit of investment is underpinned by fairly modest expectations, as Kojo feels that even £1,000 profit from a long-term investment would make it worthwhile. This does not seem to align with the model of a sophisticated financial subject who seeks to maximize returns (Mitchell and Lusardi, 2012) but is in line with the social and income constraints he is experiencing.

Second, while Kojo has the 'behavioural disposition' (Prabhakar, 2021, p 27) to plan long-term, as sought after in financial capability campaigns, following the norms of financial self-governance results in exploitative financial relationships. Income constraints, which are intensified by family pressures to send home remittances, and a life trajectory which is not recognized within the current pension system, means that the measures he has taken are unlikely to result in adequate income when retiring, yet reduce his disposable income during his working life. Before having access to a workplace pension (which he was offered only two years prior to the interview), Kojo set up a health insurance policy that included a private pension element with contributions of only £40 per month, putting more pressure on himself ("you have to continue paying, you see, if you don't pay your money is gone"). Similarly, after having accessed a workplace pension, he can only afford minimum contributions, which means in the context of relatively high management fees for a UK workplace pension scheme and the short time period of contributing (Morton, 2021), Kojo will receive a rather low amount of pension income during retirement while also not receiving the full UK or Dutch state pension. Kojo's active engagement with financial products thus fails to make a real difference to his long-term wealth while at the same time it creates income sources for financial institutions.

What these three cases reveal is that individuals who experience multiple dimensions of constraints subsume the logics of financial self-governance into the reasonings and rationales already established in their everyday life. 'Individual dispositions and social circumstances, together, shape the use of money' (Bandelj et al, 2017, p 51) instead of decisions being taken based solely on individual dispositions and constraints. These actions are not non-strategic behaviours (Clark, 2014) nor irrational mental shortcuts (Altman, 2012), but are necessary to cope with the constraints experienced. However, it is notable that these strategies, while offering practical solutions, often result in intensifying the disciplining mechanism of financial self-governance without providing adequate income during retirement.

Concluding remarks

In recent years, financial literacy research and education campaigns have refocused their attention to encourage lower income, women and people from minority ethnic backgrounds to adopt financial self-governance, seeking to nudge them into conforming to norms of conduct. While critical political economy and economic geography have highlighted the limits of financial literacy due to the fact that women and people with different life trajectories face limitations within the asset-based welfare system, everyday financialization has unveiled that individuals do not simply adopt the financialized subject position of the rational investor; instead everyday rationalities become enmeshed with logics of finance, culminating in variegated forms of everyday financialization (see Chapter 2). This chapter has combined these two insights and explored how structural and normative constraints build part of active meaning-making processes, ultimately challenging current advances of contextual financial literacy.

Situating counter-conduct within the unequal context of asset-based welfare reveals that rather than being passive victims of constraints, being outside the current pension system forms part of 'the will not to be governed, thusly, like that' (Foucault, 2007, p 75). Interviewees experiencing constraints quite rationally deconstruct the understanding of pensions as universally beneficial. As suggested in Chapter 3, the current asset-based welfare system disadvantages individuals who have an interrupted working life, rely on several jobs, are self-employed and/or have lower income possibilities, resulting in them feeling less able to rely on pensions for their long-term financial security. The inflexibility and inaccessibility of pensions prohibits them from seeing pensions as a viable investment option, culminating in them rejecting the idea of making voluntary contributions and opting for savings products instead. When having access to pensions, instead of trying to deepen their financial knowledge as expected by finance rationality and pursued by financial education campaigns (Altman, 2012; Bucher-Koenen et al, 2016; Montgomerie and Tepe-Belfrage, 2019), individuals who experience constraints tend to accept the default option of a workplace pension scheme. The interplay between everyday rationalities and constraints thus results in trying to achieve the first two elements of the three-pronged asset-accumulation strategy, namely savings accounts and homeownership, while disengaging from the third: pensions.

Illustrating the complex and meaningful ways in which individuals entangle financial subjectivities with constraints calls for a more inclusive understanding of financially responsible behaviour, opposing the dichotomy of rational/

irrational behaviour (Clark, 2014; Pellandini-Simanyi and Banai, 2021). The adopted behaviour, while deviating from those expected of rational investors, should not be understood as irrational (bounded rationality [Strauss, 2008]) or unsuitable for the complexity of the environment (environment-consistent rationality [Lavoie, 2015]) but seen as a response to the normative context generally and the structural context of workplace pensions specifically. Not having a similar access to pensions as someone with a full-time job hinders the adoption of asset norms and reduces the ability to continuously engage with workplace pensions. Since one would need to put substantially more savings aside to receive the same level of pension income as someone with a full-time job, it could be argued that it would be financially responsible to contribute to pensions if they are offered, and thereby not lose out on employers' contributions, but to not necessary actively engage with them. Distancing oneself from pensions and instead concentrating on savings which align more with work and family situations, and, interestingly, which often have tax-free allowances, are logical reactions to the pension system's in-built assumptions. Savings are thus not used in a non-strategic manner nor lie outside a financialized subject (Langley, 2008; Clark, 2014) but are part of seeking to achieve financial security.

Linking insights on constraints within capitalist systems (Fraser, 2017; Hamilton and Darity Jr, 2017) with everyday pension decisions (Pellandini-Simanyi et al, 2015; Lai, 2017) has unveiled how experiencing multiple dimensions of constraints intensifies the disciplining mechanism of the inherent unequal capitalist relationship. While interviewees who struggle with processes of social reproduction and/or experience a different work trajectory, both not recognized in the current pension system, perceive pensions not as a viable option, interviewees who are exposed to multiple dimensions of constraints seek to fulfil asset norms including pensions despite their limited means. Due to their inaccessibility, setting up additional pensions is employed as a self-governing measure to ensure one conducts regular savings. However, despite seeking to follow norms of asset accumulation and contributing to pensions even when not being automatically enrolled, their future retirement income will be insufficient. Moreover, it reduces the current income and increases the profit opportunities for the financial institutions. Context-specific financial education, which has acknowledged socio-economic differences, puts emphasis on individual responsibility (Lusardi, 2015; Clark et al, 2021), ultimately depoliticizing the underlying contradictions and constraints in a pension system that is built on assumptions of a typical male, well-earning life trajectory, and thus, without tackling systemic inequalities, ensures that individuals who experience constraints continue to meet financial commitments.

8

Managing Contradictions
and Constraints

As shown in the previous chapter, structural and normative constraints in interplay with the uncertainty of financial investments and job insecurity inhibit the everyday asset manager subject from performing, resulting in amending asset norms to one's own needs. While the resistances discussed previously have been 'quick to compromise' (Foucault, 1978, p 96) in response to the contradictions inherent in asset norms, namely accumulating assets despite being critical, and/or 'necessary' to cope with constraints, namely disengaging from pensions, others may 'play the role of adversary' (Foucault, 2003, p 280). Put differently, a discourse of the systems' inherent contradictions and constraints is omnipresent in interviewees' statements, yet the resultant counter-conduct occupies 'different tactical positions' (Foucault, 2003, p 208), ranging from a weaker form, that is a 'will not to be governed, thusly, like that' (Foucault, 2007, p 75), to a stronger one, reflecting the will 'not being governed quite so much' (Foucault, 2007, p 45).

Five variegated financial subjects (see Figure 8.1)[1] emerged from this interplay between conduct and the 'plurality of resistances' (Foucault, 1978, p 96). Whereas the calculative investor develops a highly diversified asset portfolio and enjoys investing, taking over responsibility for financial management is not seen as a positive by the majority of interviewees, but as a necessity in order to mitigate potential future risks ("you can't assume everything is there for you" [Amy]). Individuals therefore look within constructed asset norms and adjust these to their own needs, culminating in either avoiding direct investments in financial assets (everyday asset manager), focusing on relationships when investing (relational asset manager) or giving preference to property or business investments (independence seeker). A stronger form of counter-conduct then seeks to subvert norms by aiming to avoid asset accumulation (non-asset manager). Due to the everyday asset manager having been discussed extensively in previous chapters, given its

Figure 8.1: Variegated financial subjects in the UK

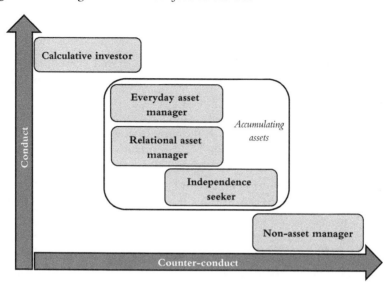

dominance, this chapter focuses on the other varied financial subjects and considers their interplay with experiencing constraints, representing an extension to the previous chapter's discussion on workplace pensions and their inherent constraints. Beyond coping with constraints in pension savings, interviewees actively seek to save for retirement and redefine asset norms in line with their context.

These insights extend previous perceptions of variegated financial subjectivities (Coppock, 2013; Lai, 2017) by introducing a typology of distinct financial subject positions that recognizes the impact of contradictions and constraints on the active meaning-making process. This typology moves beyond solely identifying behaviour as deviating from one of the two components of asset norms (as encountered in Chapter 2), namely accumulating financial assets and internalizing finance rationality, and views actions taken as financially responsible actions in line with the experienced contradictions and constraints.

The calculative investor

Calculative investors draw on the subject position of the everyday investor as theorized in the literature (Lai, 2017; Pellandini-Simanyi and Banai, 2021), positioning themselves as financial persons ("I always looked at things from a financial point of view" [Baron]) who enjoy investing ("I get a buzz off investing" [Isaac]). Belonging to the fifth income quintile or the higher end of the medium-income group, these are interviewees who have the financial means and the confidence to invest in riskier assets and incorporate the full extent of finance rationality (mirroring the picture provided for UK households where the highest-income group has the most diversified asset portfolio).

In line with the expected conduct of the theorized everyday investor subject (Langley, 2008), they speak of risk as an opportunity ("you have to speculate to accumulate" [Zara]) and aspire to use a diverse set of financial investments (see Table 8.1), including riskier investments "on the basis that [they] can afford to, obviously don't wanna lose, but can afford to lose" [Charlie]). A discourse of growth ("hoping that it will grow and give you some income and some value growth" [Theodore]) is accompanied by an aspirational discourse centring on climbing up the social ladder ("We're not unrealistic but we're aspirational" [Isaac]), where competition is established as a measure of success, even resulting in figuratively competing with parents: "better than them [her parents] yeah, we beat them, that's the goal" (Amy). Because of being confident in making investment decisions ("it's just part of our brain" [Eva]) and seeking to avoid "hidden charges" (Zara), prominence is given to investing directly, with a conviction of making better decisions than professional investors: "We had a portfolio with Santander on shares, which I have to say, up until we handed it to them, it did very, very well. We handed it to them and it was very little" (James). Weaving through these discourses is the notion that investments

Table 8.1: Balance sheet of a calculative investor

Assets	Liabilities
House	
ISAs and small savings accounts	
Building society savings accounts	
National Savings Certificates	
HSBC investment bond	
Several investment bonds	
Renewables energy fund	
Growth fund for grandchildren	
Co-funds – variety of stocks and shares and bonds	
Inheritance tax portfolio	
Self-invested pension	

Note: Strikingly, higher income interviewees felt constrained in speaking about finance since doing well is equated with the possibility of losing friendships over finances ("Everyone wants you to do well as long as you're not doing better than they are" [James]), as can also be seen in a lot of high-income earners not wanting to share exact numbers corresponding to their assets as in the case of this balance sheet.

and asset accumulation are enabling mechanisms to go further ("they've given me the opportunity [to be] pretty, pretty well secure" [Peter]), putting arguments forward for less state regulation: "it's a bit too much nanny stating" (Zara).

Interestingly, in line with the media and governmental discourse, interviewees seem to advocate financial education, where the belief is expressed that people should be empowered by "educating [them] better in what their options are and then let them choose what they want to do" (Zara). More specifically, calculative investors appear to talk from a position of superiority, distinguishing between 'us' to whom finance comes natural ("it's just part of our brain" [Eva]) and 'them' who don't understand finance ("most people don't understand money management" [Fern]). This 'exclusion governing discourse' (Foucault, 1972, p 11) goes as far as victimizing those who intentionally behave financially irresponsible ("there's a wealth of information and yet people spend more time going on to Paddy Power or Foxy Bingo" [Peter]) or unintentionally ("they don't go down the path with every intention of going down that path ... they're smart friends but they still wouldn't know" [Fern]). As a consequence, having internalized the calculative investor subjectivity in contrast to the normal approach of engaging with finance seems to require discursive justification. By asking the question "we are sad, don't we" after explaining the enjoyment in selecting shares, the 'others', the ones who do not follow this approach, are depicted as being 'normal':

'so we always get the FT weekend and on Sunday morning, we always sit down and look at our shares and decide whether we keep them or sell them or when we've going to sell them, what are we going to buy instead, that's kind of a little Sunday morning thing, tea or coffee, bacon butties and the FT, we are sad, don't we?' (Zara)

Apart from finance rationality leading to directly investing in stocks and shares, clearly differentiating calculative investors from saver subjects, it results in an 'improbable' counter-conduct (Foucault, 1978, p 96). As discussed in previous chapters, a welfare system focused on individual asset accumulation 'isn't outside power or lacking power' (Foucault, 1978, p 131) but enables the dismantling of publicly funded welfare measures and creates new profit opportunities for the financial sector. Although calculative investors draw on an agency discourse in the form of individual responsibility and believe in asset accumulation as a mechanism of personal growth ("it's about growing value" [Theodore]), the second component of the underlying power relationship is critically reflected upon. It is realized that by investing in financial assets, financial institutions gain profit and might not put the interest of their customers first ("any sort of financial product are just an absolute value for the bank" [Eva]). A continuous reference is made to hidden charges: "most of the money are in the SIPPs and shares we've chosen and that we look after because in those tracker funds you are paying the management fees and then the tracker funds are taking a fee as well but you don't see the breakdown" (Zara).

This distrust of financial products ("I've known about malpractice in the personal finance" [Habib]) and having confidence in managing investments results not only in the adoption of traditional diversification and developing 'a portfolio of financial market assets' (Langley, 2006, p 923), as expected of the investor subject, but also in their investing in non-financial assets. Due to its "tangible" (Eva) character and not being managed by someone else who is "out to make their own money" (Baron), a property portfolio is developed. To diversify the risk of changing house prices, properties in different locations are chosen, for instance, the domestic market is identified as risky ("we see sort of domestic property markets likely to continue dropping" [Eloise]) and investments in foreign properties are conducted ("my property in Australia, they're investments" [Peter]). Consequently, a highly diversified asset portfolio is established which, in line with theoretical expectations of finance rationality, is not exposed to a home bias and includes several pension investments: "I got a mixture of personal, I've got a mixture of company run and I've got a defined-benefit scheme, so it's a bit, it's a bit, of a mixture, I don't have all my eggs in one basket" (Peter).

As a result, calculative investors develop "a good cross-section of shares, property, pensions, insurances" (James). Property investment should not be seen here as deviating from the investor subject as discussed in the literature (Langley, 2007; Clark, 2012) but forms part of a financialized subjectivity. Tackling the distrust of financial institutions with the help of further diversifying the asset portfolio aligns with the governmental discourse of individual responsibility. Individual solutions are searched for and a belief in the importance of self-reliance through conducting investments in place of relying on the state is reinforced. The interplay between conduct and counter-conduct thus intensifies prevailing forms of governance.

The constrained everyday asset manager

In contrast to the calculative investor, the everyday asset manager, as shown in Part III, distances him/herself from the investor subject due to its contradictions and redefines asset norms into the three-pronged asset-accumulation strategy. The previous chapter has shown how interviewees who experience constraints struggle to conform to this subject position and as a consequence disengage from the third element of the asset strategy: pensions. Beyond coping with structural and normative constraints originating from the landscape for pension saving, the constrained everyday asset manager actively seeks to tackle these by utilizing investments deemed as more connected to the real-life context, as shown here in the case of women who have caring duties.

Feeling disillusioned with pension schemes due to ignoring the gendered processes of social reproduction – which have been intensified by the dismantling of the welfare state (Fraser, 2017; Mezzadri et al, 2022) – combined with their lack of accessibility and flexibility has resulted in carers actively engaging with savings and investment strategies which are perceived as giving them control over their money ("good to have control of your money" [Saskia]). According to finance rationality, insufficient savings in workplace pensions could be balanced out by higher risk/return investments such as personal pensions and stocks and shares investments, as presumed in the third tier of the UK pension system (see Chapter 3). Yet, it is notable that women are not turning to riskier investments to balance the lack of savings in workplace pensions due to their caring duties, but to products that they feel are more accessible or flexible alongside or instead of workplace pensions, seeking security over returns: "security and knowing I've got enough that I save and it doesn't have to be a huge amount" (Pippa).

Gaining control through accumulating accessible savings ("having a reasonable amount of savings" [Aldona]), instead of saving into a pension, is seen as an enabler to provide financial security even in times of difficulty: "I wanted to be able to access the money when I needed it ... I wanted to have a fairly liquid position when I need to access money I could" (Fleur). While interviewees recognize the trade-off between investing for the long-term and being able to access money in the more immediate future ("Do I have something I can't get access and get a better rate of interest or do I need something that I can dip in now, so every now and again." [Imogen]), they often choose the latter. In fact, participants frequently invest in financial assets classified in the literature as safe or fairly safe (Guiso et al, 2002; Lowe, 2010) including, besides savings accounts, investments such as premium bonds ("I was very safe, I would invest in premium bonds because you know they're very safe" [Vibha]) or endowment policies ("I got an endowment policy" [Rita]). These sorts of assets appear more controllable and accessible than long-term, locked away investments ("invested in bonds ... if we were short of money, I could get them out" [Clementine]) but also provide lower returns.

The underlying reasoning given for this predominantly safe asset strategy often came back to the gender-normative context discussed in the previous chapter in interplay with a relational context: "Shares and stuff because some people make it sound very easy, but I don't think my mind is that kind of mind, that you need to do that thing successfully. My husband could do this because he has amazing analytical skills" (Ioana). A discourse of being less financially inclined than the partner is being drawn upon ("he is meticulous and he gets fascinated" [Elsie]), reinforcing gender-normative constraints. Similar to the justification for disengaging from pensions (see Chapter 7), gender norms with regard to finance interact with norms of caring duties (Bargawi et al, 2021; Mezzadri et al, 2022), with reference being made to not having enough time to inform oneself sufficiently when taking on riskier investments in an environment of uncertainty: "you have to be so in tune with financial markets and to be honest it doesn't really, I don't have the time for even looking into that sort of things" (Agnes).

Even though financially risky investments are generally avoided ("I don't want to do anything that is risky with money" [Darcy]), carers willingly pursue non-financial investments that are theoretically defined as risky, namely a mortgaged main residence and/or buy-to-let property when having the financial means to do so: "so at the time we were buying that rental property that (endowment policy) matured and I ended up with another £16,000 ... So now I'm investing in property" (Rita). As discussed in Chapter 5, mortgaged properties are illiquid assets with high entry and exit costs, becoming highly risky when it is the main residence and/or not part of a diversified asset strategy, as shown by the balance sheet in Table 8.2 where the interviewee overly relies on property due to having only recently gained access to pensions. Here the property is the main residence, thus the interviewee would need to sell it, and the proceeds would depend on the house price and market at the time of selling (downsizing is unlikely due to it being a small property), or the interviewee would have to release equity. Despite this, women's contextual experiences provide a meaningful rationale for investing in property.

First, property investment feels less detached from everyday life, being more accessible than pensions and providing a platform for dealing with one's own life circumstances. The home is considered to be not just stable, but also a source of financial security, where the flexibility of property helps to reduce retirement and income worries.

'My home is, you know, my centre, is my security. ... so it's about security and knowing I've got enough that I save and it doesn't have to be a huge amount it just has to be enough that I am not worried. So, because I lived on minimum for many, many years.' (Pippa)

Table 8.2: Balance sheet of income-constrained everyday asset manager

Assets		Liabilities	
House	£158,000	Loan for roof panels	£10,000
Pension pot value	£30,000	Credit cards	£3,000
Savings	£5,000		

The interviewee had bought her council house and had had several income-constrained periods in the past for which reason she was not able to contribute continuously to pensions and was not always offered one. Besides flexibility, property investment helps to tackle income constraints by means of shared ownership (as also shown in the previous chapter): "I couldn't afford the deposit by myself, so shared ownership was the route that I needed to take to be able to afford somewhere" (Layla).

Second, in contrast to pensions which are controlled by financial institutions and bear an inherent uncertainty, property is seen as more controllable and less risky. Being simultaneously an investment and a home makes it appear less risky than financial investments because, although it may depreciate in value, people can still derive value from it as a place for the family, providing a tangible connection to their life:

> 'A house is less risky because I know what I bought it for I know ... it will never gonna get lower than that again, so it feels like a fairly sound proposition and obviously gain by living in it whereas just financial investments to me it's just smack of a little bit of risk.' (Darcy)

Even buy-to-let properties, which are categorized according to finance theory as risky (Guiso et al, 2002), are perceived as controllable and a viable means to overcome a low pension income due to part-time work: "it's not a huge pension, it will be pocket money ... I'm investing in property" (Rita).

These variegated financial practices, where women develop financial practices intertwined with their gendered context, should not be considered irrational, but rather represent self-conduct in line with existing constraints. Women want to provide financial security for the future in line with the three-pronged asset-accumulation strategy of the everyday asset manager, yet are limited by constraints inherent in asset norms. They thus accumulate assets more suited to their context and employ the structural and normative constraints inherent in asset-based welfare to justify redefining asset norms, revealing a 'necessary' form of counter-conduct (Foucault, 1978, p 96). The paradox is, however, that the resultant self-conduct deepens gender wealth inequalities as the asset strategy employed will not enable them to overcome the income and wealth gaps. Ultimately, the systemic failure to provide for social reproduction and accommodate women's needs in pension systems forces them to disengage from pensions and turn to financial alternatives which are low risk/return but provide accessibility, and/or to overly rely on risky non-financial assets, thereby jeopardizing the long-term financial wellbeing of women. Men, however, are able to fully benefit from the pension system across their working lives and are more likely to be able to fulfil the three-pronged asset-accumulation strategy before investing in further financial assets.

This is worsened when experiencing multiple dimensions of constraints. Being financially constrained not only in pension savings but asset accumulation more generally, and hence being inhibited from investing in alternative savings and investments, the disciplining mechanisms outlined in Chapter 6 are intensified, as shown in the case of Amidah (introduced in Chapter 7) and Namono. Similar to Amidah, Namono has moved to the UK, earns a low income, has a patchy work history and is a single mother without sufficient support for her four children because she has not been able to divorce her husband despite having been separated for 17 years. Strikingly, despite these constraints, Amidah and Namono seek to save and invest: "I would love to invest in something, I would love to see my money grow ... but it's all dependent on time because I have to work as well, I have to look after the children." (Namono). Finding oneself unable to meet norms of conduct results in utilizing budgeting strategies such as switching to "a big shopping once a month, learned it from money advice" (Amidah) and reducing the shopping list of even essential items ("I look at my current shopping list, if I don't need something, if I can improvise, I don't buy" [Namono]). Additionally, relational earmarking, where money is assigned to categories which reflect important social relationships, is employed as disciplining mechanism (Zelizer, 1994). They set up savings accounts for children even when income is limited ("I've opened for my son his account ... because when I put it in his, I won't get it out, it will just stay there" [Amidah]) because the relational meaning attached to it being an account for children makes them less likely to tap into these in contrast to their own savings account:

> 'I won't lie to you from time to time when I'm very broke I have to draw them out [savings], if necessary, if they're needed elsewhere, yeah, but I do actively have the desire to save and do try and put into my children's account and when problems come and when I'm very broke I dip into my savings.' (Namono)

Despite seeking to conform to asset norms by disciplining oneself to save ("I constantly look to ways to manage the little I have better") and even following guidance by financial education campaigns ("I've done evening course at college, I've done, I do courses on FutureLearn [a digital education platform]" [Namono]), these interviewees remain in a detrimental position concerning long-term savings (see for instance Table 8.3). Namono, who is 50 years old, is currently only making minimum pension contributions, which total £1,750 per year. Even if she could increase her contributions to the maximum, as indicated on government-sponsored website MoneyHelper (£4,279 per year), the retirement income would only result in an annual income of £1,248 and she would not be eligible for a full state pension

Table 8.3: Balance sheet of income-constrained relational asset manager

Assets	Liabilities
Pensions (estimation based on contributions and the MoneyHelper site)	£17,500
Savings	£1,000
Current account	£500
Car	£1,000

due to having experienced breaks in her career, creating a similar situation to that of Kojo, where active engagement with finance fails to make a real difference to the long-term wealth.

The relational asset manager

As the name of the subject position indicates, the relational asset manager is brought to life by the 'importance ... granted to relationships' (Foucault, 1984, p 42). In line with the everyday asset manager, relational asset managers distance themselves from the investor subject. Yet, rather than being borne out of a criticism of asset norms and the accompanying dismantling of the welfare state, it is driven by a lack of confidence emanating from gendered norms of being less financially inclined ("I am not good with numbers" [Ruby]). Due to finance being perceived as too confusing ("very confusing, lots of confusion ... it's just a mine field" [Pippa]) and uncertain ("you just don't know what's really gonna happen" [Beatrix]), relational asset managers accept the responsibility to accumulate assets but are unwilling to actively engage with investments ("finance doesn't interest me, only as much as I've got it get it sorted" [Harriet]).

On the one hand, since "the jargon is very confusing" making it "quite scary" (Darcy), advice from family and friends is sought when making decisions and choosing financial advisors ("I did ask a lot of my friends who they went with" [Saskia]). Putting emphasis on recommendations from family and friends makes it less scary over time ("It's become less scary. I know a number of people who work in the financial sector and so I'm a lot more comfortable going to them to ask for advice" [Izzy]), leading in some cases to success and in others to losses ("I did go to a financial advisor through a friend of mine who actually, I think, gave me the wrong advice" [Beatrix]). On the other hand, the concept of feeling outweighs unfeeling here (see Chapter 6), reflected in the customer service received outweighing any lack of substantive asset management:

'I always been able to get hold of Gemma ... when I walk into the bank, she says Hello, so I am a friend ... they're pleasant in a way that banks have gone very distant … I don't think they manage them particularly well. They don't ring me and say Good Lord and smashing an offer.' (Eleanor)

Taking time to explain a mortgage is taken as a selection criterion: "I didn't bother to do a lot of comparisons … they gave me two hours and sat down and we went through everything in fine detail" (Pippa). Relationships, not finance rationality, become the dominant force in making financial decisions, representing a necessary form of counter-conduct. Because of not feeling confident enough, involving help from someone else allows individuals to conform to norms of conduct: "If I had to do it entirely by myself, I would not have had this spread of stocks and shares. Because I don't think I'll be confident enough" (Harriet).

Interviewees having adopted the subjectivity of the relational asset manager seek to tackle inequalities arising from caring duties by employing gender-normative roles within the household. Being aware that one is in a disadvantageous position due to caring duties, they try to counter-balance the loss in pension values by means of intra-household negotiations, arguing for additional investments while leaving the decision in what to invest in to the partner, as shown in the case of Ai ("That tells us how clueless I am with finances, I leave it pretty much to my husband" [Ai]). Reflecting a rather robust understanding of the role of unpaid work within the household (Fraser, 2017), Ai outlines how much it would cost if her unpaid work were to be provided externally ("it would easily come up to a combined salary of £3,000 a month, wouldn't it? A taxi driver, a cook and a childminder and a child psychologist when needed") and approaches her husband to set up an alternative to pensions:

'We had a chat about a couple of years ago when I said the money that I'm not earning as a salary because I could be working … plus the lack of savings and the fact that I do not save for my retirement … Then I explained to him that I felt a bit insecure because if anything happens, I do not have much in terms of savings … and he addressed it and he thought *if I put a chunk sum onto your, if we open an ISA [Individual Savings Account], because that was the most interesting from savings and we do every year put the maximum amount we can count, would you feel more reassured?* I said yes and we would go for it, the maximum amount before it gets taxed.'

Since carers earn irregular incomes, more flexible and lower risk options such as savings accounts are often seen as viable solutions when discussing counter-balancing the lack of pension savings. Even though the chosen assets are tax efficient, for instance ISAs provide a tax-free allowance, they do not include employer's contributions, provide lower long-term returns when taking into consideration inflation and do not include tax reductions such as personal pensions. Moreover, this results in income being assigned differently within the household, further disadvantaging carers and reinforcing gender-normative roles of managing household finances (see Chapter 7).

Relationships not only shape one's own asset strategy but also enable family members to achieve financial security through asset accumulation. Instead of employing an 'individualistic attitude' of growth and competition (such as wanting to outperform family members, as in the case of the calculative investor), conduct of the relational asset manager 'entails an intensification of the values of private life' (Foucault, 1984, p 42). When being a landlord and renting out to friends, the tenant is at times included in the will for inheriting the house: "I actually rent that out to a friend of mine ... if I was to die that house goes to him" (Beatrix). Prominence is given to helping friends and family, undeterred by the aspect that this might be misused:

'He [the son] moved back in because he broke up with his girlfriend, so he's come back home to save a deposit up. That was April, I've been paying out him rather than him saving a deposit up, that's the situation and he's gone on holiday for the second time this year.' (Pippa)

This sometimes leads to buying flats for family members who are not perceived as being good in dealing with money, which is excused as not being disciplined enough: "There's a house, my daughter has the top flat and her dad, my ex-partner, has the bottom flat ... I'm doing him a big favour and he could have over his life saved money, but he's not a saver. Some people are, some people aren't" (Florence). The caring responsibility outlined in Chapter 6 with regards to helping children to save for a deposit by letting them move back to the family house and supporting asset ownership within marriage is deepened further here, having bought flats for the daughter and ex-partner. This focus on helping others is even reflected in their balance sheets, as illustrated in Table 8.4, where assets are earmarked according to family members.

The combination of valuing relationships in interplay with moral understandings of family support can also culminate in a collective approach to asset accumulation which is not recognized in the individualistic model of finance rationality, as illustrated in the following case. Aditi and her sister, who both earn a relatively good income, had put their finances together with their parents to buy a family home:

'My mum and dad are too old for finance, so they couldn't have finance and as we were in work, full-time work, my sister and I decided to buy it from our savings, obviously from gifting from our parents and then we took out a mortgage with our salaries ... it was an interest-only mortgage but then we overpaid ... there is a certain amount you can overpay by, so only overpaid by that much, so we wouldn't incur the penalty fee. It was the only way that we could probably afford the house, yeah we wouldn't be able to buy it separately.'

Aditi suggests that her parents did not have access to financial products so she and her sister used savings that their parents had given to them to resolve this access issue and obtain a secure home for their parents. Pulling together the family finances has enabled them to put up a higher deposit and get a better mortgage collectively. It is perhaps surprising that they have ended up with an interest-only mortgage within a shared homeownership contract ("70 per cent of the house value"), as these are generally considered higher risk than a conventional mortgage. This is potentially a result of constraints faced in the mortgage assessment process; however, by overpaying up to the full amount that does not incur a penalty they reduce the long-term burden of the mortgage, which is a sophisticated strategy to overcome the constraints they face.

Whereas the subjectivities of the relational asset manager echo previous research where emotions and relationships are shown to outweigh economic considerations (Lai, 2017), they emanate mainly from the subject position of the relational asset manager instead of being a wider phenomenon. Moreover, the importance of relationships should not be perceived as a form of rejection of the investor subject due to not internalizing finance rationality (Pellandini-Simanyi et al, 2015) or due to focusing on care more than on

Table 8.4: Balance sheet of a relational asset manager

Assets		Liabilities
House	£387,000	Interest-only mortgage against the house, though taken out to buy my daughter's flat £134,000
90% share of flat in Hastings (ex-husband)	£83,000	
100% of value of daughter's flat	£132,000	
1 1/2 acres of land in Essex, value £50,000 to £500,000 depending on whether it gains planning permission		
Savings	£130,500	
1/3 share of deceased mothers' house in London, awaiting sale	£310,500	
Money still owed for business sale	£29,500	

Note: The balance sheet was anonymized but otherwise kept as provided by the interviewee to show the impact of relational meanings on asset accumulation.

one's own retirement planning (Lai, 2017). Instead, the mutually constitutive relationship between conduct and counter-conduct is productive in assuming responsibility for one's own financial security and helping family members to become self-reliant. Arising from the complexity of financial products, the relational asset manager invokes relationships to accumulate assets. When being constrained in accumulating assets, gender-normative roles are drawn upon to achieve asset ownership which fits their specific context, seeking to overcome the constraints they face. This avoidance of finance rationality can be argued to be rational since it reduces the time spent in understanding financial investments which remain inherently uncertain. In the case of the everyday asset manager and the relational asset manager, the practices and discourses of interviewees thus reveal a weak form of counter-conduct operating as 'handles in power relationships' (Foucault, 1978, p 95), enabling them to smoothen the contradictions inherent in norms of conduct.

The independence seeker

In comparison to the previous two subject positions, the independence seeker takes up a more active or 'savage' (Foucault, 1978, p 96) form of counter-conduct. A desire for independence 'vis-à-vis … the institutions to which they are answerable' (Foucault, 1984, p 42) is the driving force in shaping this subject position which in turn alleviates two contradictions inherent in asset-based welfare. On the one hand, seeking to escape the disciplinary technology of labour appears to solve the contradiction between investing and rising job insecurity and to provide a way to deal with constraints arising from caring duties. On the other hand, wanting to avoid financial institutions helps to address the inherent uncertainty of financial products by giving more importance to non-financial assets and tackles structural constraints inherent in the pension system. As will be shown later, in both approaches, the independence seeker employs an agency discourse to resist governance mechanisms, in contrast to the calculative investor, who talks from a position of opportunity when employing the discourse.

Besides increasing profit opportunities for financial institutions and enabling the dismantling of the welfare state, a welfare system focused on asset accumulation also intensifies capital–labour inequalities. As discussed in Chapter 6, everyday asset managers make sure they work hard in order not to lose their job in an insecure work environment and increase work hours to ensure financial security. Yet, even then job insecurity militates against the ability to save on a continuous basis. Interviewees internalizing the subjectivity of the independence seeker aim to liberate themselves from this inherent contradiction of asset-based welfare ("I'm free of what my timetable is and how much I want to work" [Ai]). The agency discourse of freedom, choice and gaining control is dominant here: "Being in charge of yourself and being able to say, Yes, I'll do that bit of work, or, no, I won't do that- fantastic" (Theodore). Employing metaphors such as wanting to avoid becoming 'kind of great machines of society' can be thought of bolstering this form of counter-conduct:

> 'School, I see as training young kids to be kind of great machines for society … It's always, you know, you have to be able to do your mathematics and your English and your science because you need to be, I don't know whatever it is, a profession which … is safe.' (Akio)

Prominence is given to breaking free from the disciplinary technology of labour and accumulating assets ("I always worked for myself and invested in myself"), even when this means being responsible for losses ("I look for me own advice and if I fall flat on my face it's my fault" [Richard]). On the surface it thus appears to be a liberating subject position, overcoming the contradiction between job insecurity and asset accumulation.

However, upon further analysis, being self-employed is rather restrictive and disciplining. On the one hand, having a business limits asset accumulation. Because income is received in lumps, pensions are excluded from the asset strategy as discussed in Chapter 7. Also, wanting to put enough money away for unexpected expenses in the business puts a strain on asset accumulation. This goes as far as not identifying savings as yours: "in my head that's not my money", using expressions such as "tax man" distances oneself from its ownership (Emily):

> 'So I don't invest because, and my family, they go mad because they're like *You've got 25 grand and you won't put it into anything* because I want it there for if the tax man comes to me and says you owe this or you owe that, I want to be able to access it. I've got 25 grand in a pot but in my head that's not my money.'

Nevertheless, to realize asset ownership, interviewees drawing on notions of entrepreneurial subjectivity work "very long hours" (Akio).

On the other hand, business debt becomes entangled with personal finance ("well the personal debt was basically to fund the business" (Paul; this can also be seen in Table 8.5 where both are listed on one balance sheet). A focus on business growth ("want to push on and make money"), where a standstill is seen as the worst-case scenario ("we were running faster and faster to stand still" [Richard]), results in using personal debt in the business.

In case of difficulties, this debt functions as a disciplining mechanism in which individuals have to "work damn hard" (Paul) to pay it off. Despite wanting to gain freedom ("I didn't want to carry on doing the same thing for the next 20 to 30 years" [Ida]) by escaping the disciplining mechanism of

Table 8.5: Balance sheet of an independence seeker (I)

Assets		Liabilities	
Business houses	£315,317	Business liabilities towards owner	(£256,007)
Cash bank (business savings)	£26,000	Net value business	£59,310
Private savings	£50,000	Retained earnings	£29,000
House 1 Value	£200,000		
House 2 Value	£300,000		
Car	£4,000		

Note: This balance sheet was anonymized but otherwise kept as provided.

work and revolting against the intensification of capital–labour inequalities through asset accumulation ("I think money was invented by the capitalists to keep the working masses under control" [Frank]), the interplay between personal and business finance culminates in rising pressure and in an increase of work hours.

A similar conflicting relationship can be found in the case of carers, who often aspire to become self-sustaining business owners instead of being inhibited in their career trajectories due to having to take breaks from employment (see Chapter 7): "give it a go with the business because I have a very entrepreneurial mind ... something that will generate a decent amount of income for us to live on, to be employment free" (Ioana). Until they are able to "eventually generate a bit more income out of it [the business] because [they] do like to think of [their] retirement eventually" (Ai), a second stream of income is searched for. Mothers who are part of a couple, married or cohabiting set up a business in addition to their part-time employment ("the most recent investment I made has been setting up a bakery" [Nancy]) or diversify their businesses when being self-employed mothers ("I have taken on a second activity" [Ai]), thus, putting more pressure on themselves. Seeking to set up one's own business results in moving unknowingly towards creating a work trajectory which is excluded from the current asset-based welfare system and, instead of fairly safe assets such as bonds, adopting an asset category which is classified as risky in the finance literature (Guiso et al, 2002; Lowe, 2010). Yet, in contrast to the also risky classified defined-contribution (DC) pensions and stocks and shares investments, interviewees do not perceive business assets as risky assets because they fall under their own control rather than under the control of the financial sector.

The second contradiction inherent in asset-based welfare which is tackled by the independence seeker is uncertainty. Because of not being able to mitigate uncertainty with the help of financial investments ("they're out of my control" [Millie]) and having a strong distrust of financial institutions ("I'm really anti-pension ... I don't trust either the government or financial institutions" [Akio]), the independence seeker seeks to gain independence from them. Rather "than the alternative of ploughing your money into something that has let people down" (Millie), they not only avoid direct investment in financial products, as in the case of the everyday asset manager, but aim to also reduce the reliance on managed financial products ("Do not touch pensions ... You're better off buying gold bars and keep them in Switzerland and then wait for 40 years" [Paul]). Emphasis is put on "[wanting] a retirement fund where [they] have some control" (Millie) in contrast to financial investments which have been hit by "big pension and mis-selling scandals" (Nadeem) and regulation changes ("Gordon Brown comes along and taxed the dividends and all the figures on the pension growth ... came nowhere near what the projection was" [Paul]). Evidential discourse based on experience and metaphorical expressions such as "down the tube" are prevalent here:

'My mum invested in Heineken, that went down the tube, my brother invested in Equitable Life, that went down the tube, and I am like well then what's the point ... I am not gonna put 70 quid a month into something for the next years only to be told that some CEO is, you know, banging some secretary and it's all gone tits up and you haven't got any money.' (Isabella)

For the purpose of being "financially independent no matter what happens" (Isabella), preference is given to tangible assets: "something you can rely on either for retirement, some kind of safety net, it could be a home, it could be a business, it could be jewellery" [Adhira]). Property in particular is seen as a viable alternative investment when experiencing non-traditional work trajectories and having no access to pensions ("so as far as for me the best pension is property" [Nadeem]) due to its being more flexible and controllable: "property, it's something that is undeniable, it's controlled by me" (Millie).

The combination of being adjustable to one's own life circumstances and being able to control property is illustrated in the case of Vibha, introduced in the previous chapter. Vibha has not been able to sufficiently save in a workplace pension, is currently going through a divorce and is 59 years old, so she needs an investment that could provide for security in retirement in a more immediate timeframe. As a consequence, Vibha rejects pensions as a viable investment and plans to invest in property with the help of the divorce settlement money, since it is an investment which is perceived as generating an income quickly and reliably ("investment in property but stocks and shares no"). Investment in property then provides some stability in her life ("people will always need to rent whether it's good economic conditions or bad") while also giving her control of an asset that will relieve her worries during income-constrained periods. To enter the property market, despite being income-constrained, she employs peer-to-peer lending and circumvents the traditional banking system:

> 'People are lending to each other, so we don't touch the banks … He's got redundancy money and he takes a little bit every year so as not to go over his tax bracket, and I said *Why do you do it?* He said: *Because I have to pay tax otherwise. Well, you could lend me the money, and I can pay you 8 per cent interest.*'

However, the trust in non-financial assets produces unbalanced asset compositions, reflecting characteristics of the 'leveraged investor' (Langley, 2008, p 242) who takes on debt to accumulate property. As shown in Table 8.6, a focus on property when not having had access to workplace pensions has resulted in one interviewee having taken on a high-valued buy-to-let mortgage in addition to a mortgaged main residence (both considered high-risk financial products) with both mortgages being based on a sole income, as the interviewee is single and also relatively close to retirement (50 years old). Perhaps most importantly to note here is that the concomitant high debt levels tend to be ignored by means of drawing on an agency discourse ("it's giving me financial freedom"). Despite emphasizing that "once you've got a mortgage … you are trapped", variable, interest-rate only mortgages are described as liberating in contrast to constraining: "they give you a bit more flexibility and freedom" (Millie). Finance is seen as negative even though it is at the same time acknowledged that accumulating wealth is a necessity ("you need to look out and do something for you" [Nadeem]) to be free, revealing the strong promotion of subliminal messages in the construction of asset norms. The independence seeker thus challenges existing governance mechanisms of conduct without rejecting their underlying premise of asset accumulation, creating their own versions of financial subjectivities and practices, yet, reproducing the very system they aim to challenge.

The discussions presented thus far challenge an understanding of resistance as opposing, revealing how forms of counter-conduct are deeply embedded within mechanisms of governance. Instead of embracing finance, an awareness

Table 8.6: Balance sheet of an independence seeker (II)

Assets		Liabilities	
House value Wallingford	£665,000	Mortgage	£305,270
Flat in East London	£810,000	Mortgage	£375,000
No savings and only recently joined workplace pension and not officially worked enough for the state pension			

of the system's inherent constraints and contradictions is omnipresent in interviewees' statements, manifested in wanting to be 'led differently ... towards other objectives than those proposed' (Foucault, 2004, p 265) and culminating in differentiated asset trajectories. Some individuals avoid direct investment in financial assets (everyday asset manager), others leave financial decisions to others (relational asset manager) and yet others give prominence to non-financial investments (independence seeker). These asset strategies, or diverse 'values of personal conduct' (Foucault, 1984, p 41), are not irrational but represent logical responses to contradictions and constraints inherent in norms of conduct. Through problematizing governance mechanisms and amending asset norms to one's own needs, contradictions and constraints immanent in norms of conduct are smoothened and asset accumulation enabled, albeit with much more complex outcomes than theoretically expected. Besides variegated subjectivities and practices deviating from a theorized investor subject, the discussion has revealed that counter-conduct is necessary for everyday financialization to take place.

The non-asset manager

In contrast to the previous subject positions, where individuals want to 'be conducted differently' based on 'other procedures and methods', the non-asset manager seeks 'to escape directions by others' (Foucault, 2004, p 259) and rejects asset accumulation as a means to provide financial security ("I just don't have that relationship with money" [Imogen]). Suspicions are stronger concerning whether institutional changes are in the interests of ordinary people ("It's a façade, it's a scam" [Daniel]). While the everyday asset manager and independence seeker also display a distrust of finance and distance themselves from financial investments, non-asset managers question the benefits of conducting any form of investment ("you can't be one of those blinking persons that thinks you work and pay their mortgage off when they're 60 because that don't work, they're in for a shock" [Daniel]). This subject position is driven, on the one hand, by fear of losing money ("worry about it, perhaps losing money" [Claudia]) and, on the other hand, by having to give up ethical values when wanting a decent return ("if you actually want a return on it, you probably have to wave goodbye to ethics" [Harry]). Consequently, they take up an 'adversary' resistance (Foucault, 1978, p 95) in two distinct ways, building upon the deviations from the investor subject discussed in the literature: 'passive saver' (Lai, 2017, p 927) and 'revolver' (Langley, 2008, p 16).

The passive saver ("it is essential to save something every month" [Adhira]) is someone who subverts the discourse of asset accumulation as a means of welfare and works from a basis of deconstruction. Within this subjectivity, a clear difference is made between homeowners and homebuyers, as shown in the case of Claudia:

'The house isn't your own anyway even when you've got a mortgage, obviously you're paying it off and hopefully, you know, you live long enough that it will be yours in the end but the downside of that is, you know, you risk in other ways. If you lost your job, yeah, you gotta worry over the mortgage and having the house taken from you completely and then there's the other aspect of it. If anything goes wrong in the house, you are responsible for it, the maintenance of it whereas if it's rented, you know, all that's taken away from you and if you decided to move the flexibility obviously is there with renting whereas it isn't with selling or buying.'

Contrasting previous discussions in the literature which have argued that passive savers retreat to property investments (Langley, 2007;Clark, 2012), non-asset managers reject investments in non-financial assets due to realizing the incorporated risks such as losing your house and the extra burden of maintenance costs. Also, buy-to-let properties are seen as additional work and the possibility of losing money rather than posing the possibility of earning income.

'Buying something that won't be able to sell afterwards or rent afterwards ... or need a lot of maintenance ... being stuck, paying the mortgage living somewhere or trying to get tenants in somewhere and me myself being somewhere else so I'd rather not do that. I'd rather just stick to what I have.' (Adhira)

A distinction is made between owning assets to live in and accumulating assets beyond one's direct needs, resulting in financial asset accumulation even being depicted as burdensome: "we purposefully tried not to accumulate a lot of things" (Daiyu). As can be seen here, the non-asset manager reworks the agency discourse into a resistance discourse by emphasizing flexibility and freedom when providing reasons for not wanting to buy a house. Flexibility such as being able to move around and not having the responsibility of maintaining the house are dominant here. It is realized even when employing tactical ways to cope with contradictions in financial investments such as investing in property that these cannot reduce but instead intensify uncertainty and risk losing money ("worry about it, perhaps losing money" [Claudia]).

Interviewees identifying with the non-asset manager tend to earn a low income and/or belong to a lower income household, rent their accommodation, focus on rainy day savings and disengage from pensions but sign up for them if they are offered. Due to having several different jobs, the interviewees' pension savings are often patchy and relatively low, which is given as a reason to disengage from them (see Chapter 7). The passive saver thus focuses on savings and refrains from being actively involved in asset accumulation, referring back to the need to have sufficient income to be able to risk investing, even when investing in a house: "I don't consider myself to be an investor, you know, to be earning enough to be, you know, like thinking about that really" [Claudia]). Deviating from what is expected of the everyday asset manager, in this case by refraining from investing in property when being income-constrained, reflects a quite robust understanding of the risks involved in mortgaged main residences and buy-to-let properties (Guiso et al, 2002; Lowe, 2010).

The revolver relates back to the subject position of the consumer by wanting to express their autonomy with the help of debt-financed consumption and exploiting numerous credit card offers. The contradiction between being expected to become an everyday investor while at the same time being called upon to be a consumer subject who uses consumer credit to finance their lifestyle (Langley, 2008) is solved here by withdrawing from the everyday investor subject. Debt is seen as having the potential for financing their lifestyle:

'I had probably four or five bank accounts, credit cards, which had anywhere between £5 and £10,000 on them ... use that money to go on your holidays ... I was quite good at it and I never, I never missed payments or anything but I did have, I had loads of debt but I managed to also, well you rob Peter to pay Paul. You take money out to give to something else and you balance it off.' (Chris)

Describing it by use of figurative speech "rob Peter to pay Paul", the revolver feels confident in managing these different credit cards by means of rolling over debt ("I kind of use one to pay the other" [Chris]) and exploiting interest rate differentials by diversifying credit cards as much as possible ("the system is there to be exploited" [Daniel]). Since "it's always manageable and [they] can still pay for things, and cover the payments on it", they are not 'scared of debt', resulting in having several forms of debt, for instance two credit cards with a debt of up to £10,000 each and then still taking on a loan for a sofa and a car, as shown in the case of Harry: "I bought a sofa which came to about two and a half grand, I paid fifteen hundred quid out of my Christmas money and a thousand of it on six months interest free credit ... I've had to take out another loan this month because my wife's car died."

Because "banks basically are not in it for you", interviewees diversify credit cards and shop around for the best deal: "I found them exceedingly unhelpful and I thought you know what I can afford to pay this debt for a little while longer and that's when I started to shop around" (Imogen). Exploiting the system is justified by portraying financial people as inherently exploitative and profiteering on a much bigger scale ("people exploit the system on a much bigger scale than me" [Daniel]).

What the subject position of the non-asset manager shows is that power relationships do not represent a relationship where one is solely 'trapped' but there 'are always possibilities of changing the situation' (Foucault, 1997, p 167). Non-asset managers reject not only financial but also non-financial investments due to realizing the risks involved in investments ("I don't like the risk element, I don't like it at all" [Claudia]) and distance themselves from actively planning ahead ("get your salary and live your life … I don't look too much into the future, I just look in the now" [Adhira]). At the same time, 'resistance is never in a position of exteriority in relation to power' (Foucault, 1978, p 95). Finance rationality is adopted in a wider form by employing extensive strategies to exploit the financial system and contributions to workplace pensions are made "because the government has more stringent, you know, laws on that" (Imogen). Yet, pensions are not actively chosen but rather one does not opt-out ("I pay in and the company pays in and I paid, I mean I never tested to see what else is there" [Chris]), showcasing passive engagement with workplace pensions ("it's a pound for every, I don't even want to say because I'm probably completely wrong" [Claudia]).

Concluding remarks

Integrating a holistic view of asset accumulation and anchoring the empirical insights within the analytical frame of counter-conduct has allowed me to show that far from fully succumbing to asset norms (everyday investors [Martin 2002]) or rejecting asset norms (domestication of finance [Pellandini-Simanyi et al, 2015]), interviewees react as discerning actors and develop different ways of dealing with asset accumulation. While it is true that some place a stronger emphasis on property (Langley, 2008) or focus mainly on savings (Lai, 2017), this should not be seen as a rejection of a financialized subject position but as representing varied financial subjects, allowing for multiple financial practices and rationales based on the context in which they arise. Seeking to provide financial security themselves rather than relying on the welfare state even when experiencing contradictions and constraints results in practices which reflect in one form or another elements from asset norms. The interplay between conduct and counter-conduct is thus productive in constructing a multiplicity of financial subjects. Even when outwardly rejecting asset accumulation, the non-asset manager still adopts a wider form of finance rationality, being good in managing different debt products and contributing to pensions.

Running through the variegated financial subjectivities and practices is a continuous reflection upon governance mechanisms of conduct and their inherent contradictions and constraints. The subject position of the everyday investor assumes that a person is able to conduct continuous investments over their lifetime. Yet, as highlighted in the previous chapters, this position appears contradictory in a world of rising job insecurity and even if individuals invest as theoretically expected, financial investments remain uncertain. To differing degrees, interviewees' statements reflect a rather robust understanding of these contradictions and respond to them by adjusting asset norms to their needs. Uncertainty of financial investments is tackled by choosing lower risk investments when not earning sufficient income to risk more (everyday asset manager), investing in property when displaying a strong distrust of financial investments (calculative investor, independence seeker) and/or transferring responsibility onto someone else when lacking confidence in dealing with finance (relational asset manager), and the contradiction between investing on a regular basis and job insecurity is addressed by being self-employed (independence seeker).

The inherent contradictions of asset norms are intensified when experiencing structural and normative constraints within the pension system. Here it has been revealed that interviewees experiencing constraints within their asset accumulation as a result of low income, caring duties and/or experiencing work trajectories which are not recognized in the current pension system are not merely victims of these but redefine asset norms in line with their lived experiences. Instead of being less financially literate or not planning ahead (Lusardi, 2015; Clark et al, 2021), distancing oneself from pensions and instead concentrating on other forms of assets which align with their context, often with tax-free allowances, are logical reactions to the pension system's in-built assumptions, which ignore everyday constraints. Constrained individuals aim to determine their future through adjusting asset strategies to their life positions, seeking out alternative safe investment channels, such as savings accounts, premium bonds or property, which they feel they can alter in case of changing circumstances. Again, while practices deviate from the 'ideal financialized subject' (Pellandini-Simanyi and Banai, 2021, p 787), rationalities or subjectivities conform to norms of financial self-governance and thus form part of variegated financialized subjects.

Bringing in an understanding of resistance being immanent in power technologies has unveiled that counter-conduct, or 'the pursuit of a different form of conduct' (Foucault, 2004, p 265), is necessary for everyday financialization to take place. The interplay between feeling trapped in having to provide financial security for themselves and amending asset norms in response to the inherent contradictions and constraints of asset norms results in governable subjects where self-conduct, that is, 'the way in which one conducts oneself' (Foucault, 2004, p 258), enables an asset-based welfare state based on individual responsibility. Adjusting asset norms allows individuals to express agency, give meaning to asset accumulation and smoothen its inherent contradictions; yet doing so reinforces a system that increasingly responsibilizes its citizens for their financial welfare without tackling its inherent inequalities. Investing in lower risk but also lower return investments is a logical reaction to constraints but does not solve wealth inequalities; instead it increases the disciplining mechanism (pressure on oneself) without improving the position within the regulatory mechanism (asset ownership). For instance, carers want to conform to norms of self-governance despite being constrained, even voluntarily signing up for workplace pensions, trying to improve their financial literacy and investing in perceived safer investments, yet the measures chosen will not be sufficient to tackle the unequal starting points within the pension system. The interplay between conduct and counter-conduct is productive in constructing a multiplicity of financial subjects.

9

Conclusion

With the growing importance of personal pension management to provide financial security in the future, amid increasing instability in financial markets and a cost-of- living crisis following the COVID-19 pandemic, this book has explored how individuals engage with the pressure to plan for retirement. Since the 1980s, a 'regime of truth' (Foucault, 1980, p 131) has been established in which it is seen as normal that individuals take over responsibility over future risks by building a diversified financial asset stock, guided by finance rationality, on which they can draw upon during periods of income shortfalls. Putting emphasis on 'values of personal conduct' (Foucault, 1984, p 41), people should embrace risk willingly, actively engage with financial products and adopt financial strategies such as diversification. This change in behaviour is incentivized by 'a weakening of the political and social framework' (Foucault, 1984, p 41). Pensions, sick pay and unemployment benefits have been continuously reduced and labour market regulations weakened. Consequently, the United Kingdom has one of the lowest social service provisions and one of the weakest employment protections among OECD countries, creating an environment where it is costlier for individuals not to provide financial security themselves. And yet, individuals do not invest as expected, reflected in under-saving and under-diversifying.

Instead of questioning the ability of asset-based welfare measures to deliver financial welfare, measures have been implemented which attempt to bring everyday practices closer to theoretical assumptions, such as automatic enrolment in workplace pensions and financial education targeting people across the social strata (Roberts, 2015; Bucher-Koenen et al, 2016; Montgomerie and Tepe-Belfrage, 2019). These measures seek to increase pension savings and reduce the employment of *irrational* heuristics, reflected in a lack of engagement with investment tools and sub-optimal investment choices (Altman, 2012; Mitchell and Lusardi, 2012; Elliehausen, 2019). Even with such measures in place, there remains a persistent wealth inequality. More critical studies have therefore argued that financial inclusion initiatives, instead of empowering individuals, operate as a disciplining mechanism (Langley, 2007; Loomis, 2018). Putting responsibility on the individual without recognizing the unequal starting points inherent in a capitalist welfare state puts more pressure on labour while creating new profit opportunities for financial companies; it also enables the dismantling of the welfare state (Belfrage and Kallifatides, 2018; Huber et al, 2020). Even when being able to conform to the norms of asset accumulation, the inherent uncertainty of financial investments and rising job insecurity militates against the ability to perform the role of the everyday investor subject (Munro, 2000; Erturk et al, 2007; Langley and Leaver, 2012).

Despite attention being given to the inequalities in the capitalist welfare state, less is known about how people who face inherent contradictions and constraints engage with these. Studies on everyday financialization have either focused on how discursive and institutional practices construct the ideal of the investor subject (Grey, 1997; Maman and Rosenhek, 2019), resulting inadvertently in a similar dichotomy as financial literacy and behavioural economics research which constructs individuals as internalizing (Davis, 2009; Martin, 2002) or rejecting the investor subject (Langley, 2006; Clark, 2012), or on how individuals are transformed through governance mechanisms while integrating their own rationalities (Pellandini-Simanyi et al, 2015; Samec, 2018) without exploring how constraints inherent in a capitalist welfare state might be part of the meaning-making process, shaping variegated financialized subjects.

This book has built on these bodies of work by exploring the socio-economic reality of everyday financial practices within a Foucauldian governmentality framework. Revealing the mutually constitutive relationship between norms of conduct and counter-conduct, or, in other words, between asset norms and resistance to these norms, helps to explain why differential subjectivities and practices emerge and continue to exist in even advanced financialized countries. This final chapter synthesizes the different levels of analysis, moving from the everyday asset manager to the variegated forms of financial subjectivities and practices, and highlights its relevance to the current literature but also to policy suggestions. Taken together, the findings presented in the book point to a rethink of the theorization of everyday financialization and what constitutes financially rational behaviour.

The everyday asset manager: unwilling but conforming

In previous decades, the UK government has been promoting private asset ownership (regulatory mechanism) while reducing publicly funded welfare programmes (disciplinary mechanism), seeking to widen capitalist aspirations to the wider public. Conservative and Labour governments have aimed to create a society with more capitalists, that is, more self-reliant entrepreneurs, while othering *irresponsible* benefit receivers and non-investors (see Chapters 3 and 4). To make norms of asset accumulation desirable, governmental and media discourse have incorporated an agency discourse depicting asset accumulation as the opportunity to gain freedom through hard work. At the same time, growing money and job insecurity has been accompanied by a non-agency discourse of having no other choice than to provide financial security for oneself by accumulating assets and adopting financial strategies with the goal of making returns and creating income during non-working periods. Informed by Foucault's concept of governmentality and its understanding of conduct and counter-conduct, this book has sought to explore how interviewees engage with these processes of responsibilization and financialization and how they have impacted everyday practices, contributing to the literature in a threefold way.

First, combining insights on institutional changes and discourses with everyday rationalities, that is, exploring the interplay between interviewees' financial discourses and the concepts constructed in the media and governmental discourse, has illuminated interviewees' critical engagement with norms of conduct (see Chapter 4). The agency and non-agency discourses are reworked into a resistance discourse, where financial institutions are portrayed as profit-seeking institutions and the uncertainty of financial investments is put forward as a reasoning to disengage. This is quite a robust understanding of the inherent contradictions of asset-based welfare which calls on people to accumulate assets for the purpose of providing financial security during periods of income shortfall while transferring pensions risks from the employer and state onto the individual, and thus increasing profit opportunities for the financial sector without guaranteeing a pension income during retirement (Langley and Leaver, 2012; Webber, 2018). Even if individuals invest as expected by theoretical assumptions of finance rationality, uncertainty with regards to future values of financial investments remains, as can be seen in the recent pandemic where values substantially declined in 2020 (Mazur et al, 2021). Despite these contradictions, asset norms constructed through the interplay of asset-based welfare measures (regulatory mechanism) and rising job and money insecurity (disciplinary mechanism) result in the everyday asset manager feeling trapped in having to provide financial security themselves (see Chapter 4). The contradiction of investing and being critical is overcome by drawing on notions of insecurity, in other words, the disciplinary mechanism acts as enabler rather than inhibitor of asset accumulation (Munro, 2000; Langley, 2007).

Second, circumventing the underlying focus on one part of asset ownership, either homeownership or financial assets (Langley, 2007; Soaita and Searle, 2016), and adopting a holistic view of asset management has revealed that interviewees adopt a financialized subject position, albeit in the form of the everyday asset manager (see Chapters 5 and 6). Recognizing the contradictions inherent in investing results not in rejecting accumulating assets (Langley, 2007; Pellandini-Simanyi et al, 2015) but in redefining asset norms into a three-pronged asset-accumulation strategy consisting of savings, homeownership and pension. Because of being critical of asset norms and wanting to keep control in an uncertain environment, the everyday asset manager excludes financial investments which are considered high risk and includes non-financial investments which are seen as controllable due to being managed by themselves. At the same time, an elementary form of finance rationality is employed, reflected in diversifying pension income sources, giving preference to managed investments and hedging by means of insurances. An everyday asset manager thus accumulates financial and non-financial assets and adopts new modes of self-governance, extending the theorization of the everyday investor. Rather than property investment deviating from the investor subject (Langley, 2007; Clark, 2012), it is part of asset norms constituted by government initiatives and media discourse and embedded in everyday life.

Third, the empirical findings suggest that instead of becoming capitalists by accumulating assets (Martin, 2002; Weiss, 2015), asset accumulation intensifies the discipline from labour and strengthens capital–labour inequalities (see Chapter 6). By taking up the subject position of the everyday asset manager, interviewees emphasize that it is the responsibility of the household to establish financial security. In an effort to achieve asset ownership, they adopt technologies of the self in the form of non-accessible savings accounts, pursue a non-materialistic lifestyle and seek to make sure family members are financially secured. Strikingly, while within the theorization of finance rationality decisions based on emotions and relational meanings are perceived as disturbance, driving 'economically irrational decisions' (Bandelj et al, 2017, p 43), it has been shown here that employing the 'variety of social relations rather than individuals' (Zelizer, 1994, p 25) enables asset ownership by means of earmarking and employing relationships to achieve asset ownership. Perhaps more importantly, the findings have revealed that the disciplinary technology of labour not only constructs asset norms but is also deepened by asset norms. Interviewees emphasize that they increase work hours, choose a job solely based on income and make sure that they work hard to be able to accumulate assets. The evidence provided here suggests that asset accumulation in itself, rather than only debt commitments (Karacimen, 2015), puts more pressure on labour and restricts everyday practices. Households live the contradiction of accumulating assets and being disciplined at the same time, reflecting a mutually constitutive relationship between asset norms and everyday practices.

The constrained asset manager: willing but constrained

Not only contradictions inherent in asset norms impact active meaning-making processes in everyday retirement planning but also structural and normative constraints intersect with these. This book has thus analysed the underlying rationales and strategies utilized within the context of individuals facing limitations in the existing asset-based welfare system. In doing so, it joins the collection of authors that have challenged a pension system based on the concept of finance rationality when limitations are in fact built into the system (see Chapter 2). In contrast to these existing studies, however, the insights provided here reveal that rather than being solely victims of contradictions and constraints inherent in a capitalist welfare system, simply constrained by the unequal system or rejecting everyday financialization, governable subjects are aware of the systems' underlying constraints and seek ways to cope with them. Integrating insights on variegated financial subjectivities into discussions on contextual factors has helped to explore three constraints in retirement planning: income, gender and occupational constraints.

First, this book has highlighted the importance of income in constructing the everyday asset manager (see Chapters 5 and 6). Far from being irrational when not taking on higher risk investments (Clark, 2010; Lusardi, 2015), interviewees quite rationally make a distinction between the everyday investor who can afford to take on more risk and adopt a sophisticated diversification and the everyday person who is limited in asset accumulation. The realization that one would need to risk substantially more of a family's income than a higher income earner when investing in riskier financial assets translates into adjusting asset norms to one's income context. Seeking to avoid jeopardizing the family's security, low- and medium-income earners distance themselves from the investor subject, seeing risk not as an opportunity but as the possibility to lose money, and prioritize savings and homeownership before pension investments. Counter-conduct, or the unwillingness to engage with the investor subject and its notions of risk and investments, thus helps to cope with the inherent limitations of conduct, namely the intersection between the uncertainty of investments and the need to have sufficient income and wealth to adopt sophisticated diversification. Yet, adjusting asset norms to one's own context not only results in smoothing contradictions inherent in asset-based welfare, but also intensifies inequalities between capitalists and labour. Instead of adopting a diversified asset portfolio which results in accruing capital income in the future and enables one to move up the social ladder as expected of the everyday capitalist, medium- to low-income earners predominantly rely on safe financial assets generating lower returns than higher risk assets and focus on debt-financed homeownership, a risky asset which at the same time acts as their main living base.

Second, having illustrated the complex and meaningful ways in which women entangle financial subject positions with constructions of gender has unveiled how structural and normative constraints contribute to counter-conduct (see Chapter 7), that is, 'the will not to be governed, thusly, like that' (Foucault, 2007, p 75). Inequalities arising from gendered social reproduction are intensified in pension systems that ignore these processes. Women want to contribute to workplace pensions but are constrained in their ability to do so due to normative expectations of care and the limited flexibility of pensions, resulting in them feeling less able to rely on pensions for their long-term financial security. To cope with high childcare costs and caring duties, interviewees make calculated decisions to opt out of the labour market (losing access to pensions) and disengage from pensions. Gender-normative roles of the non-financial person (Joseph, 2013; Hasler and Lusardi, 2017) are employed to justify the disengagement from pensions, as it appears to take substantial effort to inform themselves about pensions which are not accessible when needed – especially considering that their responsibility for childcare, domestic chores and the day-to-day budgeting leads to a desire for more accessible savings – and where its in-built structural constraints would cause a disruption to pension savings when having children. Women thus limit the time they spend engaging with a pension system which does not fit their context. These solutions are not errors of judgement (Strauss, 2008; Lusardi, 2015); rather, the constraints inherent in the pension system leave women with no other choice than to adjust their retirement planning due to not being able to easily pause or reduce pension contributions when taking over caring responsibilities.

Third, establishing a dialogue between the literature on everyday financial practices (Lai, 2017; Pellandini-Simanyi and Banai, 2021) and studies exploring the context of financial decisions (Clark, 2014; Hamilton and Darity Jr, 2017) has enabled an exploration of how everyday rationalities and constraints culminate in variegated financial subjects which confound understandings of rational behaviour (see Chapters 7 and 8). The current asset-based welfare system is built on a work trajectory where one continuously earns sufficient income over the lifetime, disadvantaging people who are self-employed, work part-time, or work across multiple occupations. Not having a similar access to pensions as someone with a full-time job means having to put sufficiently more aside to achieve the same level of retirement income as someone who has had full access to a workplace pension with its employer's contributions and tax benefits. Being excluded from the current asset-based welfare system results in viewing voluntarily contributions to a pension (when not automatically included) or engaging with a workplace pension (when enrolled) as not viable options. Instead, in line with their work environment, interviewees emphasize the need to have access to flexible and accessible means to invest for retirement. Here, practices deviate from the 'ideal financialized subject' (Pellandini-Simanyi and Banai, 2021, p 787) but rationalities, also referred to as subjectivities, conform to norms of financial self-governance. Rather than being irrational or passive, individuals experiencing occupational constraints plan for the future, actively engage with the limitations of the current pension system and seek out mechanisms to cope with these. Distancing oneself from pensions while pursuing flexible savings are logical reactions to the pension system's in-built assumptions which disadvantage differential work trajectories.

Strikingly, the desire to provide financial security themselves is intensified when experiencing multiple dimensions of constraints. While interviewees who struggle with processes of social reproduction or experience a differential work trajectory, both not recognized in the current pension system, perceive pensions not as a feasible option, interviewees who are exposed to multiple dimensions of constraints seek to fulfil asset norms including pensions despite their limited means. Reducing their current financial means by setting up additional pension savings and diversifying work income sources are employed as technologies of the self but also puts more pressure on themselves without guaranteeing adequate future income due to the low contribution amounts.

What these discussions unveil is the complex and meaningful ways in which individuals entangle financial subject positions with the everyday rationalities and constraints they experience, never fully succumbing to the limitations of the asset-based welfare system. Actions informed by the context are seen here as logical and aptly negotiated responses to an increasingly unequal welfare system, highlighting the contextual richness of empirical reality, instead of merely showcasing deviations from abstract assumptions, and challenging the view that individuals are less keen on saving for retirement (Strauss, 2008; Lusardi, 2015).

Variegated financial subjects: managing but governed

Embedding understandings of constraints within the context of variegated subjectivities and revealing the rationales and strategies associated with the context of individuals contributes to the theorization of variegated financial subjectivities and practices. Whereas it has been highlighted that everyday financialization is not a monolithic process, calling 'for variegated subjectivities rather than just financialized or non-financialized subjects' (Lai, 2017, p 914), studies on variegated everyday financial practices stop short of a resultant development into distinct financial subject positions. By uncovering the complex interplay between conduct and counter-conduct, this book has suggested a typology of five distinct financial subjects (see Chapter 8).

Having internalized a discourse of self-reliance and personal growth through asset accumulation, as expected by the everyday investor subject, the calculative investor employs a rather improbable counter-conduct. Reflecting critically on financial institutions, which are depicted as profit-seeking institutions, the investor subject is amended by including non-financial assets in the asset portfolio. A more critical view of the current system, while still being quick to compromise in action, can be found in the following subjects. Whereas the everyday asset manager and the relational asset manager seek to establish financial security, it does not originate from a belief in its benefits but from the pressure to accumulate assets due to a retreating welfare state and rising job insecurity. As its name indicates, a desire for independence is then displayed by the independence seeker, reflected in them taking up a stronger form of counter-conduct, seeking to reduce their reliance on the formal financial system and wanting to escape the disciplining mechanism of work. Finally, rather than amending asset norms, the non-asset manager displays the strongest form of counter-conduct and refuses to actively invest and engage with norms of asset accumulation. The unifying thread in the asset strategies introduced earlier is counter-conduct where subjects critically reflect upon governance mechanisms of conduct, realizing the contradictions and constraints inherent in asset-based welfare. Yet, the resultant variegated financial practices suggest a nuanced engagement with asset norms, displaying differing degrees of counter-conduct in line with one's context.

This book differs from existing studies which have explored 'which aspects of it [the ideal financialized subjectivity] are embraced and which are rejected' (Pellandini-Simanyi and Banai, 2021, p 787) in that the focus lies on the 'relational character of power relationships' whose 'existence depends on a multiplicity of points of resistances' (Foucault, 1978, p 95). The previously identified varied subject positions not only deviate from the theorized everyday investor subject but are also necessary for everyday financialization to take place. The subject position of the everyday investor assumes a person who is able to conduct continuous investments over their lifetime and build a sophisticated financial asset portfolio. Yet, as highlighted by previous studies, this stands in contradiction with rising job insecurity (Erturk et al, 2007; Langley, 2007) and structural and normative constraints due to income, caring duties or experiencing a differential working life (Grady, 2015; Loomis, 2018). Even if individuals invest as theoretically expected, financial investments remain uncertain (Langley and Leaver, 2012; Storper, 2014). Strikingly, interviewees' statements depict a rather robust understanding of these inherent contradictions and constraints. To differing degrees, they foreground the exploitative character of financial institutions and the accompanying uncertainty of investments, how asset accumulation enables the dismantling of the welfare state and intensifies capital–labour inequalities reflected in rising money and job insecurity, and how they feel excluded from the current asset-based welfare system.

Yet, problematizing these underlying power relationships and redefining asset norms according to one's own needs provides not only a sense of agency but also smoothens contradictions inherent in norms of conduct. Choosing lower risk investments (everyday asset manager), investing in property (calculative investor, independence seeker) and transferring the responsibility of accumulating assets to someone else (relational asset manager) are strategies to tackle uncertainty, and seeking to escape the contradiction between asset norms and job insecurity is achieved by self-employment (independence seeker). When experiencing constraints in addition to contradictions individuals look within norms of conduct and align self-conduct, that is, 'the way in which one conducts oneself' (Foucault, 2004, p 258), to these constraints, resulting in a disengagement from pensions and seeking out alternative investment channels. Individuals who are constrained due to caring duties or having adopted a work trajectory not recognized in the current asset-based welfare system, often affecting women and people belonging to minority ethnic backgrounds, seek out safe investment channels which they feel they can access in case of changing circumstances. They thus choose assets which are perceived as more accessible and controllable, such as savings accounts, premium bonds or property (constrained everyday asset manager and independence seeker).[1] Moreover, uncertainty, and the burden of norms and obligations in interplay with structural constraints result in pension practices being adapted to the personal context, with individuals seeking to improve financial literacy and employing relationships and relational meanings to navigate asset ownership (relational asset manager).

The concept of conduct and counter-conduct has brought to the forefront how the imperfections of everyday financialization are representing, on the one hand, possibilities for ruptures and, on the other hand, reproduce the very system they challenge, albeit differently in practice than theoretically suggested. These insights imply an even more pessimistic view than previously considered, where it is suggested that everyday financialization can take place without individuals willingly adopting the mindset of the everyday investor. Besides 'not even need[ing] to change people's subjectivities but [can] progress[ing] by co-opting existing moral economies' (Pellandini-Simanyi and Banai, 2021, p 787), everyday financialization cannot exist without counter-conduct. Put differently, variegated subjectivities and practices are not solely militating against a unique financial subject position but are essential for a welfare system which responsibilizes its citizens for their financial welfare. Being able to transfigure the subject position they are called upon to internalize to their own needs enables individuals to give meaning to asset accumulation and overcome its inherent contradictions and constraints. Ways of not being like that are thus deeply embedded in mechanisms of governance, assimilating tactics from within the system.

Lived finance rationality: logical but exploited

The findings outlined here suggest that there is room to conceptualize a lived finance rationality as an alternative to classical interpretations of finance rationality, an endeavour towards which this book has contributed. Moving beyond a categorization of financialized/rational and non-financialized/irrational subjects, this book has shown how multifaceted acts of counter-conduct, impacted by everyday rationalities and limitations inherent in the asset-based welfare system, shape practices and discourses that culminate in varied financialized subjects. These behaviours are not financially irresponsible due to deviating from an 'ideal financialized subject position' (Pellandini-Simanyi and Banai, 2021, p 787) but form part of a financialized subject position where people pursue asset accumulation to provide financial security themselves, albeit adjusted to the experienced contradictions and constraints. Within the conceptualization of a lived finance rationality variegated practices are thus understood as logical responses to the personal context and as necessary for everyday financialization to take place due to its inherent contradictions and constraints. Conduct and counter-conduct are inextricably interlinked within the frame of lived finance rationality. By opening up new perspectives on rationality and highlighting the active meaning-making processes when experiencing contradictions and constraints, the limitations of current policy approaches can be uncovered.

Integrating insights on variegated financial subjectivities into discussions on contextual factors (Strauss, 2008; Clark, 2010) challenges the imposition of universalizing and individualistic constructions of pension planning (Mitchell and Lusardi, 2012; Lusardi, 2015) and calls for a more inclusive understanding of financially responsible behaviour. Instead of seeking to identify deviant individual behaviour and introducing new policy measures intended to prop up the existing system, everyday financial practices should be seen as rational responses to a dysfunctional system. The contextualized insights into financial behaviours contest previous interpretations which have positioned non-conforming behaviour as being less financially literate or motivated, revealing that interviewees actively seek to prepare for retirement in ways that accommodate the contradictions and constraints they experience. They quite rationally unpick the uncertainty, rising insecurity and structural and normative constraints inherent in the current asset-based welfare system but feel that they have no other choice than to provide financial security themselves, thus adapting their financial practices to their own context. The resultant variegated financial practices and discourses deviate from expectations of the theorized everyday investor subject, but should nevertheless be understood as logical reactions to an unequal welfare system.

This broader understanding of the variegated outcomes of financialization as embedded in a landscape of retirement inequality points to the need to move beyond the space and context-specific financial education initiatives that have recently been put forward (Clark, 2014; Clark et al, 2021). Everyday pension practices reveal that constraints to pension planning do not exist due to someone being younger, being single and having just started a career, that is, someone who in the future will earn more income and through this can adopt a more sophisticated investment strategy (Clark, 2010), but due to persistent income and wealth inequalities and individuals experiencing a differential life trajectory than that expected by the built-in assumptions of the current pension system. Despite recognizing differing contexts, the uniform benefit of pensions and education programmes seeking to establish equal instead of equitable access is not questioned within contextual financial education initiatives, again individualizing systemic problems (MaPS, 2019; FinCap, 2021; Lewis, 2023a). In contrast, lived finance rationality, defined as variegated financial practices and discourses shaped by the context in which they originate, shows that inequalities cannot be solved by means of individual solutions in an asset-based welfare system which excludes large parts of society. Even when following advice from financial literacy campaigns by planning long-term, taking up additional pension investments and putting more pressure on themselves by means of self-governing measures, the uneven outcomes of the current pension system are not overcome. And while automatic enrolment has made it easier to access a workplace pension scheme, the issue of structural constraints – namely breaks in employment, falling below the income threshold, being self-employed – is still not accounted for. Despite variegated everyday financial practices originating from the imperfections inherent in the pension system, the current pension policy framework remains dominated by theories and conceptualizations rooted in a male, well-earning life trajectory, marginalizing plural life trajectories and aiming at nudging people to become more knowledgeable in finance.

That finding one's own unique financial approach, as illustrated in the three sections of findings noted previously, is criticized within financial literacy campaigns seems rather striking in a pension system which promotes individual responsibility. However, it is less surprising when taking into consideration how norms of asset accumulation have intensified the power imbalances embodied in capital–labour relationships. Financial institutions have benefited from introducing increasingly complex products – generating huge fee incomes for the financial sector without ensuring the adequacy of future pension incomes (Ayres and Curtis, 2015; Webber, 2018) – and the increasing everyday financialization has enabled the dismantling of the welfare state (Belfrage and Kallifatides, 2018). Measures such as automatic enrolment in pension schemes and financial education campaigns seek to ensure that individuals who struggle with the pension system's immanent imperfections continue to meet financial commitments without having to rely on the state. Interestingly, recent policy initiatives have 're-implanted, and taken up again in one or another direction' (Foucault, 2004, p 282), forms of self-conduct in mechanisms of conduct. To 'bring the most unfavourable in line with the more favourable' (Foucault, 2004, p 91), individuals are called upon to first invest in pensions before investing in property and higher taxation rules have been introduced for buy-to-let properties (Brown, 2024; Lowe, 2023).

Perhaps more importantly, variegated financial practices, despite seeking to cope with the system's imperfections, reinforce capital–labour inequalities. Having combined insights of the everyday financialization literature (Langley, 2007; Lai, 2017; Pellandini-Simanyi and Banai, 2021) with insights from studies exploring the inherent capitalist relations (Karacimen, 2015; Fraser, 2017; Hamilton and Darity Jr, 2017) has unveiled how variegated financial practices and discourses intensify inequalities inherent within the capitalist welfare state rather than creating 'mini-capitalists' (Blakely, 2019, p 69) as proclaimed by the governmental and media discourse. While these unique asset strategies are perceived as more suited to one's real-life context, reflecting a robust understanding of immanent contradictions and constraints, they do not overcome the inequalities in the landscape of finance. Instead, they enable the capitalist welfare system and intensify the disciplining mechanism of financial self-governance without providing adequate income during retirement. Taking on lower risk assets due to imperfections in the system is less effective in delivering adequate incomes in retirement and reinforces the disadvantage compared to higher income earners who can continuously contribute to pensions and build a diversified financial asset portfolio. Also, an overreliance on pensions within the financial asset category exposes medium- and lower income households to the uncertainties of the financial markets while at the same time they increase the pressure on themselves by means of self-governance mechanisms. Or even worse, non-financial investments increase the fragility of balance sheets, such as in the case of mortgaged property, and expose owners to risky assets, and this can reinforce relations of social reproduction in case of difficulties, as shown during the Global Financial Crisis (Montgomerie and Young, 2011; Roberts, 2013). The systemic failure to acknowledge imperfections immanent in the asset-based welfare system forces individuals who deviate from the ideal of an everyday investor to take these paths which unintentionally serve to reinforce inequalities.

Recognizing differential employment paths could therefore be a first step in making the system more inclusive, for example, by extending access to workplace pensions to groups currently excluded. Yet, these measures would not go far enough to address socio-economic inequalities in the asset-based welfare system, as highlighted again in the current cost-of-living crisis. Hence, there is a need to establish equitable starting points for pension savers in the medium-term, balancing out inequalities due to occupational constraints, unpaid care work and income constraints, and reducing the reliance on the capitalist welfare state for financial security in retirement in the long-term. The concept of lived finance rationality is helpful here due to not only highlighting unique approaches to asset accumulation but also due to showing how these emerge from the interplay between experiencing constraints and the pressure to provide financial security. By moving beyond understanding everyday financial practices and rationalities as financially irresponsible or irrational and instead perceiving them as financially responsible when adjusted to the context helps to detect the limitations of the current system and encourage the development of policies in line with the context. Too often the focus in policy and industry lies on improving financial wellbeing by seeking to change behaviours while ignoring the legacy of its inherent assumptions of a well-earning, non-interrupted working life. Removing the inherent biased assumptions from systems that provide for financial wellbeing in retirement and instead making sure that the system can accommodate varied experiences over the life-course would make pensions more inclusive and improve long-term outcomes.

When it comes to thinking of practical solutions to tackle differences in pension planning, devising a means by which pension contributions are not solely contingent on the terms and conditions of employment would go further to help individuals who do not follow typical career paths. One possible solution in addition to extending access to workplace pensions could be to subsidize this access to make it more equitable, tackling inequalities due to breaks in employment and the inherent uncertainty. A further solution could take the form of a government subsidized lifetime Individual Savings Account (ISA) specifically for people who work part-time, across multiple employment contracts or are self-employed. These measures combined would mean that when someone has to take a break in employment, the employer would continue contributing to the pension and the government would help with additional savings for the lost employees' contributions, which would incentivize both companies and the state to create an environment where individuals are not forced out of the system. In the long-term, the reliance on defined-contribution (DC) pensions, which have lower employer contribution rates than defined-benefit (DB) pensions (Cribb and Karjalainen, 2023), should be reduced and policy makers should bear in mind that, while encouraging individuals to plan more is certainly a good idea, this will not overcome the unequal starting points and/or tackle normative constraints, as highlighted in caring duties and lower savings goals. It is thus necessary to accompany any policy measures with a goal to change mentalities about traditional gender roles within households, for instance, by devising policies which make it more attractive for both partners to take over caring duties and by refraining from labelling non-conforming behaviour as being less financially inclined.

APPENDIX A

Income Thresholds and Interviewee Profiles

Income thresholds for the interviews were defined based on income deciles defined in the Wealth and Assets Survey (WAS). The middle-income group comprises gross income deciles 3–8 and the high-income group 9–10 income deciles. The goal was to interview a diverse sample of the population including women and men, retired, employed and self-employed people, as well as individuals from different ethnic backgrounds. While no specific quotas per category were set, interviewees that have not yet been represented sufficiently were prioritized. For this purpose, two waves of interview collection periods were conducted so that a more targeted approach could be implemented in the second wave. The first wave took place from mid-July to mid-November 2016 and the second one from mid-January to mid-May 2017. Recruitment of the interviewees was undertaken in a threefold way: (1) running adverts in community centres, local supermarkets, websites and social media; (2) participating in community-related events such as a summer festival as well as specific events organized by NGOs, for instance, an event for immigrants or financial events such as an investment-focused event; (3) employing snowball sampling which relied on referrals by either interviewees or personal networks. This was deemed beneficial because of finance being a sensitive topic. Through using networks, trust was established before the interview and participants talked more openly about financial aspects.

Interviewee profile was diverse with regard to age, income, wealth, employment and gender. Interviewees' average income was £31,003 (mean income in 2016–2017 was £33,500 [HMRC, 2022]), ranging from £8,600 to £110,000 annual income with 59 per cent of interviewees belonging to the low- or lower medium-income group. The wealth structure depicts a similar trend as in the WAS, with more than half of UK households having a total net wealth of £262,000 compared to 56.4 per cent of interviewed households, however, this includes again a huge wealth disparity ranging from a negative net wealth (asset minus liabilities) of £5,100 to a positive net wealth of £3,070,000. The youngest participant was 24 and the oldest 88 years old and 60 per cent were female and 40 per cent male. In line with the national average, 13.3 per cent of the interviewees were self-employed (the figure for the UK as a whole is 13 per cent [ONS, 2022b, 2024]) and 23.5 per cent were from a different ethnic background than White British with 19 per cent having a different ethnic background than White, compared to 25.6 per cent and 18.3 per cent in England and Wales (ONS, 2021a).[1]

The WAS which supports the interview data is a longitudinal survey conducted every two years and currently consists of eight waves with the latest wave being 2018–2020. At the time of the analysis, the most recently released wave covered 2014–2016 (Wave 5). Whilst Wave 6 has been released since then and covers the years 2016–2018, a cross-check of some of the key descriptive statistics has shown that there were no major changes between Waves 5 and 6. Since this analysis is meant to provide solely a wider context, the analysis therefore continues to rely on Wave 5.

Analysis and Approach to Data

To analyse the interview data as well as the documentary evidence, a pluralistic approach including thematic and discourse analysis – the two main forms of discovering themes from qualitative data – was applied (Hesse-Biber and Johnson, 2015). Both thematic and discourse analysis include an initial familiarization and thematic coding of the data. The main difference between them is 'not the initial process of analysis but the analytic concepts' (Taylor, 2001, p 39). While discourse analysis searches for discursive patterns in themes representing a 'certain style, a certain constant manner of statement' (Foucault, 1972, p 33) constitutive of social phenomena, thematic analysis treats themes as an end in itself (Taylor, 2001). Employing a pluralistic approach enables an integrated exploration of language in use where discursive dependencies (discursive patterns which are constitutive of social phenomena) are put into relation to non-discursive (Foucault, 1991). By means of discourse, financial subjects are constructed, yet it is also a tool of resistance. Exploring subjects' discourses therefore opens up the possibility of unpacking different dimensions of financial subjectivities. Thematic analysis then reveals 'the places where it [discourse] implants itself and produces its real effects' (Foucault, 2003, p 28) in terms of financial practices.

By means of a Foucauldian discourse analytic approach, it is shown how discourses surrounding asset norms come into being, 'establishing what subsequently counts as being self-evident, universal, and necessary' (Foucault, 1991, p 76), and how interviewees position themselves within these discourses. This includes an analysis of discursive formations which normalize a way of behaving and analysing metaphors which is also widely used in Foucauldian discourse analysis (Jacobs and Manzi, 1996; Talib and Fitzgerald, 2016) and has entered financialization studies (Soaita and Searle, 2016). Discursive formations and 'metaphors enable one to grasp precisely the points at which discourses are transformed' (Foucault, 1980, p 70) and a way of acting is normalized – for instance, when being used to mitigate contradictive forces and provide justification for practices. The thematic analysis then shows the effects of discourse, that is, the impact of asset norms on everyday life. Following Bryman and Bell (2007), interviews were thematically analysed in three main steps: inductive coding of interviews; combining codes into coherent themes and distinguishing between common and uncommon themes; and integrating themes into wider theoretical aspects. This analytic approach offers valuable insights into how financial practices are reflected in conceptualization of asset norms while being sensitive to the asset composition.

Notes

Chapter 1

[1] Whilst the focus of the book lies on the UK, the move towards asset-based welfare has been part of a wider global shift since the 1980s. The arguments and insights presented here can help to explore processes of financialization in other capitalist societies and countries which have adopted asset-based welfare policies.

[2] Social reproduction is understood here as 'the affective and material labour that goes into all the activities constituting the maintenance and sustenance of the household and broader community' (Zulfiqar, 2021, p 742).

[3] Responsibilization is a term coined in the literature to express the transfer of responsibilities from one economic agent to the other (Wakefield and Fleming, 2016).

[4] In line with a qualitative document review (Gurney, 1999), the document analysis is not aimed at providing generalizable insights but attempts to map how norms established in the media are entering interviewees' discourses. This does not exclude the possibility of further existing discourses in a wider range of newspapers not mentioned by interviewees.

Chapter 2

[1] Population is not a 'multiplicity of individuals' where the goal is to single-out non-conforming individuals and make them conform, but the goal is to create norms for the overall population (Foucault, 2004, p 64).

Chapter 3

[1] Regimes of truth develop an understanding of what is acceptable and inacceptable including evaluative elements rather than clear distinctions between true and false statements.

[2] This number is likely to be an underrepresentation of the actual number of self-employed people due to being based on a self-reported survey (ONS, 2022b).

[3] As a result of deregulation, mis-selling scandals occurred and, subsequently, the Financial Services Authority, whose aim was to overlook financial service offers, was set up and later split into macro-level regulation by the Bank of England and micro-level regulation by the Financial Conduct Authority.

[4] This scheme is still in place today offering a discount up to £136,400 inside and £102,400 outside London.

[5] The conceptual founder of asset-based welfare, Michael Sherraden, advised the Labour government.

[6] While it is recognized that millions of people use credit to pay for essentials, the goal is to educate people on budgeting and saving techniques instead of tackling the structural reasonings for debt (MaPS, 2024).

[7] There might be an argument that price effects have impacted this development, yet data from WID (2018) based on constant prices shows that this is a general development of private gross wealth.

Chapter 4

[1] Here, fun shares relate to everyday activities and include, for example, investing in theatre productions.
[2] This reflects a higher share of buy-to-let property than UK households and can be partly explained by having focused on medium- to high-income households that adopt this strategy to cope with structural constraints immanent in workplace pensions.

Chapter 5

[1] This is higher than the average of income deciles 3–10 of UK households (40.8 per cent) which is partly due to 52.6 per cent of interviewed households being from the South East which had, at the time of the interviews, a median net property wealth of £170,000 compared to £100,000 in England as a whole (ONS, 2018b).
[2] The coefficient ranges from 0 to 1 with 0 representing equality and 1 depicting inequality.
[3] Distribution of wealth per income deciles is shown here solely with the help of UK households due to the relatively low number of interviewees per decile category.
[4] This reflects a higher share of buy-to-let property than UK households overall and can be partly explained by the interviews having focused on medium- to high-income households who have used this as a strategy to cope with structural constraints immanent in workplace pensions.

Chapter 7

[1] Some 49 per cent of UK pension savers are in pension schemes which are considered expensive (Morton, 2021).

Chapter 8

[1] These variegated financial subjects are not understood as monolithic or devoid of contradictions but it is possible that interviewees draw on discourses and/or practices from several subject positions. Interviewees nevertheless have tended to move more towards one specific subject position. Due to having collected the balance sheets of interviewees it was possible to make sure these reflect financial practices rather than being solely discursive.

Chapter 9

[1] While the content of the resultant pension strategies often overlaps with those of individuals who are not constrained (for example, property as a form of investment), the fundamental logic behind them is related to the constrained subject positions in play, enveloping structural and normative experiences.

Appendix A

[1] The identification of participants' ethnic background was based on self-identification, meaning interviewees stated their ethnic background when discussing asset management.

References

ABI Analysis (2017) *UK Insurance and Long-Term Savings: Key Facts*, London: Association of British Insurers.

Agunsoye, A., Monne, J., Rutterford, J. and Sotiropoulos, D. (2022) 'How gender, marital status, and gender norms affect savings goals', *Kyklos*, 75(2): 157–83.

Ailon, G. (2019) '"No one to trust": the cultural embedding of atomism in financial markets', *The British Journal of Sociology*, 70(3): 927–47.

Aitken, R. (2003) 'The democratic method of obtaining capital: culture, governmentality and ethics of mass investment', *Consumption Markets & Culture*, 6(4): 293–317.

Alcock, P. and May, M. (2014) *Social Policy in Britain*, New York: Macmillan.

Allen, C. and Rebillard, C. (2021) 'The unequal COVID saving and wealth surge', IMF Blog, Available from: https://www.imf.org/en/Blogs/Artic les/2021/11/09/the-unequal-covid-saving-and-wealth-surge [Accessed 10 December 2021].

Allon, F. (2014) 'The feminization of finance: gender, labor and the limits of Inclusion', *Australian Feminist Studies*, 29(79): 12–30.

Altman, M. (2012) 'Implications of behavioral economics for financial literacy and public policy', *Journal of Socio-Economics*, 41(5): 677–90.

Anstead, M. (2007) 'The best way to handle money when George was "an ostrich"', *The Daily Telegraph*, 3 November.

Anxo, D., Fagan, C., Cebrian, I. and Moreno, G. (2006) 'Patterns of labor market integration in Europe: a life course perspective on time policies', *Socio-Economic Review*, 5(2): 233–60.

Archer, F. (2006) 'Take stock of the benefits from a swift shift into shares', *The Daily Telegraph*, 23 December.

Ayres, I. and Curtis, Q. (2015) 'Beyond diversification: the pervasive problem of excessive fees and "dominated funds" in 401(k) Plans', *Yale Law Journal*, 124(5): 1345–835.

Bandelj, N., Boston, T., Elyachar, J., Kim, J., McBride, M., Tufail, Z. and Weatherall, J.O. (2017) 'Morals and emotions of money', in N. Bandelj, F.F. Wherry and V.A. Zelizer (eds) *Money Talks: Explaining How Money Really Works*, Princeton, NJ: Princeton University Press, pp 39–56.

Bandelj, N., Wherry, F.F. and Zelizer, V.A. (2017) *Money Talks: Explaining How Money Really Works*, Princeton, NJ: Princeton University Press.

Bargawi, H., Alami, R. and Ziada, H. (2021) 'Re-negotiating social reproduction, work and gender roles in occupied Palestine', *Review of International Political Economy*, 29(6): 1–28.

Barnard, C., Deakin, S. and Hobbs, R. (2003) 'Opting out of the 48-hour week: employer necessity or individual choice?', *Industrial Law Journal*, 32(4): 223–52.

Barrett, C. (2016) 'BoE's Andy Haldane admits to pensions bafflement', *Financial Times*, Available from: https://www.ft.com/content/724cb536-1d4b-11e6-a7bc-ee846770ec15 [Accessed 20 October 2020].

Barros, G. (2010) 'Herbert A. Simon and the concept of rationality: boundaries and procedures', *Brazilian Journal of Political Economy*, 30(3): 455–72.

BBC News (1999) 'Fall and rise of PEP', Available from: http://news.bbc.co.uk/1/hi/special_report/1999/04/99/isa_age/309787.stm [Accessed 1 July 2018].

Becchio, G. (2019) 'Behavioral economics, gender economics, and feminist economics: friends or foes?' *Journal of Economic Methodology*, 26(3): 259–71.

Beggs, M., Bryan, D. and Rafferty, M. (2014) 'Shoplifters of the world unite! law and culture in financialized times' *Cultural Studies*, 28(5): 976–96.

Bekaert, G., Hoyem, K. and Hu, W. (2017) 'Who is internationally diversified? Evidence from 401 (K) from 296 firms', *Journal of Financial Economics*, 124(1): 86–112.

Belfrage, C. and Kallifatides, M. (2018) 'Financialisation and the new Swedish model', *Cambridge Journal of Economics*, 42(4): 875–99.

Bell, T. (2021) *The Covid Certainty: More Savings for the Rich, More Debt for the Poor*, Resolution Foundation, Available from: https://www.resolutionfoundation.org/comment/the-covid-certainty-more-savings-for-the-rich-more-debt-for-the-poor/ [Accessed 10 December 2021].

Benartzi, S. and Thaler, R. (2007) 'Heuristics and biases in retirement savings behavior', *Journal of Economic Perspectives*, 21(3): 81–104.

Bergman, N., Scheele, A. and Sorger, C. (2017) 'Variations of the same? A sectoral analysis of the gender pay gap in Germany and Austria', *Gender, Work and Organization*, 26(5): 668–87.

Berry, M. (2016) 'The UK press and the deficit debate', *Sociology*, 50(3): 542–59.

Blair, T. (1997) 'Speech at the Aylesbury Estate, Southwark', 2 June, Available from: https://web.archive.org/web/20070626045507/http://archive.cabinetoffice.gov.uk/seu/newsa52f.html?id=400

Blair, T. (2000) 'Knowledge 2000 Conference, *The Guardian*, 7 March, Available from: https://www.theguardian.com/uk/2000/mar/07/tonyblair

Blair, T. (2002) 'Speech on welfare reform', *The Guardian*, 10 June, Available from: https://www.theguardian.com/society/2002/jun/10/socialexclusion.politics1

Blair, T. (2004) 'Speech given at Labour Party conference', *The Guardian*, 28 September, Available from: https://www.theguardian.com/politics/2004/sep/28/labourconference.labour6

Blakely, G. (2019) *Stolen: How to Save the World from Financialisation*, London: Repeater Books.

Blau, F. and Graham, J. (1990) 'Black–White differences in wealth and asset composition', *Quarterly Journal of Economics*, 105(2): 321–39.

Bonefeld, W. and Holloway, J. (1996) *Global Capital, National State and the Politics of Money*, Basingstoke: Macmillan.

Booth, A. and Nolen, P. (2012) 'Gender differences in risk behavior: does nurture matter?' *The Economic Journal*, 122(558): F56–F78.

Boshara, R., Emmons, W. and Bryan, N. (2015) *The Demographics of Wealth: How Age, Educations and Race Separate Thrivers from Strugglers in Today's Economy*, St Louis, MO: Federal Reserve Bank of St. Louis.

Bozio, A., Crawford, R. and Tetlow, G. (2010) *The History of State Pensions in the UK: 1948 to 2010*, London: Institute for Fiscal Studies.

Brignall, M. (2006) 'Equity release schemes', *The Guardian*, 28 January.

Brown, G. (1997) 'Budget speech', 2 July.

Brown, J. (2024) 'Understand the new rules governing tax relief on landlord properties.' Available from: https://www.moneysupermarket.com/landlord-insurance/buy-to-let-tax-relief/ [Accessed 12 August 2024].

Bryan, D. and Rafferty, M. (2014) 'Political economy and housing in the twenty-first century: from mobile homes to liquid housing?', *Housing, Theory and Society*, 31(4): 404–12.

Bryan, D., Martin, R. and Rafferty, M. (2009) 'Financialization and Marx: giving labor and capital a financial makeover', *Review of Radical Political Economics*, 41(4): 458–72.

Bryan, D., Rafferty, M. and Jefferis, C. (2015) 'Risk and value: finance, labor, and production', *South Atlantic Quarterly*, 114(2): 307–29.

Bryman, A. and Bell, E. (2007) *Business Research Methods*, Oxford: Oxford University Press.

Bucher-Koenen, T., Alessie, R., Lusardi, A. and Van Rooij, M. (2016) *Women, Confidence and Financial Literacy*, Luxembourg: European Investment Bank Institute.

Burgess, K. (2002) 'Star managers' culture reaches new heights: investors are increasingly putting their faith in the ability of individual fund managers to buck the falling markets', *Financial Times*, 22 July.

Burr, R. (1984) 'Beware of your best friend's broker: what to do with middle-aged wealth', *The Guardian*, 22 September.

Burn-Murdoch, J. (2022) 'Britain and the US are poor societies with some very rich people.' *Financial Times*, 16 September.

Buxton, J. (1987) 'Shake-up for Edinburgh', *Financial Times*, 12 September.

Caldwell, K. (2013) 'How to avoid the seven deadly investment traps', *The Daily Telegraph*, 22 August.

Calkin, C. (2021) 'Can equity release help children and grandchildren climb the property ladder?', *Financial Times*, 27 May.

Campbell, J. (2006) 'Household finance', *The Journal of Finance*, 61(4): 1553–604.

Campbell, J. and Cocco, J. (2003) 'Household risk management and optimal mortgage choice', *Quarterly Journal of Economics*, 118(4): 1449–94.

Cannon, R. (1985) 'Not quite one of the family: financial implications of modern relationships', *The Guardian*, 28 December.

Cannon, R. (1987) 'Indigo as you please: the money show', *The Guardian*, 5 December.

Carruthers, B. G. (2017) 'The social meaning of credit, value, and finance', in N. Bandelj, F. F. Wherry and V. A. Zelizer (eds) *Money Talks: Explaining How Money Really Works*, Princeton, NJ: Princeton University Press, pp 73–88.

Chandler, B. (1993) 'FT quarterly review of personal finance', *Financial Times*, 29 January.

Chaudhuri, S.R. and Xu, X. (2023) *Living Standards and Inequality*, London: Institute for Fiscal Studies.

Chzhen, Y., Gromada, A. and Rees, G. (2019) *Are the World's Richest Countries Family Friendly? Policy in the OECD and EU*, Florence: UNICEF.

CIPD (2015) *Employment Regulation and the Labour Market*, Lancaster: The Work Foundation.

Clark, G. (2010) 'Human nature, the environment and behavior: explaining the scope and geographical scale of financial decision-making', *Geografiska Annaler: Series B, Human Geography*, 92(2): 159–73.

Clark, G. (2012) 'Pensions or property?', *Environment and Planning A*, 44(5): 1185–99.

Clark, G. (2014) 'Roepke lecture in economic geography: financial literacy in context', *Economic Geography*, 90(1): 1–23.

Clark, R., Lusardi, A., Mitchell, O. and Davis, H. (2021) *Financial Well-Being among Black and Hispanic Women*, Washington, DC: Global Financial Literacy Excellence Center.

Coggan, P. (1993) 'FT quarterly review of personal finance', *Financial Times*, 22 October.

Coppock, S. (2013) 'The everyday geographies of financialisation: impacts, subjects and alternatives', *Cambridge Journal of Regions, Economy and Society*, 6(3): 479–500.

Cowie, I., West, R.-M., Simon, E. and Wall, E. (2008) 'The best thing to do is take the long-term view as the effects of the credit crisis start to ripple through the economy', *The Daily Telegraph*, 11 October.

Crafts, M. (2023) 'Life insurance', Pinterest, Available from: https://www.pinterest.co.uk/pin/786441153654251972/ [Accessed 1 May 2023].

Cribb, J. and Karjalainen, H. (2023) 'How important are defined contribution pensions for financing retirement?', Institute of Fiscal Studies, Available from: https://ifs.org.uk/publications/how-important-are-defined-contribution-pensions-financing-retirement [Accessed 7 September 2023].

Cribb, J., Emmerson, C., Johnson, P., Karjalainen, H. and O'Brien, L. (2023) 'Challenges for the UK pension system: the case for a pensions review', Institute of Fiscal Studies, Available from: https://ifs.org.uk/publications/challenges-uk-pension-system-case-pensions-review [Accessed 1 May].

Cumbo, J. (2015) 'Who has their eye on your pension?, *Financial Times*, 11 December.

Curry, C. (2021) 'How to fill the dangerous UK pensions framework gap', *Money Marketing*, Available from: https://www.moneymarketing.co.uk/opinion/how-to-fill-the-dangerous-uk- pensions-framework-gap/ [Accessed 12 November 2022].

Cuthbert, M. (2006) 'Fresh pension regime puts destiny in your hands', *The Daily Telegraph*, 2 September.

Cutler, T. and Waine, B. (2001) 'Social insecurity and the retreat from social democracy: occupational welfare in the long boom and financialization', *Review of International Political Economy*, 8(1): 96–118.

Daley, J. (2017) 'The small print sleuth: forget mis-selling, the biggest danger that consumers face now is "mis-buying"', *The Daily Telegraph*, 20 May.

Darity, W. (2005) 'Stratification economics: the role of intergroup inequality', *Journal of Economics and Finance*, 29(2): 144–53.

Davies, A., Freeman, J. and Pemberton, H. (2018) ' "Everyman a capitalist" or "free to choose"? Exploring the tensions within Thatcherite individualism', *The Historical Journal*, 61(2): 477–501.

Davis, G. (2009) *Managed by the Markets: How Finance Reshaped America*, New York: Oxford University Press.

Dean, M. (1999) *Governmentality: Power and Rule in Modern Society*, London: Sage.

Dearden, L., Fitzsimons, E. and Wyness, G. (2011) *The Impact of Tuition Fees and Support on University Participation in the UK*, London: Institute for Fiscal Studies.

Devine, V. (2021) 'Want to stick to your budget? Open six bank accounts', *The Guardian*, 15 June.

DfBIS (2013) *Changes to TUPE Rules Cut Red Tape for Business*, Department for Business, Innovation and Skills. Available from: https://www.gov.uk/government/news/changes-to-tupe-rules-cut-red-tape-for-business [Accessed 10 April 2018].

DfLHC (2022) 'Department for Levelling Up, Housing and Communities', Statistical Data Sets, Available from: https://www.gov.uk/government/statistical-data-sets/tenure-trends-and-cross-tenure-analysis [Accessed 8 February 2023].

Di Feliciantonio, C. (2016) 'Subjectification in times of indebtedness and neoliberal/austerity urbanism', *Antipode*, 48(5): 1206–27.

Dibb, G. and Murphy, L. (2023) 'Now is the time to consult UK's investment phobia', *Institute for Public Policy Research*, Available from: https://www.ippr.org/blog/now-is-the-time-to-confront-uk-s-investment-phobia [Accessed 17 July 2023].

Dibben, M. (1984) 'Going by the book? Guardian family guide', *The Guardian*, 13 October.

Dickson, T. (1991) 'First clarify your aims: choosing an investment trust', *Financial Times*, 26 April.

Disney, R. (2016) 'Pension reform in the United Kingdom: an economic perspective', *National Institute Economic Review*, 237(1): 6–14.

Dixon, H. (1987) 'Home sweet secure home', *Financial Times*, 10 January.

DoH (2013) *Housing and Equity*, London: Department of Health, Housing and Finance Working Group.

Druta, O. and Ronald, R. (2017) 'Young adults' pathways into homeownership and the negotiation of intra-family support: a home, the ideal gift', *Sociology*, 51(4): 783–99.

DWP (2011) *Guidance Offering a Default Option for Defined Contribution Automatic Enrolment Pensions Schemes*, Available from: https://assets.publishing.service.gov.uk/media/5a74f32b40f0b6360e47226b/def-opt-guid.pdf [Accessed 15 August 2019].

DWP (2017) Automatic enrolment review 2017: Analytical report. Department for Work and Pensions. Available from: https://assets.publishing.service.gov.uk/government/uploads/system/uploads/attachment_data/file/668657/automatic-enrolment-review-2017-analytical-report.pdf [Accessed 10 April 2022].

DWP (2013) *Pensions: The Basics*, London: Department for Work and Pensions.

DWP (2018) *Workplace Pension Participation and Savings Trends of Eligible Employees: 2007 to 2017*, London: Department for Work and Pensions.

DWP (2019) *Pensions Dashboards: Government Response to the Consultation*, London: Department for Work and Pensions.

DWP (2021) *Your State Pension Explained*, Department for Work and Pensions, Available from: https://www.gov.uk/government/publications/your-new-state-pension-explained/your-state-pension-explained [Accessed 10 December 2022].

Edwards, J. (1987) 'Mid-life joy', *Financial Times*, 21 February.

Elliehausen, G. (2019) 'Behavioral economics, financial literacy, and consumers' financial decisions', in Allen N. Berger (ed) *The Oxford Handbook of Banking*, Oxford: Oxford University Press, pp 814–44.

Engelen, E. and Konings, M. (2010) 'Financial capitalism resurgent: comparative institutionalism and the challenges of financialization', in G. Morgan, J.L. Campbell, C. Crouch, O. K. Pederson and R. Whitley (eds) *The Oxford Handbook of Comparative Institutional Analysis*, Oxford: Oxford University Press, pp 601–24.

Erturk, I., Johal, S., Leaver, A. and Williams, K. (2007) 'The democratization of finance? Promises, outcomes and conditions', *Review of International Political Economy*, 14(4): 553–75.

Eswaran, M. (2014) *Why Gender Matters in Economics*, Princeton, NJ: Princeton University Press.

European Commission (2018) *Mutual Information System on Social Protection, and the department is Employment, Social Affairs & Inclusion*, Available from: http://ec.europa.eu/social/main.jsp?langId=en&catId=1132&new sId=9153&further News=yes [Accessed 15 June 2018].

Eurostat (2022) *Gender Pay Gap in Unadjusted Form*, Available from: https:// ec.europa.eu/eurostat/databrowser/view/sdg_05_20/default/bar?lang=en [Accessed 22 February 2023].

FCA (2022) *Keeping Pace with Rising Costs: Improving Financial Inclusion for Consumers*, Available from: https://www.fca.org.uk/news/speeches/keep ing-pace-rising-costs-improving-financial-inclusion-consumers [Accessed 1 April 2023].

Fields, D. (2017) 'Unwilling subjects of financialization', *International Journal of Urban and Regional Research*, 41(4), 588–603.

FinCap (2021) *Financial Capability Strategy for the UK*, Available from: https:// www.fincap.org.uk/ [Accessed 1 June 2022].

Finch, J. and Mason, J. (2000) *Passing On: Kinship and Inheritance in England*, London: Routledge.

Finley, S. (2021) 'Financial literacy, financial liberation: toward a critical race approach to financial education', in T. Lucy (ed) *Financialization, Financial Literacy, and Social Education*, Abingdon: Routledge, pp 113–27.

Fleming, S. (2019) 'These countries have the most expensive childcare', Available from: https://www.weforum.org/agenda/2019/04/these-countr ies-have-the-most-expensive-childcare/ [Accessed 10 August 2022].

Flynn, A., Holmberg, S., Warren, D. and Wong, F. (2017) *The Hidden Rules of Race: Barriers to an Inclusive Economy*, Cambridge: Cambridge University Press.

Folbre, N. (2020) 'Manifold exploitations: toward an intersectional political economy', *Review of Social Economy*, 78(4): 451–72.

Foucault, M. (1972) *Archeology of Knowledge*, London: Tavistock Publications.

Foucault, M. (1977) *Discipline and Punish*, New York: Vintage Books.

Foucault, M. (1978) *The History of Sexuality, Volume 1*. New York: Pantheon Books.

Foucault, M. (1980) *Power/Knowledge*, New York: Pantheon Books.

Foucault, M. (1982) 'The subject and power', *Critical Inquiry*, 8(4): 777–95.

Foucault, M. (1984) *History of Sexuality, Volume 3*, New York: Pantheon Books.

Foucault, M. (1991) 'Politics and the study of discourse', in G. Burchell, C. Gordon and P. Miller (eds) *Foucault Effect: Studies in Governmentality*, Chicago, IL: The University of Chicago Press, pp 73–86.

Foucault, M. (1997) *Ethics: Subjectivity and Truth*, New York: The New Press.

Foucault, M. (2003) *Society Must Be Defended*, New York: Picador.

Foucault, M. (2004) *Security, Territory, Population*, New York: Palgrave Macmillan.

Foucault, M. (2007) *The Politics of Truth*, Los Angeles: Semiotext(e).

Foucault, M. (2008) *The Birth of Biopolitics*, New York: Palgrave Macmillan.

Foucault, M., Gordon, C. and Patton, P. (2012) 'Considerations on Marxism, phenomenology and power: interview with Michel Foucault', *Foucault Studies*, 14: 98–114.

Fraser, N. (2017) 'Crisis of care? On the social-reproductive contradictions of contemporary capitalism', in T. Battacharya (ed) *Social Reproduction Theory*, London: Pluto Press, pp 21–36.

French, S. and Kneale, J. (2009) 'Excessive financialisation: insuring lifestyles, enlivening subjects, and everyday spaces of biosocial excess', *Environment and Planning D: Society and Space*, 27(6): 1030–53.

Frericks, P., Knijn, T. and Maier, R. (2009) 'Pension reforms, working patterns and gender pension gaps in Europe', *Gender, Work & Organization*, 16(6): 710–30.

Friedman, M. (1957) *A Theory of the Consumption Function*, Princeton, NJ: Princeton University Press.

Froud, J., Johal, S., Montgomerie, J. and Williams, K. (2010) 'Escaping the tyranny of earned income? The failure of finance as social innovation', *New Political Economy*, 15(1): 147–64.

FT (1984) 'The wooing of the small investor', *Financial Times*, 8 November.

FT (1993) 'FT quarterly review of personal finance', *Financial Times*, 16 July.

Gaffney, D. (2015) *Welfare States: How Generous Are British Benefits Compared with Other Rich Nations?*, London: Trades Union Congress.

Gammell, K. (2007) 'Silver lining investment strategies on how to profit from the stock market storms', *The Daily Telegraph*, 22 September.

Garcia-Lamarca, M. and Kaika, M. (2016) 'Mortgaged lives: the biopolitics of debt and housing financialization', *Transactions of the Institute of British Geographers*, 41(3): 313–27.

Gardner, J. (2020) 'Measuring the ethnicity pensions gap', The People's Pension, Available from: https://thepeoplespension.co.uk/mediacentre/policy-research/measuring-the-ethnicity-pensions-gap/ [Accessed 10 September 2023].

Ghodsee, K. (2019) *Why Women Have Better Sex under Socialism: And Other Arguments for Economic Independence*, London: Vintage.

Ginn, J., Street, D. and Arber, S. (2001) *Women, Work and Pensions*, Milton Keynes: Open University Press.

Giupponi, G. and Xu, X. (2024) *What does the rise of self-employment tell us about the UK labour market?* Available from: https://ifs.org.uk/sites/default/files/output_url_files/BN-What-does-the-rise-of-self-employment-tell-us-about-the-UK-labour-market-1.pdf [Accessed 8 August 2024].

Goff, S. (2008) 'Share price falls erode income drawdown plans', *Financial Times*, 1 February.

Goldstein-Jackson, K. (1987) 'Inheriting the windfall', *Financial Times*, 30 May.

Goldstein-Jackson, K. (2000) 'Hard work gains honest profits', *Financial Times*, 29 January.

GOV.UK (2018) *Get help with Savings if You're on a Low Income (Help to Save)*, Available from: https://www.gov.uk/get-help-savings-low-income [Accessed 12 December 2018].

GOV.UK (2022) *Statutory Sick Pay (SSP)*, Available from https://www.gov.uk/statutory-sick-pay/what-youll-get [Accessed 26 July 2023].

GOV.UK (2023a) *Help for Households*, Available from: https://helpforhouseholds.campaign.gov.uk/ [Accessed 13 February 2023].

GOV.UK (2023b) *30 Hours Free Childcare*, Available from: https://www.gov.uk/30-hours-free-childcare [Accessed 7 February 2023].

Grace, D., Weaven, S. and Ross, M. (2010) 'Consumer retirement planning: an exploratory study of gender differences', *Qualitative Market Research: An International Journal*, 13(2): 174–88.

Grady, J. (2015) 'Gendering pensions: making women visible', *Gender, Work & Organization*, 22(5): 445–58.

Greenfield, C. and Williams, P. (2007) 'Financialization, finance rationality and the role of media in Australia', *Media, Culture & Society*, 29(3): 415–33.

Gregory, M. (1998) 'Reforming the labour market: an assessment of the UK policies of the Thatcher era', *The Australian Economic Review*, 31(4): 329–44.

Gregory, T. (1988) *The Sale of the Century: Privatization in Great Britain*, Bethlehem, PA: LeHigh University.

Grey, C. (1997) 'Suburban subjects: financial services and the new right', in D. Knights and T. Tinker (eds) *Financial Institutions and Social Transformations*, Basingstoke: Palgrave Macmillan, pp 47–67.

Grisp, J. (1984) 'The rulebook makes for risk-taking', *Financial Times*, 10 October.

The Guardian (2006) 'How to find the best mortgage and save up to £725 on fees', 14 January.

Guermond, V. (2022) 'Contesting the financialisation of remittances: repertoires of reluctance, refusal and dissent in Ghana and Senegal', *Environment and Planning A: Economy and Space*, 54(4): 800–21.

Guiso, L., Haliassos, M. and Jappelli, T. (eds) (2002) *Household Portfolios*, Cambridge, MA: The MIT Press.

Gurney, C. (1999) 'Pride and prejudice: discourse of normalisation in public and private accounts of home ownership', *Housing Studies*, 14(2): 163–83.

Hacker, J. S. (2008) *The Great Risk Shift: The New Economic Insecurity and the Decline of the American Dream*, New York: Oxford University Press.

Halko, M., Kaustia, M. and Alanko, E. (2012) 'The gender effect in risky asset holdings', *Journal of Economic Behavior & Organization*, 83(1): 66–81.

Hall, S. (2012) 'Geographies of money and finance II: financialization and financial subjects', *Progress in Human Geography*, 36(3): 403–11.

Hall, S. M. (2019) 'Everyday family experiences of the financial crisis: getting by in the recent economic recession', *Journal of Economic Geography*, 16(2): 305–30.

Hamilton, D. and Darity Jr, W. (2017) *The Political Economy of Education, Financial Literacy, and the Racial Wealth Gap, Review*, St Louis, MO: Federal Reserve Bank of St Louis.

Hammersley, M. (2013) *What Is Qualitative Research?*, London: Bloomsbury.

Hammersley, M. and Atkinson, P. (2007) *Ethnography: Principles in Practice*, New York: Routledge.

Hardcastle, R. (2012) *How Can We Incentivise Pension Saving? A Behavioural Perspective*, London: Department for Work and Pensions.

Hardt, M. and Negri, A. (2009) *Commonwealth*, Cambridge, MA: The Belknap Press of Harvard University Press.

Harrop, A. (2021) *Statutory Sick Pay: Options for Reform*, Fabian Society, Available from: https://www.tuc.org.uk/sites/default/files/SSPreport.pdf [Accessed 7 February 2022].

Harvey, D. (2005) *A Brief History of Neoliberalism*, Oxford: Oxford University Press.

Hasler, A. and Lusardi, A. (2017) *The Gender Gap in Financial Literacy: A Global Perspective*, Global Financial Literacy Excellence Centre, Available from: https://gflec.org/wp-content/uploads/2017/07/The-Gender-Gap-in-Financial-Literacy- A-Global-Perspective-Report.pdf [Accessed 1 June 2022].

Hawthorne, J. (1987) 'Popular capitalism: laugh like a drain as it goes down the tube', *The Guardian*, 27 June.

Haynes, T. (2022) 'Money makeover: "I'm bad with money – how do I invest my £176k inheritance?"', *The Daily Telegraph*, 5 December.

Heath, S. and Calvert, E. (2013) 'Gifts, loans and intergenerational support for young adults', *Sociology*, 47(6): 1120–35.

Hesse-Biber, S. and Johnson, R. (2015) *The Oxford Handbook of Multimethod and Mixed Methods Research Inquiry*, Oxford: Oxford University Press.

Hickey, S. (2021) 'How to invest spare lockdown cash in the stock market … safely', *The Guardian*, 31 January.

Hillig, A. (2019) 'Everyday financialization: the case of UK households', *Environment and Planning A*, 51(7): 1460–78.

HM Treasury (2004) *Promoting* Financial Inclusion, London: HM Treasury.

HM Treasury (2013) *Budget 2013: Housing*, Available from: https://publications.parliament.uk/pa/cm201213/cmselect/cmtreasy/1063/106309.htm [Accessed 10 August 2016].

HM Treasury (2014) *Budget 2014: Greater Choice in Pensions Explained*, Available from: https://assets.publishing.service.gov.uk/government/uploads/system/uploads/attachment_data/file/301563/Pensions_fact_sheet_v8.pdf [Accessed 10 April 2018].

HMRC (2022) *Distribution of Median and Mean Income and Tax by Age Range and Gender*, Available from: https://www.gov.uk/government/statistics/distribution-of-median-and-mean-income-and-tax-by-age-range-and-gender-2010-to-2011 [Accessed 1 December 2022].

HMRC (2023) *The New State Pension*, Available from: https://www.gov.uk/new-state-pension/what-youll-get [Accessed 1 August 2023].

HoC (1995) *A Minimum Wage*, London: House of Commons.

HoC (1998) *Working Time Regulations 1998 – No. 1998/1833*, London: House of Commons.

HoC (1999) *Welfare Reforms and Pensions Act*, London: House of Commons.

HoC (2000) *Select Committee on Social Security Seventh Report*, London: House of Commons.

HoC (2011) *The Economic Crisis: Policy Responses*, London: House of Commons.

HoC (2016) *Trade Union Act 2016*, London: House of Commons.

HoC (2017) *Trade Union Legislation 1979–2010*, London: House of Commons.

Hollingrake, K. and Merriman, H. (2023) 'Department for Business and Trade', Available from: https://www.gov.uk/government/news/strikes-bill-becomes-law [Accessed 16 July 2023].

Huber, E., Petrova, B. and Stephens, J. (2020) 'Financialization, labour market institutions and inequality', *Review of International Political Economy*, 29(2): 425–52.

Hunt, J. (2022) *The Autumn Statement 2022*, 17 November.

Hunter, T. (2016) 'How to save – whatever your age', *The Daily Telegraph*, 21 June.

Jacobs, K. and Manzi, T. (1996) 'Discourse and policy change: the significance of language for housing research', *Housing Studies*, 11(4): 543–60.

Jacobsen, B., Lee, J., Marquering, W. and Zhang, C. (2014) 'Gender differences in optimism and asset allocation', *Journal of Economic Behavior & Organization*, 107(B): 630–51.

James, H. (2021) 'Individual pension decision-making in a financialized landscape: a typology of everyday approaches', *Journal of Cultural Economy*, 14(6): 627–43.

Jessop, B. (2003) *The Political Economy of European Employment: European Integration and the Transnationalization of the (Un)Employment Question*, London: Routledge.

Johnson, B. (2022) 'Homeownership Society', 9 June 2022.

Jones, R. (1997) 'You pays yer money and takes yer choice', *The Guardian*, 15 November.

Jones, R. (2002) 'Money: mortgage insurance', *The Guardian*, 31 August.

Jones, R. (2023) 'UK state pension age may rise to 68 in 2030s, reports say – what is going on?', *The Guardian*, 25 January.

Joseph, M. (2013) 'Gender, entrepreneurial subjectivity, and pathologies of personal Finance', *Social Politics*, 20(2): 242–73.

Kahneman, D. and Tversky, A. (1982) 'On the study of statistical intuitions', in D. Kahneman, P. Slovic and A. Tversky (eds) *Judgment under Uncertainty: Heuristics and Biases*, Cambridge: Cambridge University Press, pp 493–508.

Karacimen, E. (2015) 'Interlinkages between credit, debt and the labour market: evidence from Turkey', *Cambridge Journal of Economics*, 39(3): 751–67.

Karagaac, E. (2020) 'The financialization of everyday life: caring for debts', *Geography Compass*, 14(11): 1–15.

Kear, M. (2013) 'Governing homo subprimicus: beyond financial citizenship, exclusion, and rights' *Antipode*, 45(4): 926–46.

Keasey, K. and Veronesi, G. (2012) 'The significance and implications of being a subprime homeowner in the UK', *Environment and Planning A*, 44(6): 1502–22.

Kempson, E. and Collard, S. (2012) *Full Grid UK*, Oslo: National Institute for Consumer Research.

Kim, M. (2020) 'Intersectionality and gendered racism in the United States: a new theoretical framework', *Review of Radical Political Economics*, 52(4): 616–25.

Kim, W. (2023) 'Prices at the supermarket keep rising. So do corporate profits', *Vox*, Available from: https://www.vox.com/money/23641875/food-grocery-inflation-prices-billionaires [Accessed 2 August 2023].

Lai, K. (2016a) 'Financialisation of everyday life', in G. Clark, M. Feldman, M. Gertler and D. Wojcik (eds) *The New Oxford Handbook of Economic Geography*, Oxford: Oxford University Press, pp 611–27.

Lai, K. (2016b) 'Financial advisors, financial ecologies and the variegated financialization of everyday investors', *Transactions of the Institute for British Geographers*, 41(1): 27–40.

Lai, K. (2017) 'Unpacking financial subjectivities: intimacies, governance and socioeconomc practices in financialisation', *Environment and Planning D*, 35(5): 913–32.

Langan, S. (1997) 'Easy money personal finance for the uninformed: you grow up, sell out and get a pension', *The Guardian*, 18 January.

Langley, P. (2004) 'In the eye of the "perfect storm": the final salary pensions crisis and financialisation of Anglo-American capitalism', *New Political Economy*, 9(4): 539–58.

Langley, P. (2006) 'The making of investor subjects in Anglo-American pensions', *Environment and Planning D*, 24(6): 919–34.

Langley, P. (2007) 'Uncertain subjects of Anglo-American financialization', *Cultural Critique*, 65: 67–91.

Langley, P. (2008) *The Everyday Life of Global Finance: Saving and Borrowing in Anglo-America*, Oxford: Oxford University Press.

Langley, P. and Leaver, A. (2012) 'Remaking retirement investors', *Journal of Cultural Economy*, 5(4): 473–88.

Lapavitsas, C. (2009) 'Financialised capitalism: crisis and financial expropriation', *Historical Materialism*, 17(2): 114–48.

Larner, W. (2006) 'Neoliberalism: policy, ideology, governmentality', in M. de Goede (ed) *International Political Economy and Poststructuralist Politics*, New York: Palgrave Macmillan, pp 199–218.

Lavoie, M. (2015) *Post-Keynesian Economics: New Foundations*, Cheltenham: Edward Elgar Publishing.

Lebaron, G. (2010) 'The political economy of the household: neoliberal restructuring, enclosures, and daily life', *Review of International Political Economy:* 17(5), 889–912.

Legal & General (2023) 'Life insurance', Available from: https://www.lega landgeneral.com/insurance/life-insurance/ [Accessed 1 May 2023].

Lewis, M. (2006) 'A black and white guide to a grey area', *The Guardian*, 3 June.

Lewis, M. (2010) 'A nation educated into debt but never about debt'. Available from: https://www.moneysavingexpert.com/news/2010/03/ making-money-can-be-childs-play/ [Accessed 9 August 2024].

Lewis, M. (2022) 'Martin Lewis warns he is "virtually out of tools" to help people with cost of living crisis', *Indy 100*, Available from: https://www. indy100.com/politics/martin-lewis-out-of-tools-cost-of-living-crisis [Accessed 2 February 2023].

Lewis, M. (2023a) 'MoneySavingExpert', Available from: https://www. moneysavingexpert.com/site/about-the-site/ [Accessed 2 August 2023].

Lewis, M. (2023b) 'Pensions need-to-knows', Money Saving Expert, Available from: https://www.moneysavingexpert.com/savings/discount-pensions/ [Accessed 2 August 2023].

Lewis, M. (2023c) 'Premium bonds – are they worth it?', Money Saving Expert, Available from: https://www.moneysavingexpert.com/savings/ premium-bonds/ [Accessed 10 July 2023].

LM (1997) 'Labour Manifesto: New Labour because Britain deserves better', Available from: http://www.labour-party.org.uk/manifestos/1997/1997-labour-manifesto.shtml [Accessed 15 June 2018].

Loomis, J. (2018) 'Rescaling and reframing poverty: financial coaching and the pedagogical spaces of financial inclusion in Boston, Massachusetts', *Geoforum*, 95: 143–52.

Loretto, W. and Vickerstaff, S. (2013) 'The domestic and gendered context for retirement', *Human Relations*, 66(1): 65–86.

Lowe, J. (2010) 'Investment choices', in M. Mazzucato, J. Lowe, A. Shipman and A. Trigg (eds) *Personal Investment: Financial Planning in an Uncertain World*, London: Macmillan, pp 67–111.

Lowe, J. (2023) *The Good Retirement Guide 2023*, London: Kogan Page.

Lusardi, A, Mitchell, O.S. and Curto, V. (2010) 'Financial literacy among the young', *The Journal of Consumer Affairs*, 44(2): 358–80.

Lusardi, A. (2015) 'Financial literacy: do people know the ABCs of finance?', *Public Understanding of Science*, 24(3): 260–71.

Lusardi, A. and Mitchell, O. (2008) *Planning and Financial Literacy: How Do Women Fare?*, Cambridge, MA: National Bureau of Economic Research.

Lysandrou, P. (2016) 'The colonisation of the future: an alternative view of finance and its portents', *Journal of Post Keynesian Economics*, 39(4): 444–72.

MacErlean, N. and Insley, J. (2007) 'Remarry in haste, and you'll repent in poverty', *The Observer Money*, 4 March.

Maman, D. and Rosenhek, Z. (2019) 'Facing future uncertainties and risks through personal finance: conventions in financial education', *Journal of Cultural Economy*, 13(3): 303–17.

MaPS (2019) Money and Pensions Service. Available from: https://mone yandpensionsservice.org.uk/ [Accessed 10 October 2023].

MaPS (2021) *Financial Education in School*, Available from: https://maps. org.uk/en/work-with-us/financial-education-in-schools [Accessed 1 November 2022].

MaPS (2024) *UK Strategy for Financial Wellbeing*. Available from: https://maps. org.uk/en/our-work/uk-strategy-for-financial-wellbeing#. [Accessed 8 August 2024].

Martin, R. (2002) *Financialization of Daily Life*, Philadelphia, PA: Temple University Press.

MAS (2017) 'The Money Advice Service', Available from: https://www. moneyadviceservice.org.uk/en [Accessed 15 August 2017].

MAS (2021) *Should I Save or Invest My Money?*, Available from: https:// www. moneyadviceservice.org.uk/en/articles/should-i-save-or-invest [Accessed 20 June 2021].

May, T. (2017) 'Forward together: the Conservative Manifesto', Available from: https://ucrel.lancs.ac.uk/wmatrix/ukmanifestos2017/localpdf/ Conservatives.pdf [Accessed 7 July 2017].

Mazur, M., Dang, M. and Vega, M. (2021) 'COVID-19 and the March 2020 stock market crash: evidence from S&P 1500', *Finance Research Letters*, 38(101690): 1–8.

McMunn, A., Bird, L., Webb, E. and Sacker, A. (2020) 'Gender divisions of paid and unpaid work in contemporary UK couples', *Work, Employment and Society*, 34(2): 155–73.

Meacher, M. (1984) 'A guide for the money minefield', *The Guardian*, 29 October.

Merton, R. (2003) 'Thoughts on the future: theory and practice investment management' *Financial Analyst Journal*, 59(1): 17–23.

Meyer, H. (2021) 'How to start investing safely and profitably', *The Guardian*, 1 November.

Mezzadri, A., Newman, S. and Stevano, S. (2022) 'Feminist global political economies of work and social reproduction', *Review of International Political Economy*, 29(6): 1783–803.

Middleton, J., Bancroft, H. and Devlin, K. (2024) 'Energy companies rake in eye-watering £1bn a week as British families struggle in cost of living crisis', *The Independent*, 24 February.

Mitchell, O. and Lusardi, A. (2012) *Financial Literacy: Implications for Retirement Security and the Financial Marketplace*, Oxford: Oxford University Press.

Modigliani, F. and Brumberg, R. (1954) 'Utility analysis and the consumption function: an interpretation of cross-section data', in K. Kurihara (ed) *Post-Keynesian Economics*, New Brunswick, NJ: Rutgers University Press, pp 388–436.

MoneyHelper (2023a) 'Living on a squeezed income', Available from: https://www.moneyhelper.org.uk/en/money-troubles/cost-of-living/squeezed-income [Accessed 1 August 2023].

MoneyHelper (2023b) 'ISAs and other tax-efficient ways to save or invest', Available from: https://www.moneyhelper.org.uk/en/savings/types-of-savings/isas-and-other-tax-efficient-ways-to-save-or-invest [Accessed 10 January 2023].

Montagu-Smith, N. (2001a) 'An animated life, but entrepreneur turns back on Peter Pan, Nina Montagu-Smith meets a couple who want to work less but have made no pension provision', *The Daily Telegraph*, 23 June.

Montagu-Smith, N. (2001b) 'Saver can savour property prospect – after years of putting money away, Belinda Rowley can now consider buying her own home', *The Daily Telegraph*, 8 December.

Montagu-Smith, N. (2001c) 'Time to exercise prudence – affordable debts today may be a burden tomorrow', *The Daily Telegraph*, 15 September.

Montagu-Smith, N. (2008) 'Should you invest your Serps in a Sipp?', *The Daily Telegraph*, 22 September.

Montgomerie, J. and Tepe-Belfrage, D. (2019) 'Spaces of debt resistance and the contemporary politics of financialised capitalism', *Geoforum'*, 98: 309–17.

Montgomerie, J. and Young, B. (2011) *Home is Where the Hardship Is: Gender and Wealth (Dis)Accumulation in the Subprime Boom*, Manchester: CRESC.

Moore, J. (1992) 'British privatization: taking capitalism to the people', *Harvard Business Review*, Available from: https://hbr.org/1992/01/british-privatization-taking-capitalism-to-the-people [Accessed 10 November 2018].

Moore, R. (2014) 'Margaret Thatcher began Britain's obsession with property. It's time to end it', *The Observer*, 6 April.

Morley, K. (2014) 'Rethinking the pension', *Investors Chronicle*, Available from: https://www.investorschronicle.co.uk/2014/01/23/your-money/pensions-and-sipps/rethinking-the-pension-k0n3ymfEISJICNdalqx2fP/article.html

Morton, L. (2021) 'Check your pension changes', Available from: https://www.profilepensions.co.uk/blogs/check-your-charges [Accessed 18 February 2022].

Munro, M. (2000) 'Labour-market insecurity and risk in the owner-occupied housing market', *Environment and Planning A*, 32(8): 1375–89.

Murdoch, J. (2017) 'Economics and the social meaning of money', in N. Bandelj, F. F. Wherry and V. A. Zelizer (eds) *Money Talks: Explaining How Money Really Works*, Princeton, NJ: Princeton University Press, pp 25–38.

Nam, Y., Sherraden, M.S., Huang, J., Lee, E.J. and Keovisai, M. (2019) 'Financial capability and economic security among low-income older Asian immigrants: lessons from qualitative interviews' *Social Work*, 64(3): 224–32.

The National Archives (1995) *Jobseekers Act 1995*, Available from: https://www.legislation.gov.uk/ukpga/1995/18/contents [Accessed 15 November 2021].

Neelakantan, U. (2010) 'Estimation and impact of gender differences in risk tolerance', *Economic Inquiry*, 48(1): 228–33.

Newson, N. (2023) 'Trade unions: members and relations with the government', House of Lords Library, Available from: https://lordslibrary.parliament.uk/trade-unions-members-and-relations-with-the-government/ [Accessed 17 July 2023].

Nunn, A. and Montgomerie, J. (2017) 'Disciplinary social policy and the failing promise of the new middle classes: the troubled families programme', *Social Policy and Society*, 16(1): 119–29.

OBR (2022) *Developments in the Outlook for Household Living Standards*, Office for Budget Responsibility, Available from: https://obr.uk/box/developments-in-the-outlook-for-household-living-standards/ [Accessed 11 February 2023].

OECD (2015) *OECD Employment Outlook 2015*, Available from: http://www.oecd.org/employment/emp/oecdindicatorsofemploymentprotection.htm [Accessed 13 March 2018].

OECD (2017) *Pensions at a Glance 2017*, Available from: http://www.oecd.org/publications/oecd-pensions-at-a-glance-19991363.htm [Accessed 1 May 2018].

OECD (2018) *Trade Union Density*, Available from: https://stats.oecd.org/Index.aspx?DataSetCode=TUD [Accessed 16 June 2018].

OECD (2021a) *OECD Pensions at a Glance 2021*, Available from: https://www.oecd-ilibrary.org/finance-and-investment/pensions-at-a-glance-2021_ca401ebd-en [Accessed 7 February 2023].

OECD (2021b) *Towards Improved Retirement Savings Outcomes for Women*, Available from: https://www.oecd-ilibrary.org/sites/f7b48808-en/index.html?itemId=/content/publication/f7b48808-en [Accessed 1 March 2022].

OECD (2023) *OECD Gross Capital Formation*, Available from: https://stats.oecd.org/ [Accessed 17 July 2023].

O'Neill, M. (2023) 'How to survive the financial shocks of redundancy', *Financial Times*, 3 February.

ONS (2005) *Pension Trends*, London: Office for National Statistics, Available from: https://webarchive.nationalarchives.gov.uk/ukgwa/20160114000817/http://www.ons.gov.uk/ons/dcp171766_270744.pdf [Accessed 10 June 2018].

ONS (2012) *Pension Trends*, London: Office for National Statistics.

ONS (2015) *Ownership of UK Quoted Shares: 2014*, London: Office for National Statistics, Available from: https://www.ons.gov.uk/economy/investmentspensionsandtrusts/bulletins/ownershipofukquotedshares/2015-09-02#individuals-holdings-of-uk-shares-by-value [Accessed 11 March 2018].

ONS (2018) *Wealth in Great Britain Wave 5: 2014 to 2016*, London: Office for National Statistics.

ONS (2019) *Household debt in Great Britain: April 2016 to March 2018*, London: Office for National Statistics.

ONS (2021a) *Household wealth by ethnicity, Great Britain: April 2016 to March 2018*, Available from: https://www.ons.gov.uk/peoplepopulationandcommunity/personalandhouseholdfinances/incomeandwealth/articles/householdwealthbyethnicitygreatbritain/april2016tomarch2018 [Accessed 10 September 2022].

ONS (2021b) *Distribution of individual total wealth by characteristic in Great Britain: April 2018 to March 2020*, Available from: https://www.ons.gov.uk/peoplepopulationandcommunity/personalandhouseholdfinances/incomeandwealth/bulletins/distributionofindividualtotalwealthbycharacteristicingreatbritain/april2018tomarch2020 [Accessed 13 November 2022].

ONS (2022a) *Household Total Wealth in Great Britain: April 2018 to March 2020*, Available from: https://www.ons.gov.uk/peoplepopulationandcommunity/personalandhouseholdfinances/incomeandwealth/bulletins/totalwealthingreatbritain/april2018tomarch2020 [Accessed 1 July 2023].

ONS (2022b) *Understanding Changes in Self-Employment in the UK: January 2019 to March 2022*, Available from: https://www.ons.gov.uk/employmentandlabourmarket/peopleinwork/employmentandemployeetypes/articles/understandingchangesinselfemploymentintheuk/january2019tomarch2022 [Accessed 1 March 2023].

ONS (2022c) *Saving for Retirement in Great Britain: April 2018 to March 2020*, Available from: https://www.ons.gov.uk/peoplepopulationandcommunity/personalandhouseholdfinances/incomeandwealth/bulletins/pensionwealthingreatbritain/april2018tomarch2020 [Accessed 12 November 2022].

ONS (2022d) *Funded Occupational Pension Schemes in the UK: July to September 2021*, Available from: https://www.ons.gov.uk/economy/investmentspensionsandtrusts/bulletins/fundedoccupationalpensionschemesintheuk/july2021toseptember2021 [Accessed 1 June 2023].

ONS (2024) EMP01 SA: Full-time, part-time and temporary workers (seasonally adjusted). Available from: https://www.ons.gov.uk/employmentandlabourmarket/peopleinwork/employmentandemployeetypes/datasets/fulltimeparttimeandtemporaryworkersseasonallyadjustedemp01sa/current [Accessed 9 August 2024].

Oppenheim, P. (1984) 'Freedom of choice in pensions', *Financial Times*, 23 February.

Osborne, H. (2021) 'UK property sales at 16-year high as house prices soar', *The Guardian*, Available from: https://www.theguardian.com/busin ess/2021/apr/21/uk-property-sales-at-16-year-high-as-house-prices-soar [Accessed 12 November 2022].

Padley, M. and Hirsch, D. (2017) 'A minimum income standard for the UK in 2017', Joseph Rowntree Foundation, Available from: https://www.jrf. org.uk/a-minimum-income-standard-for-the-uk-in-2017 [Accessed 1 June 2022].

Palmer, R. (2020) 'Wealth, tax and gender: a paper for the commission on a gender equal economy', Women's Budget Group, Available from: https:// wbg.org.uk/wp-content/uploads/2020/03/Paper-2-Wealth-tax-and-gen der.pdf [Accessed 10 August 2022].

Papworth, J. (2002) 'Pay off the loan as soon as you can: it's not the most expensive debt but it's the biggest', *The Guardian*, 14 September.

Parker, G. (2023) 'What is the UK's retained EU law bill and why is it so controversial?', *Financial Times*, 17 January.

Parliament (2022) *Research Briefings*, Available from: https://commonslibrary. parliament.uk/research-briefings/sn01079/ [Accessed 7 February 2023].

Pauley, R. (1984) 'Pension rules widely disliked, survey shows', *Financial Times*, 22 June.

Peachey, K. (2023a) 'Cost of living: one in five eating food beyond use-by date', BBC News, Available from: https://www.bbc.co.uk/news/busin ess-64452348 [Accessed 12 February 2023].

Peachey, K. (2023b) 'Mortgage rates soar to highest level for 15 years', BBC News, Available from: https://www.bbc.co.uk/news/business-66153812 [Accessed 10 August 2023].

Pellandini-Simanyi, L. and Banai, A. (2021) 'Reluctant financialisation: financialisation without financialised subjectivities in Hungary and the United States', *Environment and Planning A*, 53(4): 785–808.

Pellandini-Simanyi, L., Hammer, F. and Vargha, Z. (2015) 'The financialization of everyday life or the domestication of finance?', *Cultural Studies,* 29(5–6): 733–59.

Penaloza, L. and Barnhart, M. (2011) 'Living U.S. capitalism: the normalization of credit/debt', *Journal of Consumer Research*, 38(4): 743–62.

Phillips, L. (2006) 'Breaking up is so hard to do in modern marriages', *The Daily Telegraph*, 18 November.

Phillips, L. (2007) 'Hard enough to lose a loved one without probate delays', *The Daily Telegraph*, 18 August.

Pickford, J. (2017) 'How much will I need to save to get on the property ladder?', *Financial Times*, 2 March.

Pitelis, C. and Clarke, T. (1993) *The Political Economy of Privatization*, London: Routledge.

PMI (2022) 'The cost of living crisis has significantly reduced pension saving', Pensions Management Institute, Available from: https://www.pensions-pmi.org.uk/knowledge/pmi-news/the-cost-of-living-crisis-has-significan tly-reduced-pension-saving/ [Accessed 1 August 2023].

Polillo, S. (2017) 'From industrial money to generalized capitalization', in N. Bandelj, F. F. Wherry and V. A. Zelizer (eds) *Money Talks: Explaining How Money Really Works*, Princeton, NJ: Princeton University Press, pp 89–106.

Pollard, J., Datta, K., James, A. and Akli, Q. (2016) 'Islamic charitable infrastructure and giving in East London: everyday economic–development geographies in practice', *Journal of Economic Geography*, 16(4): 871–96.

Powell, A., Francis-Devine, B. and Clark, H. (2022) *Coronavirus: Impact on the Labour Market*, London: House of Commons.

PPI (2017) *Impact of Automatic Enrolment in the UK as at 2016*, London: Pensions Policy Institute.

Prabhakar, R. (2021) *Financial Inclusion: Critique and Alternatives*, Bristol: Bristol University Press.

Pratley, N. (2021) 'August's jump in house prices is further proof stamp duty holiday was a mistake', *The Guardian*, 1 September.

Quinn, J. (2013) 'It doesn't matter if you have 10 pension pots if the default scheme is good', *The Daily Telegraph*, 24 August.

Read, S. (1997) 'High street offers poor returns in poor areas', *The Guardian*, 15 February.

Resolution Foundation & Centre for Economic Performance, L. (2022) *Stagnation Nation: Navigating a Route to a Fairer and More Prosperous Britain*, London: Resolution Foundation.

Richardson, N. (2008) 'Find a safe haven for your savings amid bank troubles, the appeal of building societies is growing', *The Daily Telegraph*, 7 June.

Roberts, A. (2013) 'Financing social reproduction: the gendered relations of debt and mortgage finance in 21st century America', *New Political Economy*, 18(1): 21–42.

Roberts, A. (2015) 'Gender, financial deepening and the production of embodied finance: towards a critical feminist analysis', *Global Society*, 29(1): 107–27.

Roberts, A. (2016) 'Household debt and the financialization of social reproduction: theorizing the UK housing and hunger crises', *Risking Capitalism*, 31: 135–64.

Roberts, A. and Zulfiqar, G. (2019) 'Social reproduction, finance and the gendered dimensions of pawnbroking' *Capital & Class*, 43(4): 581–97.

Ronald, R. (2008) 'Between investment, asset and use consumption: the meanings of homeownership in Japan', *Housing Studies*, 23(20): 233–51.

Roscoe, P. (2015) 'Elephants can't gallop': performativity, knowledge and power in the market for lay-investing', *Journal of Marketing Management*, 31(1–2): 193–218.

Ross, M. (2023) 'Number of ISA millionaires nearly triples in one year', *The Daily Telegraph*, 1 August.

Rutherford, T. (2013) 'Historical rates of social security benefits', House of Commons Library, Available from: https://researchbriefings.files.parliam ent.uk/documents/SN06762/SN06762.pdf [Accessed 7 February 2023].

Saigol, L. (1997) 'House party ends with a hangover: now flexible friends point way Ahead', *The Guardian*, 15 November.

Samec, T. (2018) 'Performing housing debt attachments: forming semi-financialised Subjects', *Cultural Economy*, 11(6): 549–64.

Samec, T. (2020) 'Normalization of mortgages in media discourse through affects and instructions', *Housing, Theory and Society*, 37(2): 180–97.

Sanders, P. and Schroder, N. (2008) *The Genealogy of Urban Form: Brisbane Case Study*, Brisbane: State Library of Queensland.

Schultz, T. W. (1961) 'Investment in human capital', *The American Economic Review*, 51(1): 1–17.

Schwartz, H. (2012) 'Housing, the welfare state, and the global financial crisis', *Politics and Society*, 40(1): 35–58.

Sherraden, M. (2015) *Assets and the Poor: A New American Welfare Policy*, New York: Routledge.

Short, E. (1984) 'Personal financial planning: portability poses difficult choices/Tax-free lump sums banished', *Financial Times*, 25 April.

Simon, E. and Farrow, P. (2008) 'Storm proof your finances – It's not too late to take some action to protect your home', *The Daily Telegraph,* 12 July.

Singer, C. (2022) '8 reasons to share the wealth', New Economics Foundation, Available from: https://neweconomics.org/2022/12/8-reas ons-to-share-the-wealth [Accessed 22 December 2022].

Singh, S. (2017) 'Money and family relationships: the biography of transnational Money', in Bandelj, F.F. Wherry and V.A. Zelizer (eds) *Money Talks: Explaining How Money Really Works*, Princeton, NJ: Princeton University Press, pp 184–98.

Skopeliti, C. and Otte, J. (2022) 'It was frightening': four Britons on returning to work after retiring', *The Guardian*, 21 December.

Smith, I., Morris, S. and Dunkley, E. (2022) 'Treasury sides with insurers to free up billions in capital', *Financial Times*, Available from: https://www.ft.com/content/3f569ce7-e4eb-4bc6-a7f6-cbf6fde9be35 [Accessed 7 February 2023].

Smith, K. (2023) 'Could an ISA be more efficient than my pension?', *The Telegraph*, 14 February.

Soaita, A. and Searle, B. (2016) 'Debt amnesia: homeowners' discourses on the financial costs and gains of homebuying', *Environment and Planning A*, 48(6): 1087–106.

Sotiropoulos, D. P., Milios, J. and Lapatsioras, S. (2013) *A Political Economy of Contemporary Capitalism and Its Crisis: Demystifying Finance*, London: Routledge.

Steiber, N. and Haas, B. (2012) 'Advances in explaining women's employment patterns', *Socio-Economic Review*, 10(2): 343–67.

Stevano, S., Mezzadri, A., Lombardozzi, L. and Bargawi, H. (2021) 'Hidden abodes in plain sight: the social reproduction of households and labour in Covid-19 pandemic', *Feminist Economics*, 27(1–2): 271–87.

Storper, M. (2014) 'Commentary on 2013 Roepke lecture financial literacy in context', *Economic Geography*, 90(1): 25–7.

Strauss, K. (2008) 'Re-engaging with rationality in economic geography: behavioral approaches and the importance of context in decision-making', *Journal of Economic Geography*, 8(2): 137–56.

Strauss, K. (2014) 'Accessing pension resources: the right to equality inside and out of the labour market', *International Journal of Law in Context*, 10(4): 522–37.

Suter, L. (2017) 'Ask an expert: Laura Suter helps answer your questions on paying tax on savings accounts and ISA regulations. And can you put your shares in your children's names?', *The Daily Telegraph*, 10 October.

Swinson, J. (2013) *Changes to TUPE rules cut red tape for business*, 5 September, Available from: https://www.gov.uk/government/news/changes-to-tupe-rules-cut-red-tape-for-business

Szymborska, H. (2019) 'Wealth structures and income distribution of US households before and after the Great Recession', *Structural Change and Economic Dynamics*, 51: 168–85.

Szymborska, H. (2022) 'Rethinking inequality in the 21st century: inequality and household balance sheet composition in financialized economies', *Journal of Post Keynesian Economics*, 45(1): 24–72.

Talib, N. and Fitzgerald, R. (2016) 'Micro–meso–macro movements: a multi-level critical discourse analysis framework to examine metaphors and the value of truth in policy texts', *Critical Discourse Studies*, 13(5): 531–47.

Tan, E. (2014) 'Human capital theory: a holistic criticism', *Review of Educational Research*, 84(3): 4111–445.

Taylor, S. (2001) 'Evaluating and applying discourse analytic research', in M. Wetherell, S. Taylor and S. Yates (eds) *Discourse as Data: A Guide for Analysis?*, London: Sage and The Open University, pp 5–48.

Taylor, S. (2013) *What Is Discourse Analysis?*, London: Bloomsbury.

TDG (2022) 'Don't fall for these 6 equity release myths', *The Daily Telegraph*, 9 August.

TDG (2023) 'Don't fall for these 6 equity release myths', *The Daily Telegraph*, 18 August.

TG (2007) 'Are you throwing your money down the drain?', *The Guardian*, 25 September.

Thaler, R. (1990) 'Anomalies: saving, fungibility, and mental accounts', *Journal of Economic Perspectives*, 4(1): 193–205.

Thaler, R. and Benartzi, S. (2004) 'Save tomorrow: using behavioral economics to increase employee saving', *Journal of Political Economy*, 112(S1): S164–S187.

Thaler, R. and Shefrin, H. (1981) 'An economic theory of self-control', *Journal of Political Economy*, 89(2), 392–405.

Thaler, R. and Sunstein, C. (2021) *Nudge: Improving Decisions about Health, Wealth, and Happiness*, New Haven, CT: Yale University Press.

Thatcher, M. (1974) 'The owner-occupier's party', *The Daily Telegraph*, 1 July.

Thatcher, M. (1975) 'Speech to Conservative Party Conference', 10 October, Available from: https://www.margaretthatcher.org/document/102777

Thatcher, M. (1979) 'Conservative General Election Manifesto 1979', 11 April, Available from: https://www.margaretthatcher.org/document/110858

Thatcher, M. (1981) 'Speech launching Business Opportunities Programme (Small Businesses)', 5 May 1981, Available from: https://www.margaretthatcher.org/document/104642

Thatcher, M. (1983) 'Speech to Conservative Party Conference', 14 October, Available from: https://www.margaretthatcher.org/document/105454

Thatcher, M. (1984a) 'Speech to 1922 Committee ("The Enemy Within")', 19 July, Available from: https://www.margaretthatcher.org/document/105563

Thatcher, M. (1984b) 'Speech to Conservative Party Conference', 12 October, Available from: https://www.margaretthatcher.org/document/105763

Thatcher, M. (1985) 'Speech to Conservative Central Council', 23 March, Available from: https://www.margaretthatcher.org/document/106000

Thatcher, M. (1986) 'Speech to Conservative Party Conference', 10 October, Available from: https://www.margaretthatcher.org/document/106498

Thatcher, M. (1987a) 'Interview for Woman's Own ("no such thing as society")', 23 September. Available from: https://www.margaretthatcher.org/document/106689

Thatcher, M. (1987b) '1987 Conservative Party General Election Manifesto', Available from: http://www.conservativemanifesto.com/1987/1987-conservative-manifesto.shtml

Thatcher, M. (1988) 'Speech opening British Day at World EXPO 1988', 5 August. Available from: https://www.margaretthatcher.org/document/107313

Thorniley, T. (2001) 'There's no place like home – so hang on to it', *The Daily Telegraph*, 24 January.

Tidbury, M. (1987) 'Looking at your own performance', *The Guardian*, 5 December.

TNA (2010) *Billion Pounds Package for Housing*, Richmond: The National Archives.

TUC (2022) *Cost of Childcare Has Risen by over £2,000 a Year since 2010*, Trades Union Congress, Available from: https://www.tuc.org.uk/news/cost-childcare-has-risen-over-ps2000-year-2010 [Accessed 7 February 2023].

Van der Zwan, N. (2014) 'Making sense of financialization', *Socio-Economic Review*, 12(1): 99–129.

Vincent, M. (2007) 'Don't leap into the unknown', *Financial Times*, 3 November.

Vlachantoni, A., Feng, Z., Evandrou, M. and Falkingham, J. (2014) *Ethnicity and Occupational Pension Membership in the UK*, Southampton: Centre for Research on Aging.

Wakefield, A. and Fleming, J. (2016) *Responsibilization*, Sage Knowledge, Available from: http://sk.sagepub.com/reference/the-sage-dictionary-of-policing/n111.xml [Accessed 20 August 2016].

Warwick-Ching, L. (2007) '1986: British Gas privatisation and the search for Sid', *Financial Times*, 24 November.

Waters, R. (1990) 'A bitter portfolio – hindsight: the cautionary tale of one angry investor', *Financial Times*, 26 October.

Watts, N. (2013) 'Osborne distances himself from Thatcher legacy over disability benefits', *The Guardian*, 2 April.

Webber, D. (2018) *The Rise of the Working-Class Shareholder: Labour's Last Best Weapon*, Cambridge, MA: Harvard University Press.

Weiss, H. (2015) 'Financialization and its discontents: Israelis negotiating pensions', *American Anthropologist*, 117(3): 506–18.

White, M. and Lakey, W. (1992) *The Restart Effect: Evaluation of a Labour Market Programme for Unemployed People*, London: Policy Studies Institute.

WID (2018) *The World Inequality Database*, Available from: www.WID.world [Accessed 23 March 2018].

Wood, J. (2017) 'The integrating role of private homeownership and mortgage credit in British neoliberalism', *Housing Studies*, 31(4): 1–21.

Woodroffe, S. (2007) 'Why I put my money in managed funds', *The Guardian*, 12 September.

Worsfold, D. (1987a) 'Money raising begins at home', *The Guardian*, 20 June.

Worsfold, D. (1987b) 'Take some of it with you', *The Guardian*, 13 June.

Wright, M. (2001) 'Give your dependants their independence', *The Daily Telegraph*, 5 January.

WTW (2022) *Global Gender Wealth Equity Report*, London: Willis Towers Watson.

Zelizer, V. (2011) *Economic Lives: How Culture Shapes the Economy*, Princeton, NJ: Princeton University Press.

Zelizer, V. (2012) 'How I became a relational economic sociologist and what does that mean?', *Politics & Society*, 40(2): 145–74.

Zelizer, V. A. (1994) *The Social Meaning of Money: Pin Money, Paychecks, Poor Relief, and Other Currencies*, New York: Basic Books.

Zulfiqar, G. (2021) 'The social relations of gold: how a gendered asset serves social reproduction and finance in Pakistan', *Gender, Work and Organization*, 29(3): 739–57.

Index

References to figures appear in *italic* type; those in **bold** type refer to tables. References to endnotes show both the page number and the note number (182n1).